A Wolf Called Romeo

NICK JANS

A Wolf Called
ROMEO

HOUGHTON MIFFLIN HARCOURT
Boston · New York

For information about permission to reproduce selections from this book,
write to Permissions, Houghton Mifflin Harcourt Publishing Company,
215 Park Avenue South, New York, New York 10003.

www.hmhco.com

Library of Congress Cataloging-in-Publication Data
Jans, Nick, date.
A wolf called Romeo / Nick Jans.
pages cm
Includes bibliographical references and index.
ISBN 978-0-547-85819-7 (hardback)
1. Romeo, –2009. 2. Wolves — Alaska — Biography. 3. Human-animal
relationships — Alaska. 4. Poaching — Alaska. I. Title.
SF422.82.R66J36 2014
636.9773092 — dc23
[B]
2013048435

Book design by Greta Sibley
Map by Laurie Craig

Printed in the United States of America
DOC 10 9 8 7 6 5 4 3

All photos courtesy of the author, with the following exceptions:
page 108, Romeo and Jessie: David Willson; page 121, Romeo and
Brittain: Hugh Lade; page 146, Harry and Romeo: Joel Bennett;
page 219, Peacock and the suitcase bear: Alaska Trial Court
evidence file; page 220, Park Myers in court:
Michael Penn/*Juneau Empire*

Lines from Henry Beston's *The Outermost House: A Year of Life
on the Great Beach of Cape Cod* reprinted with permission,
estate of Catherine Beston Barnes.

In memory of Greg Brown

1950–2013

A friend to all living things

For the animal shall not be measured by man.
In a world older and more complete than ours, they move
finished and complete, gifted with the extension of the
senses we have lost or never attained, living by voices
we shall never hear. They are not brethren, they are
not underlings, they are other nations, caught with
ourselves in the net of life and time.

HENRY BESTON
The Outermost House

ROMEO'S TERRITORY

1. The Big Rock
2. Tern Island
3. West Glacier Trail Parking Lot
4. Rifle Range
5. Skater's Cabin
6. Skater's Cabin Road
7. Nick and Sherrie's House
8. Mendenhall Campground
9. Mendenhall Lake
10. Mendenhall Glacier
11. To Herbert River and Amalga Harbor
12. Mendenhall River Mouth
13. Mendenhall Wetlands
14. Juneau Airport
15. To Downtown Juneau
16. Mount McGinnis
17. Bullard Mountain
18. Thunder Mountain
19. Montana Creek
20. Montana Creek Road
21. Glacier Highway/Egan Drive

CONTENTS

ACKNOWLEDGMENTS

The hard work of writing, though solitary, is never done alone. I am indebted to all who encouraged and aided me in this book, seven years in the living, and three in the making. Special thanks to Harry Robinson for being so generous with his memories; to Corry Donner, who read every word not once, but many times with a keen eye and good judgment; to my wife, Sherrie, who pushed me toward the telling and lived the story along with me; Tina Brown, Joel Bennett, and Vic Walker, steadfast friends throughout; Laurie Craig, map artist nonpareil; Susan Canavan at Houghton Mifflin Harcourt, who believed; and Elizabeth Kaplan, agent extraordinaire, who guided me. Special thanks to researchers Dr. Vic Van Ballenberghe and Patrick Walsh, who reviewed the manuscript's scientific content. I also offer heartfelt thanks to many who shared their experiences and knowledge, including John Hyde, Michael Lowman, Ryan Scott, Neil Barten, Doug Larsen, Matt Robus, Lem Butler, Chris Frary, Pete Griffin, Ron Marvin, Jon Stetson, John Neary, Kim Turley, Denise Chase, Lynn Schooler, Nene Wolfe, Arnie Hanger, Elise Augustson, Sue Arthur, Harriet Milks, Alaska State Trooper Dan Sadloske, Dr. William Palmer, and dozens more I've no doubt overlooked. I extend my profound respect to the many researchers who have illuminated the world of wolves, and to the Inupiaq hunters, especially Clarence Wood and Nelson Greist, Sr., who tried to teach me what they knew.

First meeting, Romeo and Dakotah

PROLOGUE

"Are you sure about this?" my wife, Sherrie, breathed. She glanced over her shoulder toward the comforting glow of our house on the lakeshore, then gazed ahead where a black wolf stood on the ice in the gathering twilight. Bundled against the Southeast Alaska cold, we'd taken along just one of our three dogs—our female yellow Lab, Dakotah, who'd always been perfectly mannered and under voice control around wildlife, from bears to porcupines.

Despite some understandable jitters, Sherrie was so thrilled she was about to jump out of her skin. After all these years of trying and not seeing, there it was: her first wolf. Perfect, I thought, and easier than it ever should be. But as we walked farther out on the ice, things changed. The wolf, instead of watching from the tree line as he had several times with me, angled toward us at a trot. Then he broke into a bounding lope, snow flying beneath his paws, jaws agape. I drew Sherrie toward me and reached for Dakotah's collar. My vision sharpened, and synapses crackled. I'd seen my share of wolves over the years, some point-blank close, and hadn't quite shifted into panic mode. But anyone who claims he wouldn't get an adrenaline jolt from a running wolf coming straight in, with no weapon and no place to run, and loved ones to defend, is either brain-dead or lying.

In a few heartbeats, the wolf had closed the distance to forty yards. He stood stiff-legged, tail raised above his back, his unblink-

ing stare fixed on us — a dominant posture, less than reassuring. Then, with a moaning whimper, Dakotah suddenly wrenched free of the two fingers I'd hooked through her collar and bounded straight at the wolf. A tone of desperation sharpening her voice, Sherrie called again and again, but there was no stopping that dog. The Lab skidded to a stop several body lengths short of contact and stood tall, her own tail straight out, and as we watched, mouths open, the wolf lowered his to match. With the two so close, I had my first clear idea of just how large the wolf really was. Dakotah, a stocky, traditional-style female Lab, weighed in at a muscular fifty-six pounds. The black wolf towered over her, more than double her weight. Just his head and neck matched the size of her torso. A hundred twenty pounds, I figured. Maybe more.

The wolf stepped stiff-legged toward Dakotah, and she answered. If she heard our calls, she gave no sign. She was locked on and intent, but utterly silent — not at all her normal happy-Lab self. She seemed half-hypnotized. She and the wolf regarded each other, as if each were glimpsing an almost-forgotten face and trying to remember. This was one of those moments when time seems to hold its breath. I lifted my camera and snapped off a single frame.

As if that tiny click had been a finger snap, the world began to move again. The wolf's stance altered. Ears perked high and held narrow, he bounced forward a body length, bowed on his forelegs, then leaned back and lifted a paw. Dakotah sidled closer and circled, her tail still straight out. The eyes of each were locked on the other. With their noses a foot apart, I pressed the shutter once more. Again, the sound seemed to break a spell. Dakotah heard Sherrie's voice at last and bounded back toward us, turning her back, at least for now, on whatever call of the wild she'd just heard. We watched for long minutes with Dakotah softly whining at our sides, staring toward the dark, handsome stranger who stood staring our way and whining back, a high-pitched keening that filled the silence. Half-stunned, Sherrie and I murmured back and forth, wondering at what we'd seen and what it meant.

But it was getting dark — time to go. The wolf stood watching our retreat, his tail flagging, then raised his muzzle to the sky in a drawn-out howl, as if crushed. At last he trotted west and faded into the trees. As we walked toward home in the deepening winter evening, the first stars flickered against the curve of space. Behind us, the wolf's deep cries echoed off the glacier.

With that first close meeting one evening in December 2003, a wild black wolf became part of our lives — not just as a fleeting shape in the dusk, but as a creature we and others would come to know over a span of years, just as he came to know us. We were neighbors, that much is certain; and though some will scoff, I say friends as well. This is a tale woven of light and darkness, hope and sorrow, fear and love, and perhaps, a little magic. It's a story of our time on this shrinking world, one I need to tell — most of all, to myself. Late at night, it fills the spaces between heartbeats, nudges me awake. By speaking, I hope not to be rid of it, nor even to understand, but just to set down all the facts, the musings, and unanswered questions as best I can. Years from now, at least I'll know that I did more than dream, and that once upon a time, there was a wolf we called Romeo. This is his story.

Romeo's signature — left rear drag marks

1

WOLF!

December 2003

I was taking my usual afternoon ski on Mendenhall Lake on an early-December day, right behind the house. Ahead, the blue bulk of the Mendenhall Glacier loomed, framed by a ragged sweep of snow-laden peaks — McGinnis, Stroller White, the Mendenhall Towers, Bullard, and Thunder Mountain — glowing in blue winter light. My nearest company was a hiker nearly a mile away. Concentrating on my skiing form, I almost missed the line of tracks that intersected my trail. Even at a quick glance, there was something about them that made me skid to a halt and double back for another look.

It couldn't be.

It was.

Prints that would cover my palm, larger and more diamond-shaped than a dog's, front and rear paw prints almost an exact match, all laid out in that flowing pattern I'd seen so many times in my two decades living in the Arctic wilderness, a thousand miles to the north. I brushed my hand lightly across one track. Crisply etched, yet feather soft — just a couple of hours old, at most.

A wolf. Right there, at the edge of the city limits of Juneau, the state capital. Of course, this was Alaska. But even in The Great Land, one of its last strongholds anywhere on the planet, *Canis lupus*, the gray wolf, is spread thinly across the country — according to the state's own estimates, between seven thousand and twelve thousand, averaging out to fewer than one fiftieth of a wolf for each of Alaska's half-million-plus square miles. Most Alaskans, even those living in ultra-remote villages, spend a lifetime without ever seeing one, or even catching the echo of a howl. Here in Juneau, third largest city in the state, with a population of over thirty thousand, outdoors people and biologists talked of a pack that ran the ridgelines from Berners Bay south across the Mendenhall Icefield, as far as the Taku valley, an enormous sprawl of dense rain forest, sawtooth mountains, snowfields, and crevasse-riddled glaciers. My wife Sherrie and I had heard faint howls now and then from the deck of the home we'd just built, perched on the edge of suburbia and the wild, and counted ourselves lucky. A fresh wolf trail down on the lake, the most popular winter playground for the entire city, was big news.

I spent minutes studying the tracks, which meandered from near the West Glacier trailhead toward the maze of trails, beaver ponds, and brushy woods known as Dredge Lakes. The animal, besides showing enormous feet even by wolf standards, displayed a clear, habitual drag of his left rear paw, which made a distinctive furrow. On my homeward loop I kept my eyes open, half expecting the trail to have been an illusion. But it was still there. I followed the tracks into the tree line and found overlapping, older prints leading to circular depressions where the animal had bedded down. He'd been hanging around at least since the most recent snow, a few days before.

Back at the house, I blurted the news to Sherrie. Though she nodded, I knew she didn't quite believe me. Couldn't it have been a wandering dog? Or a coyote, like we'd seen before, out on the lake? She'd moved from Florida to Alaska fifteen years earlier and traveled thousands of miles across the almost unimaginable vastness of the state, trying and hoping to spy a wolf, without ever having caught so much as a flicker of fur. Now, we had fresh tracks right here, a half mile from our door, and a twenty-minute drive from the governor's mansion. To tell the truth, I still didn't believe it myself, even when I returned for another look.

Two days later, I lounged in the hot tub on our back deck in a cloud of steam, working out the kink in a sore shoulder, when I spotted a dark shape moving far out on the ice. Even at a distance, that straight-backed, floating trot practically shouted wolf. I jumped out, toweled half-dry, and threw on ski gear. Ten minutes later, our three dogs trotting at my heels, I double-poled out along the lake's west shore. I knew the dogs—constant companions, our own pack—would stay close, and I carried a leash for our youngest, just in case. I didn't hope to more than see the wolf as a distant mirage, and only if I were lucky.

Just around the bend from what area regulars call the Big Rock, a ten-foot-tall, glacier-deposited granite boulder jutting from the shallows at the head of a bay along the west shore, I met two rattled women with their dogs. They'd just been followed for a quarter mile, they said, by a huge black wolf. Staring and intent, it had edged into unnervingly close range behind them—twenty feet, they gestured—then finally moved off, after they waved and shouted. "Where?" I asked. They pointed north up the lake and hurried back toward the parking lot, dogs close at their heels. I skied on, and three-quarters of a mile up the lake, against the trees, I spied what must have been the same animal, standing, staring back over his shoulder.

Wolf! A wild-edged thrill swelled in my chest, strong as the time I'd met my first, more than two decades before. My two Labs and blue heeler clearly understood this was no stray husky. Even mild-mannered Gus, the black Lab ex–Seeing Eye dog we'd recently adopted, raised his hackles and rumbled a growl. Dakotah, our gorgeous, almost-white female Lab, whined. Chase, the yearling blue heeler, who was bred to guard the herd against such creatures, raised a sharp, desperate alarm as the wolf trotted into the brush.

Though the odds were slimming by the moment, I raced back to the house, gathered my camera pack and tripod, and shut the heartbroken dogs inside with noses pressed against glass. I panted back out to the creek mouth where the wolf had disappeared. There he stood, a dark shape along the snow-deep shore. He must have seen me coming, but instead of loping off, as I'd expected, he slowed to a walk, sniffed around, and curled up for a snooze near an alder clump. Starting with that sighting from a hot tub, of all places, the whole se-quence of events seemed to be tilting toward the surreal.

Out in the open, I figured I didn't have a chance to get within picture range. Still, I attached my biggest telephoto lens, ditched my skis, shouldered my tripod, and post-holed on foot through knee-deep snow, meandering, fighting down the urge to look toward him. As ecologist Dr. Tom Smith had once reminded me, an unknown an-imal staring at and approaching another communicates three pos-sible messages: I want to displace you; I want to eat you; I want to mate with you — all alarming overtures. And I knew that the wide, staring eye of a camera lens, with the photographer leaning behind it, radiating quiet excitement, only intensifies the perceived threat.

I plodded on with head lowered, pausing and sitting for long minutes whenever he looked my way. At a couple hundred yards, he yawned, stretched, and moved off a few paces, then lay down again. Though even the most ethical wildlife photographers occasionally write themselves a personal exemption slip in cases of extreme op-portunity, and the wolf wasn't acting stressed or going far, I resisted the temptation to push too far inside his personal envelope of space. We completed a slow-motion interspecies two-step for an hour, most of that time with me sitting, eyes averted, or sometimes turn-ing my back and increasing the distance, until finally I was within eighty yards, thanks in part to the wolf angling toward me at least twice. Setting up, I fought to hold steady against my breathing as I squeezed off a series of shots in blue, fading light — the wolf gazing across the lake, then lifting his muzzle and howling against a back-drop of snow-draped trees. Then he faded into the hemlocks, and I headed home in the twilight, feeling like some *National Geographic* rock star.

Back home, Sherrie had just returned from work and errands. When I told her, of course she went bonkers. *What do you mean? You really . . .* Of course, she wanted to go straight out, right then. Just about pitch-dark, I pointed out. Black wolf, black night, and cold to boot. But we'd give it a shot tomorrow evening, soon as she got home.

We stood out in the yard, listening for howls, and heard nothing. Maybe he had already drifted back into the country, gone for good.

The next day, I was out alone on the lake at first light, believing the odds of another sighting were slim. But damned if the wolf didn't appear as if on cue, right where he'd been before: back along the trees in the bay behind the Big Rock, just off the West Glacier Trail. He seemed far more wolflike this time, though. He didn't show the same willingness to be approached. I sat back and studied him with binoculars. This guy (now confirmed a male, as I saw him lift his leg to scent-mark a snow-covered log) wasn't just any wolf. Out of my hundred-some hard-won sightings in the Arctic, he stood out — perfectly proportioned from his broad head to his deep-barreled chest. Exactly how big was hard to say without some sort of reference to measure against, but he was clearly some shade of huge. Gorgeously furred in glossy black, he seemed groomed, as if he'd just returned from collecting best in breed at Westminster. All in all, I'd never seen a more perfect example of the species.

Once you know what to look for, there's no mistaking a wolf for a dog. It's more than a matter of size or weight. Wolves are built differently — longer legs, straighter spines, thicker necks, brushier tails, and thicker, multilayered coats. A wolf's gliding, economical movements, like its tracks, are distinctive, too. However, the true measure of distance between wolves and dogs lies in the eyes. A dog's may display intelligence and engagement, but being caught in a wolf's unblinking gaze is like standing in the path of a laser. That startling intensity bores in and seems to take the very measure of your being. This black wolf's deep amber irises held all that force, but something more radiated from him that I'd never sensed in any other wild wolf: a relaxed acceptance of my presence. Most wolves I'd encountered, even those that approached me out of curiosity, were probing, on edge, ready to lope for the horizon at the least flicker of suspicious movement, the least waft of wrong scent. In fact, most wild wolves I'd encountered ran at the first hint of human presence, sometimes a distance of a mile or more, and went to incredible lengths to remain unseen. On the other hand, some wolves, whether habituated ani-

mals in protected areas or naturally wild, may all but ignore unob-
trusive humans and go about their business as if the watchers were
invisible. In rare instances, a wolf — usually a younger animal, or one
who has never encountered people before — may investigate us with
bold curiosity. Tracking wolves alongside Inupiaq subsistence hunters in the western Brooks Range, and watching them as a photographer, writer, and naturalist, I'd witnessed that full range of behavior
firsthand. But something about this wolf was different. He lay there
watching, neither agitated nor unengaged. It was if he were studying me almost as much as I was him, trying to figure out what I'd do
next. And regardless of what the wolf had on his mind, what I would
do, along with the rest of my kind, was a perfectly good question.

One thing was certain. Sherrie needed to see this wolf, for my sake
as much as hers. After all, I'd promised her a wolf sighting on our
first date years before, and though we'd come close several times, I'd
never quite been able to deliver. You can't plan on seeing wolves, any
more than you can falling in love. By the time she got home from
work, dusk was heaving in, a dark line of cloud riding the horizon. I
didn't have to tell her to hurry as she bundled into her parka, snow
pants, and boots. We took just Dakotah along for company — Chase,
the blue heeler, was just too reactive toward any unknown canine if
it got too close, and gentle Gus made the perfect babysitter — and
headed out onto the lake. Twenty minutes later, just a few hundred
yards from our back door, we met the black wolf in the winter twilight — the encounter that began this story. Years later, knowing what
I do now, I close my eyes and feel the image of that instant eddy
around me like a gust of windblown snow. There would be no going back.

Over the next week, whatever we knew as normal life screeched
to a halt. Sherrie went to work gnawing on her knuckles, called
for updates and sightings, and hurried home to get out on the lake
for a few minutes before dark. I blew off chores and writing dead-
lines; dishes stacked up in the sink; we ran out of eggs. There was no
time to waste. Judging from the signs I'd seen in the snow, the black

wolf had already stuck around longer than anyone could expect. Of course, we were so damn excited that we were tempted to blab to all our friends and let them in on the deal: *Come on over, see the wolf!* We knew people who'd be thrilled to see stale tracks, let alone a two-second flash of their maker.

We decided the fewer who knew, the better. One word in the wrong circle, and the whole thing could turn into a one-ring circus with a bad end. We kept the news to our downstairs tenant and close friend, Anita (she took her two dogs for daily walks on the lake and needed to know), and my old pal Joel Bennett, a respected wildlife filmmaker whom I'd helped guide to caribou and wolves years ago in the Kobuk valley. Both were sworn to secrecy. Each would meet the wolf with us first, and many times later on their own, and with others.

On those first morning forays, of course I left the dogs shut in back home; pals or not, trained or not, it's a no-brainer that wildlife photography and canines don't mix. I wanted to be totally focused, and even a well-controlled dog is just another moving object that can only make getting into range—or far better, having the subject approach you—more difficult. Wild animals can count, so to speak, and don't like being outnumbered. Too, canines register as predators on most animals' radar. In fact, dogs are a documented factor in what biologists call agonistic (aggression-related) encounters between humans and a number of species, including grizzlies, moose, and wolves. All that aside, I'd always had the best luck and the most profound experiences alone, without even a human companion.

A cold front had settled in. Coupled with the on-rolling winter solstice, that translated to sun above the mountains for just a few hours and morning temperatures hovering below zero—mild compared to my former Kobuk valley home far to the north, but cold all the same. Both my camera gear and frost-damaged fingers complained, but I dug in and made both work as best I could. After all those years of frozen sweat and busted gear in the Arctic, I had just three wolf pictures worth showing. The rest, gleaned from a couple of dozen chances, amounted to rapidly retreating furry butts you had to pick out of the slide with a magnifying loupe. Even with a big lens and top-notch gear, you need to be a few dozen yards away from any animal for a decent portrait; and wild wolves are notoriously difficult subjects. Most of my wolf encounters had been measured in heartbeats; I might as well have been watching smoke peeling downwind. This was something else entirely.

The black wolf had already won my undying gratitude for not pulling a Houdini every time he saw me. Still, he seemed to possess an incredible instinct for disappearing whenever the light got close to decent, and for keeping at just the outside edge of photographic range. I had to balance my desire to get the perfect shot with not wanting to displace him. Squinting down the bazooka barrel of my 600 mm Nikon manual focus lens, further stopped down by a 1.4 multiplier, trying not to steam up the viewfinder or jiggle the tripod, I squeezed off long-range shots at agonizingly slow shutter speeds, adding to a growing pile of slides that featured a dark, decidedly unsharp silhouette in a blue-white landscape. Though my early photography efforts with him were largely failures from a professional perspective, I was beyond thrilled to watch a wolf, any wolf, but increasingly, *this* wolf — see how he moved, where he went, what he did.

One of those first days, I sat hunkered on the lakeshore just after dawn, watching from a distance, hoping the wolf would decide to angle my way, as he had before. Suddenly he swung his head, staring down the lake, ears cocked. A skier approached — a woman with a husky mix trotting at her heels. The wolf loped toward them. I watched, half holding my breath. A few days before, the *Juneau Empire* had run a front-page article about wolves eating dogs within the city limits of Ketchikan, a couple hundred miles to the south. Notwithstanding that friendly seeming overture with Dakotah, I wondered if I could be in for a live replay. Wolves were wolves, and I had no illusions about what they did for a living. Maybe that's why he was here — he'd developed a taste for fresh leg of kibble-stuffed spaniel.

The wolf closed in and the dog charged out to meet it head-on. Nose to nose, they stood, tails out, backs stiff. Though the husky mix was solidly built, the difference in size was startling. The wolf could have grabbed his sixty-pound cousin crosswise in his jaws like a bratwurst, given a spine-snapping shake, and trotted away with his prey dangling. Both animals tensed.

And then it started. The wolf bowed, then launched skyward off his haunches with all the weightless grace of a ballet dancer, hung in the air, executed a half pirouette, and floated earthward. Hesitant and clumsy by comparison, the dog joined in. As I watched open-mouthed, they switched to pawing and mouth-fighting like year-lings, interspersed with the wolf's gravity-defying leaps and spins. There was an artistic exuberance to his movements that went beyond play. Celebration was more like it. Or a dance. The woman leaned on her ski poles and watched, rapt but relaxed, oddly unconcerned about either her or her dog's safety.

In the Arctic, friends of mine talked of single, unaggressive wolves shadowing traveling sled dog teams or hanging around their cabins for periods ranging from a few minutes to a number of days, especially in the early-spring mating season, when young adult wolves commonly disperse from their natal packs to form their own. These wanderers naturally seek their own kind, and dogs will do in a pinch, especially for a young, lonely wolf. My friend Seth Kantner had a female black wolf show up at his Kobuk River cabin several times, apparently trying to make friends with Seth's big, semiferal sled dog, Worf—though the dog would have none of it; whenever she appeared, he gathered all his bones in a pile, lay on them, and growled. The ancestors of the Inupiat I lived among encouraged occasional interbreeding in their sled dog bloodlines. Probably it was also unavoidable, when a wolf slipped into a group of tethered dogs and found a receptive mate. You can glimpse echoes of wolf in many upper Kobuk and Noatak huskies, especially the few remaining larger, old-style work animals — dogs like Worf.

In fact, this wolf's very color was a testament to the intermingling of wild and domestic canids. Cutting-edge research on genetic markers by an international team of biologists, funded by the National Science Foundation in 2007, has positively linked the black, or dark-phase, color in wolves (common in North America, extremely

rare in Europe and Asia) to interbreeding with domestic dogs belonging to early Native Americans thousands of years ago, no doubt
including not just wolves coming near humans to breed, but a few
escaped dogs gone feral, à la Jack London. Wolf-dog hybridization
continues to this day, both by human design and natural chance.
Thus, this black wolf was a living, breathing expression of the longtime, ongoing genetic feedback between the species.

All well and good. Mating between viable species, understandable. Hanging around for a while, sure. A little sniffing and socializing,
why not? But *playing?* This dances-with-dogs bit seemed like some
Disney subscript. Then, abruptly, the dog lost interest and wandered
off to nose something, as if they weren't quite speaking the same language, and it had tired of thumbing through the phrase dictionary. It
trotted back toward the woman, the wolf moved away, and I skied forward. The woman waxed casual and New Age about the whole deal.
Oh, she assured me, they'd been meeting the wolf on and off for days
now, and from the first, he had "offered himself in play." Was this the
first wolf she'd ever seen? Oh, yes. He was quite an "old soul."

Old soul my ass, this stuff just didn't happen — not in Alaska, not
anywhere. I might as well have witnessed a talking rutabaga. But it
was no use trying to impress upon her the rarity of her experience,
and after all, the philosophy behind her attitude reminded me: what
was, simply *was,* and you might miss the moment wondering how
or why. My old Eskimo hunting companion, Clarence Wood, once
snapped me out of my tendency toward overanalysis with a narrow-
eyed squint and disgusted mutter: "Too much think about bullshit."

But I was far less interested in the woman's interpretation of
events than in the wolf, which had by then faded back to the willows
on the lakeshore, a half mile away. Just on the ice edge, he lay down,
head up, front paws out — a calm, receptive position. The woman
with her dog skied on down the lake, and I eased in the general direction of the wolf, closed the distance inside a hundred yards, set
up tripod and camera, and started shooting once again. Of course, I
knew that trying to get a decent image of a reclining wolf at that distance in murky light was as futile as trying to root a marmot out of

a rock pile. But even a second-rate chance at a free-ranging wolf is rare enough that I burned through three rolls of professional film (I hadn't quite gone digital yet) in twenty minutes. All were destined for the trash bin, but I kept squeezing off shots. Most pros I know would have done the same.

I skied home, thoughts folded inward. I'd just caught my first glint of light on the mystery. Maybe dogs were the main attraction for this guy, rather than just a sideshow. There hadn't been as many skiers and pets out as usual due to the cold and the relatively new ice of the lake, and I'd been going early and late to deliberately avoid human traffic. Surely there had been interactions between the wolf and other dogs, maybe fitting the same pattern with Dakotah and the New Age woman's husky mix. On the other hand, he didn't go loping up to just anyone. I'd already seen plenty of dogs and people cross the lake with no wolf appearing, or with him just watching from a distance, much of the time without even being seen, or maybe mistaken for a dog (which he was, repeatedly). But for some reason, he'd approached those two women and their dogs a few days before; Sherrie, Dakotah, and me the next day; and this woman and dog at least several times. According to body language, all seemed like social encounters, lacking the least overtone of aggression. If he approached, and how close, would probably depend on recognizing individuals and on circumstances—physical cues, mood, and nuances only he would understand. If nothing else, wolves are masters at decoding intentions. That general thought was another reminder: I needed to slow down even more, lean back, and ease my grip on what I wanted—or at least, thought I did.

A few days later, the wolf was *still* out there, and Sherrie and I believed all the more that he'd evaporate the next nanosecond. Christmas vacation was coming on, and we had reservations for a week on a Mexican beach. Canceling out was Sherrie's idea. There was no sense, she told me, in going anywhere when we had this, right here and now. You'd have to know her, with her frost-sensitive Florida roots and sagging tolerance for rain forest darkness, to understand what she was giving up. I'd already dug out my snorkeling gear and flip-flops. Yet it was an easy call for both of us. Puerto Vallarta would still be there a year from now. The wolf wouldn't. This was already damn near the wildlife viewing opportunity of a lifetime. Just seeing him a few times more, we told each other, would make staying worthwhile.

One thread of conversation elbowed out all others those days: the wolf. What was going on with him? Where had he come from, and how had he ended up here? Sighting a single wolf wasn't at all unusual. In fact, more than half of my wolf encounters over the years, as well as most of the thousands of track sets I'd crossed, had been lone animals — though probably single only for a brief period. By their nature, wolves are social creatures, bonded to a tight-knit family group with whom they hunt, socialize, collectively raise young, and defend pack territory. Despite that cohesion, individual wolves or pairs frequently break off to hunt solo, or patrol the pack's territory for anywhere between a few hours and a few days. This wolf could easily have wandered down out of the mountains on a solo ramble and was about to rejoin his group.

Too, he could have been one of those young, solitary dispersers, a wolf on the move, looking for a mate and territory, to start a pack of his own. This wolf certainly seemed adolescent, in both action and body — gangly, a bit goofy if you knew what to look for, and with unworn teeth. He wasn't a wolf born this past spring (he wouldn't be on his own yet, or so large at six or seven months). That made him at least a year and a half, and probably no more than a year or, at the most, two years older than that — a spot-on profile for a dispersing wolf, having left home as our own subadult children do.

Not only young wolves, but also grown adults, established pack members, have been known to break away, for reasons we can only guess at. Some individuals will strike out on their own, traveling huge distances on an apparent whim. Alaskan studies utilizing tracking collars have recorded lone, dispersing animals (the large majority of them young males) routinely covering distances of three hundred to four hundred linear miles. Alaska Department of Fish and Game research biologist Jim Dau says, "The data suggests a high probability that some dispersers may travel five hundred miles or more." As a recent lower-48 example, consider wolf OR-7, whose solo, GPS-recorded rambles through western Oregon and northern California have made national news and garnered him his own following. The glacier wolf was likely to have come a far shorter distance. On the other hand, he was hardly your usual Alexander Archipelago wolf — the relatively diminutive subspecies of *Canis lupus* that inhabits the Southeast Alaska and British Columbia coast and offshore islands, usually topping out under eighty pounds. This wolf was more than half again as large, a fact that hinted at a different origin — from the Alaskan or the Canadian interior, where the wolves are among the largest in the world, their genetics apparently honed by hunting moose in deep-snow country. He could conceivably have emigrated a thousand-plus miles south, like me, from my old haunts in the upper Kobuk, or maybe just trotted twenty-five miles over the Coast Range and the Juneau Icefield from the Canadian side. As for his coloration, wolves range from black to nearly snow-white, with the most common color being (as the species name suggests) some shade of gray, with liberal sprinklings of tan, black, white, and brown mixed into their thick, multilayered coats. Up to 50 percent of Alexander Archipelago wolves — a notably high percentage, compared to the rest of the state — are the dark phase, ranging down to jet-black (again, an expression of that ancestral dog-wolf marker gene, possibly emphasized through natural selection for shadowy rain forest conditions). So the color of this wolf perhaps hinted at a local origin, while his size suggested a wolf from somewhere else.

All that musing aside, there was one further theory to explain the wolf's presence. In March of 2003 another black wolf — a pregnant female — had been hit and killed by a taxicab as it crossed the Glacier Spur Road, less than two miles from our door. That wolf — now in a glass case at the Mendenhall Glacier visitor center, frozen in a stiff, unwolflike pose and a glassy stare — was a possible, even probable family member. The black wolf we saw might well have chosen to stay, searching for a missing mother, sister, or mate.

No matter his origin, the black wolf had chosen a precarious hangout, on the fringe of Alaska suburbia. At his back were mountains and glacial snowfields stretching across the Coast Range and down into the dry interior of Canada; north and south, on the Alaska side of the border, remote, near-vertical coastal rain forest. He could choose any direction, yet he remained, pressing against the glass of a world filled with strange sights, sounds, and scents: cars and airplanes, boxes full of people, blazing lights and blaring commotion, and an ever-expanding maze of asphalt spilling down to tidewater. He could go almost anywhere and avoid us — for the rest of his life, if he wanted to.

It's one thing to have black bears wandering neighborhoods, snitching birdseed and scattering unsecured garbage like outsized raccoons; in Juneau, even downtown, black bear sightings are so common that most locals are alert but scarcely alarmed to find a bruin on their back porch, and far more likely to reach for a camera than a gun. Almost nobody bothers to call the cops or Fish and Game. In the history of Juneau, I can find no record of anyone ever being injured, let alone mauled, by a black bear. Brown bears, as the coastal variation of grizzlies are known, are far more dangerous, especially when surprised up close. Gus's previous owner, Lee Hagmier, had in fact lost his sight back in the late 1950s as a teenager in a brown bear attack, just four miles from our house. However, Juneauites tolerate them near the edges of town in small, polite numbers. A mother and half-grown cub had been hanging around in the Dredge Lakes area the previous two autumns with no issues beyond a couple of abbreviated bluff charges, despite dozens of humans and their dogs moving through each day. There was seldom outcry or call for any bear to be killed as a public menace.

The very word *wolf*, though, triggers waves of unreasoning, primal fear. That pervasive dread seems hardwired into our collective subconscious, from some dim, half-recalled past: *They eat us.* No matter that the phobia is built far less on fact than emotion, fanned by those who have spent little or no time observing wolves, except maybe through a rifle sight or on the end of a trap chain. But regardless of our own experience with wolves, there's something about them that pushes some rusty button in our collective psyche. Such a reflex must come from somewhere. Perhaps, millennia ago, or even further back, things were different. Added on to this fear is the economic and emotional threat to creatures we count as rightfully ours: livestock, pets, and animals we hunt for food or sport.

Immaculate predators, the very symbol of pure, uncompromising wildness, wolves and what we call civilization seem to be, in the cold terms of logic, mutually exclusive circumstances. While our mythology, folktales, and children's stories are full of kindly and beloved bears, from Winnie-the-Pooh to Yogi, their lupine counterparts are all but nonexistent. "Little Red Riding Hood," "The Three Little Pigs," and barroom stories from Montana to Ukraine paint wolves as malevolent presences, lurking on the edge of nightmare. Driven by largely apocryphal tales of man-eating packs chasing down travelers, snatching babies, and the like, wolves in most of Europe were well on their way to eradication by the time of the Pilgrims. Wilderness was a dark, evil, and fearful place, the dominion of Satan; and wolves were his minions. No surprise either that, as our forebears made their pioneering progress across the new continent, they continued in the New World where they'd left off in the Old.

Lewis and Clark, on their early-nineteenth-century march across the continent, found hoofed animals and wolves in incredible abundance, coexisting with native hunter-gatherers who revered rather than cursed the wolf. Lewis and Clark themselves described the unaggressive wolves they encountered on the great western plains, and clearly regarded them as no threat to human safety. Despite the hordes of inexperienced pioneers that soon flooded westward (no doubt taking potshots at every wolf within range), reports of wolves attacking or threatening humans were conspicuously few, even given the melodramatic liberties commonly taken in accounts of the period. However, with prey numbers dwindling due to human hunting and habitat loss, some of the remaining wolves fed on newly introduced livestock. Homesteaders and ranchers launched an all-out program of eradication, supported without question from grassroots to federal government as a great and necessary good. And apparently, simply killing wolves by all efficient means possible, including guns, steel traps, and broadcast poison bait, wasn't enough; they were often subjected to the sort of inventive torture reminiscent of the worst episodes of human genocide. Wolves were burned alive, dragged to death behind horses, fed fishhooks inside meat, set free with mouths and penises wired shut.

An indication of the unreasoning and unmitigated hatred that drove this antiwolf pogrom is captured in an 1814 account involving famed bird naturalist John James Audubon. In his travels, Audubon encountered a farmer that had caught three wolves in a pit trap he'd dug, after some of his livestock had been killed. As Audubon watched, the farmer jumped into the pit armed only with a knife, slashed the leg tendons of the wolves (who, much to Audubon's astonishment, cowered and offered no resistance), trussed them with rope, then loosed his dogs to rip apart the helpless animals as the farmer and he looked on. The lack of aggression by trapped or wounded wolves comes hardly as a surprise to me or anyone who's witnessed them in such circumstances. Far more telling is Audubon's lack of comment at the farmer's sadistic treatment of the three wolves; his tacit acceptance—from a man who would become renowned among conservationists worldwide—offers a window into the mindset of that period. In the words of social historian Jon T. Coleman, "Audubon and the farmer shared a conviction that wolves not only deserved death but deserved to be punished for living."

The slaughter continued. The last holdouts in the West were wily, notorious "outlaw" wolves with colorful names, bounties on their heads, and legendary abilities to evade capture; nonetheless, they were hunted down one by one. By the early 1940s, the carnage was all but complete. The few minor islands where wolf populations survived, including patches of northern Minnesota, Wisconsin, and Michigan, served as faint reminders of a range that once included virtually all of North America.

From the 1970s to the 1990s, rekindled interest in preserving our dwindling wild, along with our abiding fascination with wolves, led to successful reintroduction of wolves into shrunken fragments of their former range, most notably Yellowstone National Park, though not without bitter-edged controversy that shows no sign of diminishing—in fact, seems to be on the upswing at the dawn of this century, as wolf numbers and ranges expand. A vehement antiwolf message continues to be driven by contemporary western ranchers and large-scale agribusiness and supercharged by sport-hunting interests that scream wolves, left unchecked, will devour everything in their path (including themselves) until nothing is left—of course, begging the question as to why this endgame, wolf-created wasteland didn't arise many thousands of years ago. There is precisely zero scientific evidence demonstrating wolves, unlike ourselves, have ever driven any species to extinction. Of course, no antiwolf advocate points to the unrestricted slaughter and habitat reduction, not by wolves but by humans, that speeded the demise of those great herds of bison, deer, and elk reported by Lewis and Clark.

Modern, well-documented research demonstrates that apex predators such as wolves play keystone roles in keeping prey populations healthy by culling the weak and infirm. They also keep ungulate numbers in balance with habitat; wolf reintroduction into Yellowstone resulted in a stunning transformation of overbrowsed, depleted river and stream corridors, to the benefit of many species, from aspens and cottonwoods to beaver to songbirds to cutthroat trout. An added bonus was a natural form of predator control: a huge reduction in coyotes, which prey heavily on young game animals as well as livestock. But despite such positive benefits, fear-mongering and misinformation continue to drive the war on wolves in the lower 48—and Alaska, The Last Frontier, is no different.

Wolf management has long been the state's most controversial wildlife management issue, the sort of topic that leads to hard feelings, finger-jabbing, nasty letters to the editor, and occasional bar fights. Two opposing philosophies define the argument. Position A:

Wolves constitute a looming predatory menace to the game animals on which the people of Alaska depend — not to mention a threat to human safety. Keeping their numbers under control by whatever means (including shooting, snaring, leg-hold trapping, blasting them with shotguns from low-flying aircraft, and even gassing pups in their dens) is a commonsense necessity. Left to their own devices, wolves will multiply and hoover every moose and caribou out of the country. People come first, and Alaskans have a right and legal mandate to manage wildlife for their own maximum benefit. Any opposition to such a plan obviously comes from greenie-weenie, barely Alaskan, nonhunting city slickers and out-of-state, radical, pinhead lackeys of animal-rights groups.

Position B: Wolves, as top predators, are a natural part of healthy, complex, self-regulating ecosystems, and removing most of them (the plans call for 80, even 100 percent reduction in certain management units) is only bound to screw things up. Without wolves, deer and moose numbers explode in unsustainable numbers, then crash, over and over. Wolves, too, are a valued resource on which trappers and subsistence hunters depend, and a multimillion-dollar cash cow attracting throngs of ecotourists and photographers. Their presence also offers inestimable aesthetic value to many residents, even if they never manage to see one. Besides that, shooting wolves from airplanes is just plain wrong and reflects horribly on the state's image. Anyone who doesn't see things that way is a nearsighted, beetle-browed, knuckle-dragging redneck.

That's just the CliffsNotes summary. The unabridged version gets far nastier and multilayered, replete with biologists, managers, politicians, wildlife advocates, and hunters flinging mud balls made of statistics and rhetoric in each other's faces. Add in the extremists — oldschoolers who consider wolves four-legged cockroaches, and the animal-rights types who worship *Canis lupus* as imperiled überbeings — and you have the makings of a full-scale brouhaha that spills over state and even international boundaries. Wolves, by virtue of their innate canine charisma and endangered status through most of their former range, are a big deal. People far away care what happens here, a fact that rankles the many Alaskans who believe wolf control is no one's business but their own. Ex-governor Walter Hickel, decrying the interference of wolf advocates (many of them Outsiders) in the issue two decades ago, put it best, with this unintentionally comical, landmark statement: "You can't just let nature run wild."

Alaska's wolves are unique in at least one respect. At the dawn of the twenty-first century, they're still here, in meaningful (albeit human-reduced) numbers—statewide, somewhere between that seven and twelve thousand figure, according to state biologists. Thanks to the elusive, no-paparazzi nature of the species and the scale and roughness of the country, these are educated estimates at best, with a huge amount of slack built in. Some biologists figure it's more like seven thousand. But whatever the number, some folks—especially those associated with the big-dollar sport-hunting and guiding industry, who consider every hat rack–antlered moose a walking paycheck, and rural residents living in temporarily or perennially game-poor areas—think it's too many. No matter that many of the guides and rich sports who raise the most ruckus aren't even Alaska residents.

At least half of all Alaskans, whether rural or urban, native or white, bear no enmity against wolves; in fact, consider them an asset. However, those Alaskans who wield power most often, and seem to shout the loudest these days, fall into the good-wolf-is-a-dead-wolf camp. Federal exterminators conducted a no-holds-barred wolf eradication program in the territorial days of Alaska, with traps, aerial gunning, poison, and bounties. From statehood in 1959 through the 1990s, wolf-killing programs continued, but not without sometimes fierce debate and opposition. Two citizen ballot initiatives in the 1990s (my friend Joel Bennett led both) and three gubernatorial interventions brought temporary halts to the killing; but in 2003, wolf control programs resumed under newly elected governor Frank Murkowski and soon expanded to include aerial gunning by private pilot-hunter teams in areas the size of midwestern states. Southeast Alaska, where we lived, wasn't one of those enormous kill boxes—not yet.

Against the tableau of this history, I skied out from my house one day and found a huge black wolf almost in my backyard — an animal not only tolerant of humans and dogs, but almost (for lack of a better word) sociable. But odd and ominous as it all seemed, I had no way of knowing, over the ensuing months and years, just how strange the tale would turn.

Wolf kill, Brooks Range

RULES OF ENGAGEMENT

It's 1981, a mid-August evening on the spine of the Kobuk-Noatak divide, deep in the western Brooks Range: hard, wind-scraped country, gray-blue mountains and tundra valleys webbed with caribou trails, rolling away beneath a wide sky. A lean young man climbs into a sharp north breeze, a .35 caliber lever-action carbine slung over one shoulder, a second-rate film camera over the other. On a brush-verged bench on the mountain slope above him, a grizzly and a lone gray wolf skirmish in silver, slanted light — the wolf circling, dashing in to snap at the bear's rump, the bear whirling and swatting, its roars lost in the wind. The bear can't catch the wolf, and the wolf can't hurt the bear, and neither will back off. Maybe they're arguing over a kill, or the wolf might be defending a den or just deviling the bear on general principles.

He first spotted them with binoculars over a mile away, stripped off his pack, and ran toward them, across braided river channels and over cotton-grass tussocks, up the mountain through bands of frost-red dwarf birch and patches of loose shale. Sweat-drenched and shivering, he slowed as he closed the last two hundred yards through head-high willows, camera at the ready and a bullet in the chamber, though shooting wasn't his plan. He knew, too, the odds of getting a picture were thin. Neither was he answering a self-imposed dare. Of course he was afraid—alone, on the start of a solo 350-mile canoe trip, farther from another human than he'd ever been, and approaching not just a riled grizzly, but the first wolf he'd ever seen. If something went wrong, no one would miss him for weeks. He had no way of hailing the outside world, and only the bush pilot who dropped him off had any idea of where to find him. But still he moved uphill toward the bear and wolf, drawn by his heart.

I squint back through the weathered lens of three decades and smile as I watch myself scramble up that mountain, alive as I'd ever be. That one moment, reckless or not, was reason enough to have come to Alaska; I knew it then, and even more now. I'd read about and watched big carnivores in my sleep since I was a kid, growing up in a procession of landscapes where such creatures didn't exist outside zoos. Rural Maine, where I moved as a college student, learning and honing outdoor skills, still wasn't far enough. I'm going to Alaska, I told family and friends. And I headed straight toward one of the wildest chunks of country I could find on the map: the northwest Arctic, in the upper left-hand corner of the state, hundreds of miles off the road grid—a landscape defined by wolves and grizzlies, and all that came with them. There was no decision. I just went.

By the time I went loping up that hill, I'd lived in a remote Kobuk River Eskimo village for two years—still green around the edges, leaning on luck and youth to help balance out all I didn't know. Instead of going back to school as I'd intended, to become a wildlife biologist, I'd found work managing a trading post and packing for a big-game guide and had already traveled thousands of bush miles by snowmobile, skiff, and canoe and on foot. But this trip, going off by myself into deep wilderness to meet this country I'd come to love, was another step outward. The sheer aloneness of it all—not for a few days or miles, but many and far, through a landscape roamed by apex carnivores—changed the way you heard a twig crackle, appraised an eddying scent, caught the shine of something moving on a far ridge. Then, within minutes of being dropped off, the wolf and bear materialized out of the land, like a welcoming committee. Of course I ran toward them.

By the time I reached the bench where I thought I'd find the scuffle, they'd disappeared. I wasn't even sure it was the right spot. I'd underestimated the thickness of the brush, so dense I couldn't see more than a few yards. I stood, trying to hold down my breathing, straining the world through my senses. When I finally spotted the wolf, it had been watching me for some time. It stood fifty yards above me, perched on a rocky knob in its ragged late-summer coat. It lifted its muzzle and howled, less a challenge than a disgusted announcement that the klutz everyone had been smelling and hearing for the past half hour was right here. Then the wolf trotted away up the ridge, lean-ribbed and light-footed, without wasting another glance my way. I watched gray wolf merge into gray rock, then remembered: somewhere there was a pissed-off bear — maybe just beyond that alder clump. I hunkered against a rock, wide-eyed, cheap camera and peashooter rifle at the ready.

Meanwhile, the unseen grizzly had circled to get above me and downwind. When I first heard a low *wuff,* the bear was at my back, thirty feet away, sniffing the spot where I'd just stood. At my first motion, he raised his head and stared straight at me, barreled chest contracting with each huff. As I fumbled back and forth between camera and rifle, he snorted and crashed uphill and away, sparing me a decision, and perhaps a good deal more. I never did come close to getting a picture, but it doesn't matter. The moment where I met my dream is right where I can see it — now and always.

I went on from there to meet many more wolves and bears over the years, sometimes so close I could have glimpsed my reflection in their eyes, and stood wrapped in their wild scent. I lived among Inupiaq Eskimo subsistence hunters like Clarence Wood: men with frost-scarred faces, attuned to sensory nuances I could scarcely imagine, steeped in knowledge passed down across generations. They weren't just close to the natural world, they were part of it. I followed them when they allowed me, and learned what I could. I wanted to know how someone could glance at a wolf trail and declare, *Real fresh. Three of 'em. They eat good little while ago.* And more, I wanted to not only know, but feel the same seamless connection to the land, and to the animals they sought: to hunt and kill as a wolf does.

Though I scarcely came from a hunting background, my own culture's input hadn't really been that much different. The son of a career diplomat, raised in Europe, Southeast Asia, and Washington, D.C., I'd been glued to *Outdoor Life* magazine since I was eight, and graduated to the hunting tales of Ruark and Hemingway. It never occurred to me that there might be another way to relate to wild creatures besides killing them, and no one pointed me in another direction. Small surprise that my first job in Alaska was working for that hunting guide, learning the whole business from the ground up: how to find, stalk, shoot, skin, and butcher game animals, large and small. Though I soon enough discovered that guiding wasn't for me, I continued onward down my hunting path, with a developing skill set under my belt. Along the way, I picked what amounted to graduate-level seminars from the older Inupiaq men with whom I often traveled. While never an expert tracker or ace marksman, I had good eyes, strength, and persistence on my side, and always, it seemed, incredible luck whenever it came to killing. The carcasses and hides piled up over the years, more than I could count. Their flesh merged into my own. I wore and slept on their skins. Their bones and antlers decorated my cabin.

In time, Clarence became my hunting partner and close friend. Early on he told me that black wolves were different — smarter, tougher, harder to catch. And true or not, the first wolf I ever shot, nine years into my Alaska life, was black: a ninety-pound female, she and I each traveling alone on a cold, bright April afternoon in 1988, on the shoulder of Ingichuk Mountain. From the moment she fell, excitement and triumph mingled with a bitter undercurrent of self-recrimination. Back in the village, my Eskimo friends nodded quiet praise and corrected my skinning cuts. Part of the hide, tanned and sewed by *aana* (grandmother) Minnie Gray, became a parka ruff and trim that shielded my face from the Arctic cold. I gave Minnie the rest of that skin, that gift further cementing a traditional bond that had begun when I first brought her caribou meat and helped with chores. Though now a teacher at the village school, I had also become a hunter, sharing the lifestyle of the Iviisaapaatmiut—the People of the Redstone.

Minnie and Clarence both believed that animals give themselves willingly, and with the proper acts of propitiation, such as *nigiluk* (slitting the trachea to let the soul escape), are born again, in an endless cycling of souls. None of my neighbors understood my misgivings; the burden of killing what I loved—not once, but again and again—was one I would carry alone. I proved to be neither a good wolf nor a good adoptive Inupiaq—though Minnie called me "son," and introduced herself to my parents, when they came to visit, as my Eskimo mom.

But I kept going out, roaming the country on snowmobile and skis, by canoe and skiff, and on foot—tens of thousands of miles, sometimes in the company of others, often alone. Though I continued to hunt for most of what I ate and part of what I wore, more and more often I set my rifle aside and simply watched, or stalked wild creatures with a camera instead. One day I realized I couldn't remember the last time I'd fired a shot at a living thing. My time as a hunter was over. I gave away guns and hides; if I could have, I would have taken back most of my bullets. I kept a few tokens of that past life, including a row of skulls to remind me of who I'd been.

No accident, I suppose, that I ended up marrying Sherrie, bunny-hugging, card-carrying member of PETA. To give you an idea of her commitment to her beliefs, she'd dropped out of high school at age seventeen rather than dissect a pithed frog in biology class, and taken an equivalency exam instead. While I stopped far short of her eat-nothing-with-a-face ethos, I couldn't help but admire her unswerving dedication to principle; and besides that, I was smack-upside-the-head in love. I left my Arctic home and moved to the capital city of Juneau, where she worked and lived—a metropolis compared to the far country I'd roamed for two decades. With a sigh, she accepted my cooking the caribou meat my friends shipped south to me, and I her unyielding animal-rights polemics. We were united by our love of all life and the wild expanse of Alaska; now, all that seemed distilled into this flesh-and-blood wolf at our door. Though I couldn't rewrite my past, his very presence offered some sort of redemption.

So it was that our Mexican vacation took a slight curve north. Instead of sipping margaritas under a *palapa* and lounging on sun-bright sand, we spent the week after the winter solstice bundled in parkas and snow boots, shivering in the shadow of the Mendenhall Glacier. Days had waned to just a few hours of thin light. The mountains leaned in and waves of weather washed over us—deep, clear cold alternating with snow, sometimes hurling out of the twilit sky so fast we could watch it cover our tracks. At first, we skied; when the drifts piled too deep for touring skis, we plodded on foot, breaking trail with the dogs porpoising along behind us in powder over their heads. Higher up, the big snows fell. In between storms, the mountains emerged, cast in a luminous pall. The glacier itself seemed half-buried.

And the black wolf drifted in and out of view, a dark beacon of life in a still, white world. Though we'd changed plans on his account, we hardly changed our off-work routine, which included daily exercise with the dogs, usually straight out the back door, out onto the lake or adjoining trails. From the first, we decided to limit our contact—once, at most twice daily, and generally no more than a half hour at a time. After all, he had other business to attend to—not the least of which was making a living, a tough job for a single wolf. I couldn't imagine he saw us as anything more than a brief curiosity, and we wanted to keep it that way. But we did want to see this thing that would never pass before us again.

The wolf seemed to be waiting for us. When we headed out for the Big Rock, a half mile from our back door, he ghosted out of the brush, tail out and level with his back—a neutral, confident signal. As we moved up the west shore, he trotted parallel to our path, stopping where we stopped, moving when we moved. As long as we kept the dogs close, he didn't come within a hundred yards—a distance that worked for all three species. Wolves and dogs traded scent marks at a discreet distance with little eye contact, like Japanese businessmen exchanging cards. Who knew what each read of the other? We followed the curve of the sheltered bay along the lake's western shore, in the dark-curving shadow of Mount McGinnis—a less-traveled area, away from the eastern lobe of the lake with its web of trails. We tucked in behind Tern Island, just past the Big Rock, which offered a screen from most passers-by. To keep the dogs busy when we stopped, we played the game they loved best: fetch with flingers and tennis balls. Each dog had its own ball and understood taking turns. They were all so locked on to the chase that most of the time they forgot their people were watching a wolf, and a wolf was watching us back.

From the edge of the alders, the black wolf narrowed his ears and keened a piercing, fast-pulsed whine you could have mistaken for the call of some unknown bird. Dakotah perked her ears toward the dark stranger, whined back, and bounded in his direction, sometimes more than halfway; but when we called, she returned, and the wolf would follow only so far. Waving arms would bring on a startle reflex and turn him away. Fine. No matter what we'd seen, we didn't want to invite him closer. Chase informed the universe in no uncertain terms that her opinion of the marauder hadn't altered one damn bit, and wasn't about to. Gus let slip a quiet, worried mutter now and then but mostly ignored the dark shadow of his past, lurking in the brush.

When our friend Anita joined us with her two dogs, Sugar and Jonti, two more run-and-fetch maniacs, the group swelled to a crowd—three people, five barking dogs, madcap dashing around. My friend Joel tagged along a couple of times, lugging his big tripod and professional movie camera. We both knew what we had before us and, at the same time, were conscious of trying to do the right thing, the right way. No crowding or displacing. If he moved off, we'd let him go. If he came closer, we'd sit tight. The wolf would make the call.

The black wolf watched from the lake edge, seemingly puzzled but intrigued by this odd pack and its antics. When we moved farther out onto the lake, away where he wouldn't follow, and circled toward home, he trotted out behind us to sniff the dogs' scent marks and make his own replies — messages that would be read and under-stood by all who knew the world through their noses. Then he lifted his muzzle and howled to the sky, the long cry of a wolf alone.

Sometime early on, maybe the third time Sherrie and I and all three dogs went out, the balance of our understanding shifted. We'd moved in behind the island and brought out the flingers. The light was so crappy I hadn't even bothered to bring my camera pack. Sherrie was peering through the viewfinder of her camcorder, get-ting home-movie footage of the whole crazy scene — the wolf pacing back and forth along the shore, watching and whining as the dogs cut loose. A few minutes in, one of my tosses for Dakotah went awry, hit a patch of hardpack and kept rolling toward the shore. As we were wondering how to get the ball back, damned if the wolf didn't dart in, pounce, and make off with it. He pranced along the shore, tossed it in the air, batted it with his paws, and pounced again — movements any dog would understand, though the wolf added his own lupine accent. But he sure as hell knew about toys: objects with no food or direct survival value that become, through social agreement or indi-vidual whim, the focus of play.

Here was a chicken-or-egg conundrum. Was the wolf follow-ing the dogs' lead, or were our dogs engaged in a behavior inherited from their not-so-distant ancestors? After all, chasing and fetching rests just a shade away from predatory instinct, say, pursuing and catching a hare. Entirely logical to figure it's a game any wolf in the right mood would understand. Too, play makes total sense for com-plex social creatures like wolves, if viewed from a purely evolution-ary stance. Tussling, toy play, and chasing provide development of vital survival skills for young animals and help cement the social structure vital to a successful pack.

And what are dogs but our custom-tweaked, toned-down ver-sions of wolves, shaped through generations of breeding to suit our varying whims? One recent study shows a scant .02 percent differ-ence between the genetic packages of wolves and dogs. As recently as the 1990s, studies accepted by mainstream science, as well as the archaeological record, pointed to a divergence of the two species in

China or the Middle East as recently as 15,000 years ago. Since then, other studies and evidence (including a 35,000-year-old dog skull found buried in a Siberian cave along with human artifacts and a dog skeleton buried with a bone in its mouth) support canine divergence as a much earlier event, from 50,000 years to more than 125,000 years before present, and raise the strong likelihood of multiple points of domestication, spanning several continents.

Hard to imagine, but Dakotah herself was 99.98 percent wolf, including, you might suppose, the part of her that loved pursuing and catching things over and over at breakneck speed and delivering them back to her pack, in a faint echo of the chase. I've wondered if some dogs may feel a higher level of drive for such games, since it's their only outlet for genetically programmed catch-and-kill hunting behavior. A wolf in the same situation seems more relaxed, more purely at play—certainly the case with the black wolf just then, and with other wild wolves I've seen. After all, wolves hunt to live, on a daily basis; fooling around with a toy is more of a break, quite separate from the serious business of living—having fun for the sheer sake of it. To high-drive Labs and border collies, fetch is often more than just a game; it's their job, a dead serious business.

Granted, precious few wolves have regular access to tennis balls. But wolves of all ages, from captive to totally wild, do engage in play, together or alone, and often with objects that fit the definition of toys—an old antler, a ptarmigan wing, whatever suits the moment. I've been lucky to watch a few bouts of wolf play in the wild, but one stands out. About fifteen years ago, while on a solo late-winter trip into the upper Noatak valley, several wolves from a pack of twelve had approached my camp. I'd spooked two of them by trying to get a better camera angle when I should have held still. I was trudging back toward the tent, disgusted with myself, when I realized, with a start, that I had company. Half-hidden by a clump of brush, head up and relaxed, a reclining gray male stared off down the slope toward the others, pointedly ignoring my all-too-obvious presence, an underhanded stone's toss away. Finally he yawned, rose, stretched, and made casual eye contact as if to say he saw me, and couldn't possibly care. When I circled, trying to get around the brush between us, he moved off at a leisurely gait, no sign of stress.

Suddenly he stared, gathered, and pounced—on a ground squirrel or marmot, I was sure. I was witnessing my first-ever wolf making a kill! Instead, he came up with an ordinary hunk of scrub willow, two inches thick and a couple feet long—exactly the sort of stick any Lab might pick up and lug around. The wolf turned and gave me a sidelong glance, shaking his head and the stick with that familiar canine look-what-I've-got posture, an invitation to a round of keep-away. Then he paraded off down the slope like a drum major, the branch crosswise in his jaws. I sat there open-mouthed, the camera forgotten in my hands.

Toy-oriented play? No doubt of that, but something more. By virtue of my proximity (which, I think, triggered the event) and that sidelong glance, I'd been included in the game, if just for a moment—in play as a social gesture between species, like ravens and wolves playing tag. It was a foreshadowing moment that would be completed years later, in the form of the black wolf.

The tennis ball incident was far from the last time that wolf would cross into dog-human playtime—whether party crasher or welcome participant depended on perspective. Either way, he was just warming up. A few days later he snitched another ball from us that he carted off, and every now and then over the next months and years, stories would make the rounds involving the wolf, games of fetch, and episodes of toy-filching. His pattern of larceny proved what some had maintained all along: you just can't trust a wolf.

Whatever passed that day, we have a token to call us back. Years later, that yellow, fist-sized orb that the wolf stole and eventually dropped rests among Sherrie's keepsakes, bearing the puncture of a single tooth. Next to it, a tuft of Dakotah's tail hair, and a hand-sized paw print from the wolf, cast in plaster. We hold what little we have, as if it were enough.

As much as our vision of the wolf had altered, just a few minutes after the tennis ball incident it shifted once again, thanks to Chase, our then-yearling blue heeler. We had two mild-mannered, beautifully behaved Labs. Then there was Chase. Heelers (officially known as Australian cattle dogs, not to be confused with Australian shepherds) can be, well, problematic. Engineered from wild dingoes mixed with livestock dogs just a century ago and recognized by the AKC in the 1960s, they're a new breed, with plenty of variation. The most difficult examples wear their feral hearts on their sleeves without apology. No matter how close an average dog's genetic ties to wolves, heelers, by dint of their dingo heritage, and just a few generations separating them from life in the wild, take it to another level. The official breed description includes the phrase "a suspicious glint in the eye," and the AKC National Specialty show for Australian cattle dogs includes a contest in which dogs are judged for having the "most ancestral" physical traits—which leads to musings about inner, lupine remnants as well. Without doubt, many heelers are affable companions, and they're a wonderful, dynamic breed. But throw a few too many of those ancestral traits into the mix and you get a dog with issues.

Chase was one of those—a work in progress on a good day, a train wreck on the worst. We'd worked on her from when we'd gotten her at eight weeks. Though hideously bright, quick to learn tricks and all sorts of complex behaviors (how many dogs do you know who, when asked "Who's been good?" sit up on their haunches and raise a single paw, and on command, put their toys away one by one in a basket?), we hadn't yet been able to corral her borderline-psychotic tendency to rush unknown dogs with a reactive, teeth-bared charge. In her mind, I'm sure she was defending us from impending onslaught. Any canine, from a Boston terrier to a Great Dane, that came too close would get the same bum's rush. Chase, despite her blustery façade, usually ended up in abject retreat when the objects of her attack took exception—not that it stopped her the next time. Sure, she'd grow three-quarters out of it eventually, but keeping our miscreant teenage mutt leashed under those circumstances was a given. No self-respecting wolf could be expected to put up with her guff.

So there we were, minutes after the wolf's tennis ball grab—Sherrie still pointing her camcorder; me chucking balls for the Labs; the wolf trotting back and forth, watching and whining. I needed both hands for a moment and had Chase's leash end firmly under my boot — or so I thought. A sudden, unexpected tug and off she went, a snarling blur flying straight for the wolf like some thirty-pound hound of the Baskervilles, ignoring the fact she was outweighed four to one and outmatched by a factor of twenty. The wolf picked up the charge and came bounding to meet her full-on. I sprinted toward the impending collision, though I knew I couldn't get there in time. Through her viewfinder, Sherrie saw the outgoing dog and the incoming wolf, dropped the camera, and screamed for Chase. She might as well have asked a meteor to stop short of impact. The two met in an explosion of snow, the wolf wide-jawed, bounding, paws slamming down to pin our dog. In that heart-rattling instant, Chase completely disappeared under the wolf. He lowered his jaws. Just like that, our dog was gone. Dead. And I'd screwed up, in a way I could never forgive myself.

Then a blue-gray shape exploded out of the snow, headed back as fast as she'd gone in, yelping all the way. Lips pulled back in a grin any dog owner would recognize, the wolf bounded along behind her a few feet, then trailed back as Chase neared us, coated in loose snow. Though she was quivering, and her fur stiff with frozen saliva, we went over every inch and couldn't find the least ding or bruise. He could have crushed her throat with a single bite and carted her off for a snack, or administered a well-deserved disciplinary butt-whupping that would have put her in intensive care at the vet's. Instead, the black wolf, all soft paws and gums, had met force with the sort of good-humored forbearance an uncle wolf might show to pups of his own pack. Even Chase seemed to understand the break she'd been dealt. Not that she got much chance, but she didn't mess with the wolf again for years, though she continued to complain, on and off, from a safe distance.

Beyond instinctive twinges, none of us had known what to expect in those first encounters. Yet each side had put a foot forward, and a strange, almost eerie truce had passed between us. Though some arm-flappers might claim otherwise, the wolf was the one risking his life. If he could have sensed the skulls and hides of his kind that lay inside dozens of houses stretching before him — including mine, from that other life — he'd have run, tail out, for the horizon. Instead, here he was, tagging around, trying to chat up our dogs, and meanwhile radiating an incredibly laid-back, predictable demeanor toward us, the brokers of canine companionship. The word *polite* came to mind, as if he were a foreigner trying to figure out our rules of social engagement, and doing his best to avoid the least faux pas.

We kept doubling back, searching out some sort of explanation for his behavior. Was he a lamebrain, dropped on his head as a pup? An ambassador sent by the wolf nation to spy or negotiate? A shape-shifting alien? One-liners aside, we couldn't overlook a real possibility: he could be a captive wolf or part-wolf hybrid, grown into too much to handle and turned loose by his owner. While captive wolves do surely exist in Alaska, they're few in number and legal only with a difficult-to-obtain permit, issued only to a handful of wildlife parks. Wolf-dog hybrids are illegal in the state under any circumstance, subject to immediate confiscation. Either would be hard to hide in a town as small and close-knit as Juneau. Anyhow, he didn't act like a tame animal gone wild; if anything, it was the other way round. I'd seen plenty of captive wolves and several wolf hybrids, and even in their familiar enclosures, they tended toward high-strung skittishness. They just didn't act or move like the animal we saw before us — confident, at home in his world. A recently released wolf or wolf-dog cross, used to its confined routine and keepers, screened from the wild world since birth, would likely be a basket case. Then, a key point: this wolf wasn't approaching us as if expecting food, and seemed in fine condition out on his own. The most likely explanation was the simplest: Mother Nature loves to roll the dice, and out of the nearly infinite genetic combinations possible came this one-of-a-kind wolf — not the wolf we expected, maybe, but a wolf all the same. Biologist Dr. Vic Van Ballenberghe (whose studies over thirty-four years primarily as a moose biologist have of course included a great deal of overlapping wolf research and observation) observes, "All animals are individuals, with their own distinct personalities. . . .

The differences between wolves are especially striking. Some, re-gardless of how many times you encounter them, will keep their dis-tance. Others, from the same pack, are quite relaxed and tolerant from the start and remain so."

Ironically, it's just this kind of ultra-tolerant animal, the one that lay down at the edge of our firelight millennia ago, that's most likely to tweak human fear receptors. *Why isn't he afraid? He should be. If not, he's dangerous, just too close. Maybe he's got rabies. Look at the size of that damn thing. What's he thinking?* Wolves and people have never mixed well, except, paradoxically, when they have. It's a weird, dysfunctional union, considering that we invited the shadow of our fear into our homes and came to call it our best friend — all the while maintaining an ingrained, fearful distrust, sometimes verging on ha-tred, of its free-ranging forebear that lives beyond our will.

Whatever this wolf's story, and no matter how hard we tried to keep his presence under wraps, the news was bound to leak out. Ac-cording to Ben Franklin's adage, three can keep a secret if two are dead, and we were already way over the limit. Besides, we couldn't very well tell a wolf to stay in cover, not to leave tracks, not to howl — and the latter he did, sometimes for long minutes at a time, day or night. Like people, not all wolves belong on *American Idol.* Some yip or yodel, or just don't project. Predictable though it sounds, the voice sure as hell matched the wolf's physical presence: a drawn-out, sonorous note rising to a falsetto break, then trailing to hollow overtones, a cry as big and haunting as the country itself.

The Mendenhall Glacier Recreation Area was a daily destina-tion for several dozen local dog-walkers, hikers, and skiers; and, on weekends, its six-thousand-acre expanse was Juneau's favorite win-ter playground, attracting everyone from families pulling toddlers in sleds to technical ice climbers. Though it abutted near-vertical, trackless wilderness, the area's core was cut by a network of paths, ranging from meandering animal trails to wheelchair accessible to steep mountain routes to a groomed four-mile cross-country ski loop. On a mild, snow-bright Sunday, several hundred people over the course of the day might visit from any of more than a dozen access points. The combination of big snows and deeper-than-usual cold had temporarily blunted that tide, helped muffle the howling, and sifted over tracks, but we couldn't hope to keep a wolf secret, any more than kids in some fantasy could hide a unicorn in a closet. And even if we could have, he wasn't ours to hide.

The wolf did hold one card in his favor. Juneau is different from most Alaska cities, as most residents will tell you, with either an approving nod or a scowl. It's ranked as one of the greenest and most liberal-leaning towns in the entire state, the kind of place where Sarah Palin would get thumped if she ran for mayor (and where, even at the height of her statewide popularity, she lost the local gubernatorial vote). An amalgam of capital city, fishing port, and mining boomtown dating back to territorial days, Juneau seems infused by a freethinking, old-Alaska egalitarianism. It's the sort of place where people are used to ideas being hashed out in public without permanent offense being taken, and state commissioners shoot the breeze with third-generation commercial fishermen in line at the Super Bear grocery store. A deckhand for the Alaska State Ferry is as apt as a college professor to share similar environmentalist views on clearcut forestry, permits for a new gold mine, or a black wolf roaming the forested outskirts. Historically, a strong majority of Juneauites had supported management policies favoring wolves, and opposed state-sponsored predator control. The Capital City indeed may have been the only sizeable town in the entire state where a wolf might have been tolerated by enough people to afford him half a chance at survival. At ease as he was around humans, this wolf couldn't have lasted roaming the margins of the mall-spangled, helter-skelter sprawl of greater Los Anchorage, population three hundred thousand. How about Fairbanks, far to the north, way more frontier Alaska–feeling and a quarter the size? Fuggedaboudit. In fact, near most of the dozens of cities and villages scattered across the subcontinental vastness of the state, his survival would have been measured in heartbeats. Still, a solid 40-plus percent of Juneauites lean anywhere from right to hard right on the issue. Far as they were (and are) concerned, a wolf is at least a nuisance and unwanted competition for the deer, moose, and mountain goats they hunt for sport and food, if not a downright menace. So, even if a majority of residents who had an opinion saw this wolf as a good thing, or at least no cause for concern, there was a solid contingent that held opinions to the contrary.

On a clear January morning, Sherrie, the dogs, and I walked up the west shore, and instead of just us and the wolf, we found a cluster of bright parkas and cavorting dogs at the north end of the bay. And there was the wolf, not on the edge looking in, but mixing with the crowd. Anyone watching from a distance would have taken him for one of a gang of dogs playing. We leashed up and watched from seventy-five yards. The three women, all locals, shook their heads, grinned toward us and shrugged, flabbergasted. One pointed a pocket camera at the spectacle and snapped away, as if she were trying to prove to herself what she was seeing. The wolf had stepped out of the brush, one shouted, and before they even knew what it was, or there was any time to panic, everyone was wagging and chasing around. Dogs weren't listening and wouldn't come, but it all seemed fine, they said.

At least as far as canine body language went, the women were right. Though he towered over his ill-sorted counterparts, the black wolf projected all the ferocity of a pup. He whined, play-bowed, and let himself be chased, his own tail tucked low, exuding the gentle, exuberant goofiness of a yearling Lab merged into that Michelangelo-sculpted wolf body. When the women and dogs moved off down the lake, the wolf raised his tail in greeting to us, and trotted out, closer than he'd ever come. And though the fetch game went on with no ball-grabbing or dog-wolf contact — nothing as close as with the women who had just left, because we pushed back to maintain space — the wolf stopped twice as close as we were used to. Fifty yards, sometimes less than half that. If we waved our arms or took a few running steps in his direction, he'd turn and bound back a few paces, stop, and eventually drift closer. The whole scene was thrilling, of course, and great for photos (I finally got a few worth keeping), but worrisome. We weren't talking about the least flicker of aggression or discomfort—no hard stare, bristling, or lip-curling. But what if he crowded the wrong person, someone who couldn't read body language, had never met a wolf before, or took mere proximity as an excuse for self-defense, or launching a complaint to the U.S. Forest Service, or the Alaska Department of Fish and Game?

One morning before dawn, the wolf's tenor howls woke us in our bedroom, reverberating through foot-thick insulated walls and double-paned glass. We found tracks fifty yards from our back door, along the Forest Service campground road and nearby beach, by the public warm-up shelter called Skater's Cabin. In the cover of darkness, he seemed to be probing right to the edge of our neighborhood. Investigating? Hunting? True, snowshoe hares, beaver, mink, and other prey frequented the marshy ponds and second-growth woods nearby, but the howling seemed practically an announcement: *I'm here.* Whatever had prompted him, the wolf that had once held back to the lake fringes below Mount McGinnis had inched closer and showed less and less sign of leaving. Moving in was more like it—expanding the territory he'd claimed as a wolf, and exploring what it held. Whether we liked it or not, those rules of engagement were shifting beyond our control.

Waiting at our house

Spring 2004

3

ROMEO

Over the next few weeks, I skirted the edge of a waking dream. I'd look up from my first cup of coffee in the predawn light, and there the wolf would be, trotting across the frozen lake or curled on the ice, a dark speck of life that filled the land to overflowing and re-defined its very nature — as well as my own understanding of where I stood in the world, and of what might pass through it, if only I looked in the right direction. One thing to know there were wolves out there somewhere, roaming the country you called home; totally another to see one from where you ate and slept, the walls between you and the wild suddenly gone thin. Who the hell brushes his teeth while watching a wolf? More than once, I decided I must be imagining rather than seeing.

But sure enough, there was a wolf, right there and then, rather than the mere idea of wolves. And far more than the usual tokens of their passing — wind-blurred tracks, weathered bones, or a flicker of here-and-gone motion. I gazed full upon what photographer Edward Weston called "the thing itself." No wonder I spent ever more time staring out whatever window I passed, and even less wonder that I so often dropped whatever I was doing, threw on camera pack, binocu-lars, and ski gear, and was gone for hours at a time. Up to this point, almost all of my encounters with wildlife, from moose to wolverines, had been with strangers — unknown animals, a handful of which were temporarily willing to accept humans nearby. Often the truce lasted only seconds, as with a pine marten regarding me from a stream bank with relaxed, curious eyes; sometimes for hours, as when I lay on the fall-bright tundra of the upper Redstone valley, surrounded by dozens of bull caribou taking their afternoon siesta, those great-antlered heads nodding in and out, fully aware of my presence and accepting it without alarm. The world transforms itself in those moments, harks back to a past when we included ourselves in the natural world and it included us. We've long since morphed into an outlying presence that most wild creatures know as a high-level threat, either from experience or genetically programmed instinct. In rare instances, that perceived threat triggers a defensive-aggressive reaction; by far the most common response is avoidance, which may range from quiet, watchful retreat to outright panic.

Whatever the situation, and whether the connection was brief or prolonged, gradual or immediate, I'd never had the chance to get to know a large wild predator on a daily basis over a period of time — not as an anonymous organism, but an individual. Not only was I beginning to recognize specific traits and behaviors, but a distinctive, all-his-own personality; and I didn't know of anyone except a few full-time researchers who'd been dealt such a hand. Even so, biologists working with wild, free-ranging wolves conduct most of their studies from low-flying planes or at staked-out den sites, with the help of satellite or radio collars, inside a few parks and preserves or in ultra-remote areas, almost always with packs neutrally habituated (that is, nonreactive, neither afraid nor aggressive) to the scientists' presence. This was something else again. It wasn't Yellowstone or Denali National Park, not the remote Brooks Range, where I'd lived almost half my life, and not Banks Island in the high Canadian Arctic — all places where people go as I had, hoping to find wolves, often with scant success. Instead, the wolf had initiated the contact every bit as much as we had and had opened a door to another world. We hadn't dreamed of such a thing when we bought that lot overlooking the west shore of the lake in 1999, and I shoveled away wet spring snow and glacial till to pour the first concrete footings. I'd always reckoned that the best reason to build a house is a view, and we damn sure had one: full-on of the glacier rising above the lake, mountains forming a soaring, ragged frame — as it turned out, around a single, singular wolf. Just seeing him from my window had been almost reason enough to go through the ordeal of construction. Now we'd moved past that into some uncharted realm where we seemed to be as much the investigated as investigators, and what passed back and forth between us less observation than a wordless conversation between species. Without doubt, we each recognized the other, and were feeling our way forward over uncharted ground. The question was the shape of that relationship, and how far it would, or should, go.

Of course, the wolf had come to us, but that fact didn't eliminate responsibility. He was supposed to have gone weeks before — felt some distant urge, lost interest, drifted back to his world. Did he stay on because of us, or would he have chosen to stay regardless of what we did or didn't do? Could we, and should we, do what we could to send him away? Staying here, within our collective shadow, could well be a death sentence. Sherrie and I took a deep breath and acted. We ran at him, yelled, waved, and threw chunks of hard snow, which he dodged with easy grace. The next day, there he'd be again, as if nothing had ever changed. Perhaps if every person who had contact with the wolf had done the same, it might have driven him off; but in any case, the wolf showed no sign of leaving.

I found some comfort in this reflection: as far as practical matters went (and wild creatures tend toward the intensely practical, as a matter of survival), he wouldn't likely starve himself to socialize, especially with animals not his species; he must have found country to suit his needs and enough prey nearby to not just sustain himself, but make a good living. Hungry wolves, like all living things, can't afford the luxury of play, and, like humans in that same situation, do desperate things — eat dogs, who knows, maybe even attack someone. Instead, this animal appeared well fed, thick-coated, sociable, and relaxed as a wolf could be. But neither his ability to survive nor his desire to interact with dogs was less an issue than where he'd chosen to do it.

Without doubt, the wolf had become more bold and visible. He soon adopted the early-morning habit of curling up on the ice, a few hundred yards out from the Big Rock, less than a half mile from our door — a perfect, central vantage point for watching all comings and goings. Dogs and skiers appeared from parking lots and trails radiating out from that end of the lake, a steady trickle or flow of people, depending on the day, doing what they'd always done in the recreation area: play hockey in front of Skater's Cabin with the kids, train for a cross-country ski race, hook up for a dog walk with a friend. But now things had changed. There was a wolf — sometimes unseen, or a distant shape, but at other times, a huge, wild presence folks couldn't ignore, trotting out to exchange pleasantries with the family pooch. Though so far there hadn't been a whisper of trouble, it could change in the blink of a raven's eye.

When a picture of the black wolf was splashed across the front page of the *Juneau Empire,* the jig was officially up. With the flick of a camera shutter and the thunk of a printing press, whispered secret and rumor morphed into a howling, breathing, flesh-and-blood reality. The glacier wolf, as some called him, suddenly swirled into a citywide topic of conversation in checkout lines at the Super Bear grocery, the Alaskan Bar, and Thunder Mountain Café: *Yep, a wolf . . . big black one . . . out on the lake . . . went out there and saw it myself. . . . What's with that? . . . I dunno, but he sure is a big bastard.*

Now that the cover was officially blown, people started talking. We discovered we'd scarcely been so singularly sneaky; a few others had been biting their tongues just as we had, imagining themselves as guardians of their own secret wolf. He'd actually been around on and off for at least six months, a fleeting vision to most, and an increasingly regular sight to a few. A patient of Sherrie's said he'd seen a black wolf on the Dredge Lakes trails that previous late spring, trailing him and his dog. A wolf had been spotted that fall crossing the nearby shooting range, of all places, and along Montana Creek Road, a mile or two as the wolf trots from our house. Fellow Juneau writer Lynn Schooler had watched him along the lakeshore in mid-November, a couple of weeks before our first sighting. A guy I met skiing told me the wolf often had shadowed him and his two Labs on their early-morning walks. Then there was that woman down the street who had watched a dark, large husky-shepherd mix of some sort cross her yard—now she realized, not a dog at all. And we already knew of at least two other contacts besides ourselves. The stories continued to pile up, and for every one we heard, there must have been dozens more.

Strangely, that first public knowledge of a wolf in our midst scarcely seemed to alter the lake scene. Most Juneauites took his presence right in stride. This was Alaska, after all. If they saw a wolf, fine, and it became part of the outing, not a reason for coming or staying away, but an added bonus. Some people didn't bother to look and didn't care much if there was a wolf or not, as long as it didn't affect them. Others, thrilled by the rare chance they saw, embraced it and became black wolf junkies—a steadily growing, ad hoc club whose members came in all ages, shapes, and sizes. A few of those qualified as outright worshipers, holding a crown of perfection above the wolf's unsuspecting head. Others, including biologists, naturalists, hunters and trappers, professional and amateur photographers, and a wide net of citizens ranging from state legislators to store clerks to college students and mechanics, came with their own hopes to see or hear their first live wolf up close, and maybe collect a few pictures or some video footage. Overall, though, the recreation area was big enough to absorb both viewers and wolf, with room to spare. Yet another crowd perceived quite another wolf, and the first grumbles emerged: *A wolf hanging around, so near to houses, kids, and dogs? You know damn well he's up to no good. Dammit, something needs to be done.* And what that something might be was a topic of ongoing discussion, both in public and private.

Rounding out the cast of human participants at this point were the chronically oblivious. Years after the black wolf first appeared, after all the word of mouth and news features in the *Empire* and on KTOO radio, all the public hand-wringing and debate, I'd still occasionally meet local hobbits who professed their astonishment at seeing a black wolf on the lake, of all places. But people of all camps came to the lake all the same, saw or didn't see, heard or didn't hear, cared or didn't, and word percolated outward through the community, slowly but steadily driving up the number of people who decided to swing by Mendenhall Lake on a given afternoon, especially if the sun was out, trails were set, and the snow firm. The palette of reactions that would swirl around Romeo his whole life was already mixing — complex and contradictory shades, often too blurred to sort, or even name. Love and fear are, after all, closer than we think; and I felt the stirrings of both, tangled in my chest, as I worried for his safety. I imagined old Clarence Wood shaking his head at me: his traveling partner, with whom he'd hunted wolves for years, now fretting over one. I could almost hear his breathy, low voice, close to my ear: *Real nice skin. You could get 'im just like that.* And I knew there were others out there who would think the same.

Unconcerned, the black wolf trotted through whatever spaces we left vacant, off on an endless stream of lupine errands ranging from an ever-expanding agenda of dog greetings at one trailhead or another to hunting forays to naps in favorite spots to howling sessions in natural amphitheaters of his choosing, back and forth on the ice and up into the snow-drifted slopes rising above, the miles evaporating beneath those great, loose-wristed paws. His tracks led not only down well-traveled paths, but into frozen beaver swamps and alder-choked esker gullies, up dense-timbered slopes, places nobody would think of going — unless maybe following a fresh wolf trail, which is what I found myself doing with some regularity. I followed his signs stale and fresh through the willows, examined the spots where he'd bedded down, poked apart his scats, and spent long hours watching, sometimes with a wolf in sight, often not.

Decades ago, Nelson Greist, an old Inupiaq trapper who'd been raised living in caribou skin tents and hunting ptarmigan with bow and arrow, had told me that wolves in their territory are regular in their rounds and favored spots, following routes so precisely that you could sometimes predict within inches where they'd step each time they passed certain choke points—ideal spots for a trap or snare. "Follow them trail." Nelson nodded. "Then you gonna find out something." My own experience up north had long ago confirmed Nelson's rule. For example, one pair of wolves I knew by their trails but never glimpsed used to cross a certain gulley in the Mulgrave Hills north of Noatak village in the winters of 1982 to 1984 at exactly the same spot, at roughly two-week intervals. Another single animal, known to me only by tracks and scent posts (regular spots for urination), patrolled near the village of Ambler for an entire spring, and either it or a wolf with the same mental map returned the next couple of years, again in March and April, its trails intersecting my ski route at the same places every week or so.

Increasingly, the black wolf was fitting into just such a homebody pattern, though in a minuscule range—much smaller than I'd ever known or heard of. It centered on Mendenhall Lake's western shore, ranging up the slopes of Mount McGinnis, and its outskirts extended a mile or so north up the Montana Creek valley. The core area spanned eastward across Dredge Lakes, with its labyrinth of human and animal trails winding through beaver swamps and reclaimed gravel pit ponds, and along the abrupt slopes of Bullard Mountain and the three-thousand-foot ridge called Thunder Mountain (named for the rumble of winter avalanches down its furrowed north face). At the southwest corner of Dredge Lakes, just across the Mendenhall River, lay another patch of marshy young woods interlaced with Forest Service campground lanes and paths. And just beyond that lay the first line of houses, ours among them, bordering on the campground or the upper Mendenhall River. Draining the lake, cutting down through the heart of the valley, the cold, graygreen rush of the Mendenhall and the bordering Dredge Lakes and Brotherhood Bridge parklands offered a wooded corridor extending seaward through development—a grid of neighborhoods, schools, churches, business parks and malls, and finally, an industrial zone near the Juneau airport, bordering a rich tidal wetland. All in all, the wolf's core winter territory in those days totaled seven square miles or so. Hundreds, even thousands, would have been more usual.

Though such an area may seem vast from a human perspective, hardly so for a wolf. Then again, this was a single animal, not a pack, and newly moved in, so maybe limited territory made sense. Within it, his comings and goings were indeed predictable, with exceptions defining the rule. Now and then he'd disappear for a day, or several. Just when we thought he'd moved on, there he'd be, back in his same hangouts. He seemed less and less likely to hold near cover, with an escape route behind him, the way a transient wolf might do.

A wolf in new country had better be cautious. One of the leading causes of death in wild wolves is what biologists call interpack strife — a wolf being killed by wolves of another family group, on whose marked territory the outsider has trespassed. Think of the lens through which the black wolf must have seen us: an enormous, strange pack on whose ground he was encroaching, on penalty of death. By any measuring stick, ours or his, his behavior scored bold. On the other hand, single dispersing animals, if not killed or driven off, do sometimes become satellite wolves, living on the edge of a pack, scavenging not only its kills, but perhaps an aura of belonging. Or, over a period of time, a satellite wolf may gain the opportunity to sneak in and mate, or become a member of the group outright. Or perhaps the outlier entices a ready-to-disperse wolf of the opposite sex to go off to start their own pack. Bold behavior in new territory is thus biologically rewarded often enough that the trait carries forward. Exactly how each situation works out boils down to a matter of personalities, timing, and circumstance — nature again, rolling those dice. Maybe, in some strange, scrambled, or stylized way, that's what was playing out here, as it had thousands of years before, at the edge of that ancient fire: our future ally, waiting to be invited forward.

If I took dogs with me, it was usually just one — sometimes tomboy-tough, ladylike Dakotah, sometimes gentle Gus. Regardless that we'd been somewhat reassured by the wolf's forbearance with our youngest, Chase had richly earned a place on the end of a leash. I began to go out of my way to find wolf-less stretches for exercise with all three dogs, separate from my own outings. I didn't have any doubt that taking all the dogs along increased my odds of a close pass with the wolf; the more hoopla, the better he seemed to like it. I hoped, though, for more than a photo op in the midst of a bunch of gallivanting canines. Mesmerizing as it was, I wanted to know about this wolf beyond that strange scene, and know him as well. Besides, the idea of using dogs as a lure seemed somehow wrong, even if it might prove harmless with some dogs and owners; others might not be the same, and I didn't want to set an example for others to follow. A single dog, kept close, seemed a good compromise for a gradual weaning away from canine intermediaries; and, as time passed, I'd often choose to go solo to seek the wolf, on skis or foot. As it was, time alone with the wolf was already more difficult to come by.

Whether we wanted her to be or not, Dakotah was a born wolf magnet, and we could scarcely keep the two apart. From the standpoint of human aesthetics, she just plain glowed, flat-out gorgeous: deep chest, slim waist, and sculpted muscle topped off by a velvet-soft coat and thick otter tail. Her delicately dished face bore natural black eyeliner around soft brown eyes. Of course, we all think our dogs are perfect and beautiful, but to prove we weren't totally love-blind, 'Kota had been chosen from a casting call for a modeling stint on an Eddie Bauer catalog shoot in Juneau a few years before, where she got paid in treats and hugs to cavort at the glacier with equally perfect humans, and we got passed a check besides.

Beautiful as she was to us, a biological attraction didn't make much sense. Dakotah had been neutered young and was almost age nine by the time of her first encounter, hardly pumping out the come-hither pheromones on which canine mating ardor hinges. No matter how close the genetic match, she stood a species apart, her resemblance to the lupine form general at best, and a third smaller than an average female wolf. Meanwhile, there were plenty of younger wolf-ish husky mixes, some hunky shepherd types, and a scattering of Malamutes available that you'd think would have been far more alluring to a wolf.

But as inexplicable as it was, the connection between the black wolf and our dog was instant—one of a series of overlapping friendships, verging on romantic interest, that the wolf would carry on with a dozen or more canines over the years. Whatever he was or wasn't, his behavior echoed that dated meaning of the word *wolf,* stopping short of that leering, cartoon whistle.

If the black wolf caught sight of Dakotah, even at a distance, he'd bound over and commence to make a damn fool of himself—whining, pacing, and striking come-hither boy dog poses, standing tall, narrow-eared, tail up and tip waving gently. And from a distance that varied, according to the wolf's mood and the day, Dakotah would reciprocate with rapid wags, flirty play bows, and whines of her own. If we let her go, the two would bounce and prance around like hormone-addled twelve-year-olds at a junior high dance. Like chaperoning parents riding herd on hot blood, we'd call 'Kota back after a brief, occasional visit, which we allowed only with much reluctance and discussion, having given in to pathetic pleas on both sides. Afterward, the wolf would often pace behind us on our way home, gradually fall back, and stand alone on the ice, howling to the sky.

There are few sounds more naturally mournful than a wolf's cry, but the black wolf's howls at those times seemed to carry an undercurrent of utter desolation. Sometimes he seemed so desperate that he didn't stop as usual and followed us all the way home, loping ahead and angling to drive us back away from the house. Of course, the wolf recognized both us and our dogs; but now, for better or worse, he surely knew our strange, towering, wooden den as well. Sherrie said it broke her heart to shut the door with him whining and pacing at the edge of the yard. I'm sure if she'd had her way in some imaginary peaceable kingdom, she'd have coaxed him in, given him a bath and some ear rubs, and let him sleep at the foot of our bed, along with the rest of our little pack. And the way he paced and whined, seemingly pining for companionship, gave you the idea he just might go for it.

Of course, not everyone shared my wife's big-good-wolf outlook. One crusty old-timer I met one snowy day squinted at Romeo out on the ice, looked down at his spaniel, spat, and said, "Hell, I trust any wolf about as far as I can throw him," and went the other way. A woman stopped our friend Anita, coming in off the ice, and inquired whether she'd seen "that rogue wolf," in a tone that suggested it had been snatching children. Small doubt that a groundswell of pushback was building.

One morning, Sherrie pulled up the bedroom blinds, and there lay the wolf out on the ice, alone in the gray dawn, staring toward the house. *Well, there's that Romeo wolf again,* she murmured. And though at first she didn't intend it as a name, it fell into private usage and stuck because it fit. After all, she said, we knew him well enough and long enough that we needed to call him something besides "the wolf." She repeated our personal tag among co-workers and patients at the dental office, and it spread, then went viral — at least, in the pre-social-media, Juneau sense of the term.

Instead of a love steeped in destiny, it came to this: Sherrie and I dragging Dakotah, moaning and straining at the end of her leash in the half dark, the wolf pacing along parallel to us, fading in and out of the trees all the way back to the yard, and me hurling snow-balls to send him away from us. I wish we could have explained why to him. All the more heartache, when care wears the mask of cru-elty. With wolf-grumbling neighbors around the corner, and some cars hitting fifty-plus down Skater's Cabin Road, we couldn't allow him to remain, nor choose the boundary where he'd turn back. We'd steeled ourselves and made the only choice we could: keep the two apart. For that matter, Sherrie pointed out, maybe we should stop going out ourselves, or at least draw back. Just because the wolf put up with us, and this growing influx of people and dogs, didn't make it right. We debated the point over and over and reduced our forays still more, as others pushed forward to take our place.

For all his seemingly amorous advances, the black wolf never at-tempted the least hanky-panky of *that* nature with any of the hun-dreds of dogs I saw him interacting with, though he was a big male with (you'd suspect) the usual urges, and he must have met at least a few receptive females in season. Nor did I ever hear one report of randy behavior, even when some misguided woman that first sea-son brought her in-heat husky out on the ice, hoping for a union and a batch of hybrid pups. Over the years, that was always one of

the big puzzlers—no romantic overtures out on the lake, no sniffing and end-licking, and seldom any mounting, not even as a play
or dominance posture—though rude dogs attempted the latter on
occasion, yet remained unchallenged. True, wolf mating season is
just once a year, a brief window from late winter into early spring,
but male wolves and wolf hybrids are known to respond year-round
to dogs in heat. Not this guy, though his intact equipment was obvious (though far less visible than a dog's due to the wolf's dense,
multilayered coat). Whatever the reason for that suppressed mating
drive—it may have been an instinctive or hormonally triggered response as an outsider, trying to fit within the framework of a pack
that generally has just one litter a year, born to a ranking pair—it reduced one source of possible tension over the years. A good thing, in
a situation loaded enough as it was.

THE ORIGINAL MACHINE

March 2004

I skied north toward the glacier in slanted, late-afternoon light — my second five-mile loop of the day. Earlier, I'd run the dogs in the temporarily wolf-less campground, and I was on a lone speed run — as good an excuse as any to see how things were going out beyond the point. Up ahead about a mile, I spotted an already-too-familiar scene on the ice: people standing on their skis, watching as dogs raced back and forth, with the wolf alternately standing back or interacting. As I drew closer, I recognized some dogs and owners as part of a regular crew, with maybe a newbie or two mixed in. Other folks and dogs, one here, two there, far across the lake, were converging on the same spot. I'd seen my share of wolf parties by then and knew this one would probably last anywhere from a few minutes to a half hour. That's how things were going those mid-March days of 2004, just four months since we'd first met the wolf.

Romeo the wolf had progressed from fresh news to full-blown celebrity status, and we had a ringside seat as lengthening days and a stretch of postcard weather lured Juneauites to the glacier area in force. The mountains glistened white against a deep, cirrus-flecked sky; miles of ski tracks and walking trails beckoned. And there waited the black wolf, like a computer-generated effect. Surely we'd blink, and the image would shimmer and fade. But the wolf was real as the steam of his breath and his palm-sized prints etched into the snow, alive as the strange amber fire in his eyes.

He lingered in any of several locations — the Big Rock, of course, plus back toward the West Glacier Trail parking lot and several spots to the east, from the river mouth along the Dredge Lakes shore. Each place served as the sort of rendezvous area any pack might recognize, encompassing wolf-friendly features: vantage points, both visual and olfactory; access to a web of known trails; handy escape routes into dense cover; good hunting grounds and travel routes nearby. These were the arenas he had chosen as places to meet our dogs and, by default, us. Though we might have understood those same areas as *our* territory — we'd built or shaped them and made our marks on the surrounding land — they'd become the wolf's as well, defined by scents we couldn't detect, and howls with meanings we could only guess. Ready or not, the totally improbable scenario of on-demand, all-access, and even drive-up, from-the-parking-lot wolf viewing had arrived in the Capital City. Tagging along with the package came the reality-show recipe: throw a big, black wolf and a city of thirty thousand into the same pot, stir, and step back.

A growing stream of watchers and gawkers added to the usual bunch of glacier area users. Families and groups of teenagers wandered out on the lake, throwing back their heads and howling in response to Romeo's calls; furtive individuals prowled along the lake edge at odd hours, up to who knew what. Word was already spreading that all you needed was the right dog to bring the wolf up close, and the whole thing was way cool and no worries, just one big Alaska amusement park ride. Even people with zero experience around large wildlife and close to zero control of their dogs felt free to spin the wheel and see what happened. Some have-nots borrowed dogs or drafted along behind others, looking for an in, adding to the procession. There's something sexy about getting tight with big, wild carnivorous things, and that aura sucked in all kinds of people and rendered addlepated a few who should have known better. I couldn't blame them, even if I wished they'd stay home. And how was I any different, really? Around the vast majority of people, the black wolf remained aloof; though he watched from the lake's edge, he'd vanish into the brush if they pressed any closer than a hundred yards — still, an incredibly tight distance by most wolf-viewing standards.

As is so often the case, familiarity inevitably led toward contempt among certain locals. While plenty of people kept their dogs leashed or under voice command, others didn't see the harm in letting canines of varying size, shape, and temperament do whatever with the wolf: bark at it, play with it, chase it. More than a few individuals actively encouraged their pets, even fearful or snarky ones, to approach Romeo, hoping to get a paw-around-the-shoulder cameo with their dog and that dark, handsome stranger. And hey, why not line up the kids, strike a pose, and get a family picture with the wolf in the frame for next year's Christmas card? Though it might sound loony, I watched folks staging just that sort of thing with young kids by the end of that first winter, and time and again over the years. More than once when I was out monitoring the action, someone shoved a point-and-shoot my way, asking if I'd mind taking a group snapshot with the wolf in the background. Considering many, if not most, people didn't have a clue regarding wolf behavior or how to act, everything was up to the wolf — who'd take the hard fall if something went wrong. The possibility of a defensive-aggressive response to a human or dog couldn't be dismissed, especially given some of the crazy in-your-face stuff a few people were pulling: pushing ever closer, sometimes surrounding him, making sudden movements, sometimes pursuing him into the alders. Even a sociable wolf had his limits.

Meanwhile, more serious photographers in steadily increasing numbers added to the mix, lugging their gear around the lake as they angled for that elusive image of a lifetime. One local pro in particular, a talented and well-regarded nature photographer named John Hyde, began showing up on an almost daily basis and soon became a fixture at the lake. He, like I, recognized the magnitude of the opportunity and was obviously more willing to push the envelope to get his shots. While I sometimes ground my teeth, I resisted the urge to tell him his business. One thing was for sure: if Romeo had set up a photo booth and charged fifty bucks a pose, he could have made a different sort of killing than most folks might envision when they heard the word *wolf.*

Inevitably, the black wolf had created a splash point and a concentric set of ripples tough to ignore for the agencies responsible for overseeing the land and both the safety and conduct of the general public. The Mendenhall Glacier Recreation Area comprises a sliver of the gargantuan Tongass National Forest (at 17 million acres, the largest of its kind in the country, and one of the largest such areas in the world); thus the Forest Service assumes responsibility for managing the land itself and the behavior of human users. Though the federal agency reserves most supervisory and enforcement rights for itself, overlapping the state's enforcement in a manner best defined by some fuzzy-edged Venn diagram, it generally defers on wildlife management issues (for example, a certain overfriendly wolf) to the Alaska Department of Fish and Game. As far as ownership went, most of the land the animal roamed belonged to the federal government; the wolf himself, to the state of Alaska; the laws governing his management, to both entities. However, in the course of a day's wandering, Romeo might start off on federal property, stray into private holdings, trot across ground belonging to the city, amble onto a snippet of purely state-owned land, and finally return to the glacier—each an area with its own set of rules, regulations, and issues. Matters of management, public safety, and enforcement might involve the Alaska Department of Fish and Game, the Alaska State Wildlife Troopers, the U.S. Fish and Wildlife Service, the U.S. Forest Service, and maybe even the Juneau Police, all depending on what might happen and where. Despite that jurisdictional tangle, and the emotion-laden issue at hand, the action taken by all agencies regarding the black wolf that first winter can best be summed up in a single word: nothing—in the active sense of that word.

Though the wolf was a blip on the official radar, his own behavior set the tone. What the hell to do about a sociable wolf—not a momentary, but an ongoing and regular phenomenon? No one had ever heard of such a thing. Though he cast a large, dark shadow, and a few folks might wax indignant or get worked up by the sight of him so close to little Muffin or the kids, so far, he hadn't actually caused any more trouble than any mink or mountain goat, and far less than your average dumpster-diving bear. The Department of Fish and Game posted an advisory letter or two in the *Juneau Empire*, cautioning residents to keep their distance, obey common sense, and keep dogs under control; besides human and canine safety, there was the possibility of the wolf contracting canine diseases or parasites and transferring them into the wild population—people a danger to wolves, not the other way round. A few private citizens chipped in letters to the paper echoing their own concern or indignation at overfamiliar interspecies behavior. The message rang clear: people and wolves just shouldn't mix, period.

If the wolf or dogs or anyone else read the *Empire*, they showed no sign. And given the whole scenario—the size of the area; its numerous access points; the wolf's drive to pal up with canines; the number of people involved; and a growing willingness on the wolf's part to tolerate humans, coupled with the magnetic fascination so many felt for him—there was little that could have been done to shut down the contact, short of closing the whole recreation area. Close encounters were inevitable and an almost daily occurrence. "We were in uncharted territory," said Pete Griffin, who at the time held the supervisory post of district ranger for the Forest Service. "We chose to take no action because we had no cause. . . . It was a wolf in a national forest, in Alaska, which seemed appropriate enough." He squinted thoughtfully, then grinned. "Actually, I thought having him around was pretty cool. People, not the wolf, were the real management issue, and for the most part, they acted in a respectful and responsible manner." Notwithstanding a few glaring exceptions and countless minor bobbles, his point stood. So far, everything was working out better than anyone had a right to hope.

Naturally, no one consulted the wolf to see what he thought about the entire arrangement, most of all the stream of jabbering, alien beings that came and went in shining boxes, inexplicably proffering, whisking away, and ushering back playmates and potential pack members. On the other hand, his behavior explained his priorities as clearly as if he'd posted a manifesto on the Big Rock. Meeting dogs was job one; if hunting had mattered more, or the company of other wolves, or eluding people, he'd have been someplace else. That focused social drive ruled his behavior, though its presence indicated, at the same time, that his basic survival needs were being met. As always, he could disappear on a whim into places no one could follow, and either return on his own terms or keep on going. The wolf, though, continued to show little inclination to go much of anywhere, at least not in the far-ranging wolf sense of the word.

On a typical winter day, he'd be in position before first light to meet the prework and early-morning dog-walking crowd, as if he'd punched a time clock; of course, he preferred his favorites, but in a pinch, others would do. By late morning came a usual lull, when he stepped back for a nap, with a good watching point nearby. Depending on the day, he might or might not appear again to the general public until midafternoon or even dusk—just in time for the after-work rush. Since bad weather generally reduced the amount of human and dog traffic, going out in less than ideal conditions, better yet in the murk of predawn or evening, made sense. Like most wolves, Romeo was apt to be most active at the edges of light, though he might hunt, sleep, or travel at any time, if the situation beckoned.

A scattering of hardy locals figured any inconveniences a bargain. One rangy, hawk-nosed guy with a long stride and a big black Lab mix took it to a whole other level. I sometimes spotted him from the house, on his way in off the ice at first light, having been out wandering Dredge Lakes with the wolf in the dark for who knew how long, often in weather that kept everyone else home. I couldn't help admiring his tenacity but felt dark, possessive stirrings: *Where did he get off? Who the hell was he?* Though I didn't even know his name back then and wouldn't meet him face to face for several years, despite speaking on the phone and often passing within several hundred yards of each other without so much as an offhand wave, Harry Robinson and I were destined to become allies from afar and friends later, drawn together by our shared bond to the wolf. Years later, I heard his full story.

Harry and Brittain first met the black wolf about the same time we had. They encountered him not at the glacier, but three miles down the Mendenhall valley, on the less-traveled, hillside branch of the Brotherhood Bridge Trail. The trail system led through a wooded preserve along the seaward course of the Mendenhall River, set aside by the city of Juneau in the late 1980s when helter-skelter development seemed poised to gobble the entire valley floor. Bordered by neighborhoods and businesses, Brotherhood serves both as a popular recreation area and part of that central wildlife corridor linking glacier to tidewater. Harry had been taking Brittain there before work in the early-morning winter darkness, and he recalls the dog had sometimes strayed into the hillside forest above the trail and returned when he called her — though she still seemed intent on something unseen, above in the trees. Then, dog-walking with a friend, Harry encountered hand-sized paw prints in fresh falling snow, with no accompanying human tracks. Some huge, loose dog, the two men figured, as their own ranged ahead. Around the next bend in the trail lay a small meadow, and there they found their pets, playing with the maker of those tracks — not a dog after all.

"He was gangly," said Harry, "but just enormous, and he had this luxuriant silky coat, like he'd just come from a grooming salon." Brittain and the wolf seemed so relaxed and familiar around each other that Harry guessed they had probably been meeting those times she'd disappeared. "They were touching noses and rubbing against each other, like old buddies," he recalls. "He wasn't nearly as interested in my friend's dog. . . . At one point, he was standing next to Brittain and leaped right over her back, sideways. It was all pretty amazing." The two men stood mesmerized in the gray light and sifting snow, uncertain what to do and concerned for the safety of their animals. Like all of us in those early days, they were figuring things out on the fly. Finally, they called the dogs back and leashed them, at which point the wolf raised his muzzle skyward and began to howl nonstop. Not sure what that might signify—agitation building toward aggression, or who knew what—the two men retreated.

Just as I'd been, Harry was hooked at first sight. He'd been raised in a family steeped in the outdoors. From early on, his father (a nomadic jack-of-all-trades, once a hunting guide) taught him tracking, survival, and shooting skills. As a four-year-old, Harry had befriended an orphan mountain lion cub his family had taken in, and his fascination with wild country and animals of all kinds continued into adulthood. He picked up a geology degree at the University of Washington and became a part-time wilderness guide for REI in Seattle, leading trips to forgotten mines in the central Cascade Range. He also explored remote, off-trail areas on his own, where several times he caught fleeting glimpses of wild wolves (where officially there were none). He volunteered at Seattle's Woodland Park Zoo and wangled his way into spending time with the zoo's wolf pups, with whom he struck up a special bond.

In 1996, Harry moved to Juneau, following a job offer, the call of adventure, and the added cachet of romance with a longtime girlfriend who'd come north ahead of him. Though the relationship eventually faded, he stayed and settled in, picking up where he'd left off Outside (as the lower 48 is called by Alaskans)—taking long hikes in the surrounding mountains, many of those walks alone and off-trail. After he adopted Brittain at the local Humane Society, she became his constant companion—and, as events unfolded, his emissary to the heart of the wild.

He met the wolf before full light most mornings, not only at Brotherhood, but on the north end of the Mendenhall Wetlands Wildlife Refuge, an expanse of ecologically rich tidal marsh dotted with islands of trees, adjacent to residential neighborhoods, a checkerboard industrial zone, and the airport. It hardly seemed wild country in the Alaska sense of the word, except that now the icon of wilderness patrolled its area, redefining it by his presence. Harry and Brittain sought the wolf at least as much as it sought them, and they found each other on an ever-increasing basis. Though a spayed female herself (there seemed to be some sort of pattern, though with frequent exceptions), Brittain was large-bodied and tall, better matched than most dogs to the wolf in weight, though hardly in power or grace, where no dog could keep up. The two seemed to perfectly understand each other, and the wolf allowed the dog to play-bite, shoulder-slam, and generally bullyrag him. While accepting faux insults on end, Romeo offered none in return—another expression of the good-natured forbearance that seemed ingrained in his being. Harry, meanwhile, harbored no illusion that the wolf had any attraction toward him; he acted in the interest of the two canines, who seemed equally attracted to each other, as he himself was increasingly attracted to the wolf. Whether he admitted it to himself or not, Brittain's role in the relationship was gradually shifting from intermediary toward avatar. Standing by as a neutral presence that posed no barrier and remained predictably calm, Harry was included ever closer, and accepted within their circle.

Within a few weeks of the first encounter, Harry, Brittain, and the wolf shifted their meeting grounds out toward the glacier, which by then had become the wolf's territorial headquarters. Far as Harry was concerned, the Mendenhall Glacier Recreation Area offered advantages over the wildlife refuge or Brotherhood—fewer prying eyes and interference, more space to roam. The trio began meeting not only before dawn, but in the evenings as well, and vanished off-trail in Dredge Lakes for hours at a time. When he arrived at the parking lot, Harry would howl a few times (in poor semblance of the real thing, he admits), and within minutes, the wolf would appear. Bad accent or not, Romeo clearly recognized both message and messenger. Then off they'd go, the wolf leading the way through his territory to secluded nooks and glades where no one else ventured. Sometimes Harry would linger much longer than he'd intended; luckily, his work often allowed him to rearrange his schedule. And, being a single man of few encumbrances and singular focus (back in Washington State, he'd been a top-level tournament billiards player), he did all he could to nurture the relationship between dog and wolf. "Seeing Brittain seemed to mean a great deal to the wolf," Harry said. "You could tell by his reactions when he saw her, and how disap-

pointed he sometimes was when we left. I hated to disappoint him."
The black wolf — Wolfie, as Harry called him privately — became the
central focus of his life. He locked on to those hand-sized tracks before him and never turned back.

Like Harry, I traveled out alone in my share of snotty conditions —
times when it snowed so hard the wolf's back and head were piled
thick in white; or cold plunges when frost coated his muzzle and
eyelashes, and his howls rose in frozen plumes; sudden thaws, when
the lake turned to a slushy, soft-edged mess; and whiteouts, when
depth perception evaporated into a void without shadow, and every
step was uncertain. One truth was driven home by trailing him in
those conditions: the wolf lived and moved each day in a world hard
beyond our reckoning.

Out on the main lake trails on a sun-warmed late-winter day was
another matter — an odd combination plate of wilderness experience
and crowd scene, sometimes verging on a carnival atmosphere, especially on weekends. Dozens of people and dogs a week — a mixture ranging from day-in, day-out diehards to the merely curious — marched, trotted, shuffled, loped, or glided toward the lone
wolf and eddied around him as if he were a dark rock in our current.

Through it all, Romeo remained an incredible sport, even when
some little terrier mix of unfortunate ancestry committed the hubris
of curling a lip and snapping at his gently proffered nose, or a pas-
sel of jovial skiers and dogs ringed him without realizing it, cutting
off his escape route and sending an unintentional threat. Like their
owners, most dogs matched Romeo's affable nature with their own.
Some waxed cautious or fearful, others totally uninterested, and a
tiny minority hackles up from the start. If a dog turned aggressive,
the wolf, instead of bowling over the offender, would tuck his tail and
dodge it with a weightless burst or sudden leap and blend his moves
into a game. We all became accustomed to the incongruous spectacle of a cable-and-steel, 120-pound wolf striking appeasing pos-
tures before some mongrel that scarcely came up to his knees, and

engaging in submissive play with rude underlings that he could have thrashed in an instant.

And, like any celeb, the black wolf attracted his share of buzz and speculation, including the same questions we'd been asking ourselves all along. His backstory posed the central mystery. Most folks reckoned, logically enough, that he was indeed related to that black wolf killed by the taxi near the Mendenhall Glacier visitor center in April of 2003. Witnesses had heard howls from more than one wolf in the woods after she'd been struck. The dead female was carrying four pups, just weeks away from birth. Couldn't Romeo be a heartbroken mate stuck in time and space, searching endlessly for his Juliet, as one woman later cooed? Many Juneauites assumed this supposed relationship was the inspiration for the name that followed the wolf. And maybe that link explains why *Romeo* stuck, after all. It fit well enough and tied up the tale in a plausible, anthropomorphically pleasing bow. That may not have been what Sherrie had in mind when she murmured that word, less a name than an offhand thought; but we knew by then that the story had taken on its own life, traveling far beyond any of us, and the wolf himself.

Research and eyewitness anecdotes show that mated wolves do indeed form till-death-do-us-part monogamous bonds that equal any in the animal kingdom and put many human commitments to shame. Wolf researcher Dr. Gordon Haber reported a case of a male wolf finding his dead mate (killed by airplane hunters in a state-sanctioned predator control operation), burying her, and lying on top of her body for ten days. Once, nearly a decade before, I returned to the carcasses of two wolves Clarence and I had skinned, a huge black male and a gray, almost certainly alpha male and female of a pack, to find a circle of tracks and imprints, marking where a family had sat with their dead—a hard realization that haunts me still and shoved me farther along the trail I was already traveling.

As a more immediate window into the closeness of wolf relationships, consider domestic dogs and the countless recorded examples of unconditional loyalty, love, and sacrifice toward human companions: rescuing babies from fires, refusing to leave the graves of dead masters, wandering hundreds of miles to find home, and all the rest, trailing back in legend, history, and literature. The generic Latin-based appellation *Fido* ("I am faithful") was bestowed with good reason, and the source of that tendency to form, hold, and act upon such strong social bonds is rooted deep in the lupine genome. The complex group behaviors of hunting, raising young, and defending territory—the three central tasks of any successful pack—require the same close-knit dedication to family that we honor so highly in our pets. When we gaze into the adoring eyes of a canine companion, we're staring at the carefully muted and shaped soul of a wolf. A key difference between the two is that through the process of selective breeding, we've convinced domesticated dogs to transfer their allegiance to our species—not just serve us, but love us as equals, or above themselves—a trade-off, one could suppose, for our assuming dominant pack roles as suppliers of stability, food, and leadership. Many dog behaviorists subscribe to the theory that we've engineered dogs into a state of arrested adolescence—a necessary condition to effect this transfer. Wild wolves, meanwhile, look only to each other, as they always have, and we in turn look toward their shadowed forms with mingled admiration, suspicion, and dread.

The fountainhead of the wolf's incredible social cohesion is the intense tie between the mated pair that forms the nucleus of the pack; these two are, in fact, considered a pack in and of themselves. In human terms, they're family, a far more accurate descriptor than "pack," with its connotations of a loosely organized mob. Though variations and exceptions have been documented by researchers, most often there is only one reproducing pair in a pack, the dominant male and female. There's no mistaking the solicitous affection the two often show toward each other—nuzzling, gentle play, resting together, and mutual grooming. The rest of the pack, if any, is made up of nonmating pups from previous litters, with perhaps an adopted disperser mixed in. These younger animals, themselves all highly bonded to their parents and to each other, fall into a pack hierarchy from most dominant to most submissive, an order that

sorts itself out in daily interactions — play, fighting, hunting, feeding, traveling — according to prey availability, pack dynamics, physical size, and personalities. Larger wolves generally trump smaller
ones; in fact, the largest adult wolf in a pack is most often the dominant, or alpha, male. Despite receiving the doting, coparenting attention of the entire family group in early life, only a small fraction
of pups will ever reach breeding age, which is around a wolf's second
year, with actual mating often being delayed for several years more,
depending on fate, opportunity, and an individual's drive. Younger,
smaller wolves are often the first to succumb when times are hard;
since wolves are fast breeders and recover quickly from population
crashes, adults are more biologically valuable than young. A pup's
inexperience leads to errors in judgment and dooming injuries; if it
brushes near humans, its natural, sometimes bold curiosity leaves
it especially vulnerable to traps and rifles. Too, it may be killed in
fights with neighboring groups, and starvation exacts a heavy toll.

Surviving young will typically disperse sometime between one
and four years after birth, on occasion wandering huge distances
in the process of seeking mate and territory. One study found that
roughly 15 percent of wolves at any given time are solitary, though,
of course, the percentage of lone animals may vary greatly from one
population to another, according to local dynamics. Most of these
lone animals are those young dispersers; the rest, survivors from hu-
man-decimated packs or the rare wolves that inexplicably choose life
alone, as either a temporary or (far more rarely) a permanent strategy. No matter their origin, the level of mortality among these outli-
ers is much higher than that of wolves living within an average pack,
with the same dangers looming on all sides, and none of the protection that a larger, bonded group may afford. Biologist Haber once
observed that a lone wolf is a dead wolf — perhaps a bit of an over-
statement, but not by much. The odds stacked against Romeo were
steep and always had been.

Given the timing of the taxi-struck female black wolf's death near
our house, just a few weeks after mating season and several before
denning and the highly cooperative, all-absorbing business of raising

a litter, the dead female's mate would likely have been one of those nearby wolves that were heard in the woods after her death; or, if temporarily separated, he would have searched for her by howling and checking scent posts and rendezvous sites for days, if not weeks. Circumstantial evidence seemed to fit the lost mate theory: Romeo appeared in the Dredge Lakes area that following summer, just a mile or so from where the female wolf had been killed. However, his age made that scenario less likely. Few second-year male wolves get the chance to breed within an established pack; that's the hard-won right of older, more dominant animals. On the other hand, a young male seizing the chance to breed isn't out of the question, under certain circumstances, which, in fact, might have applied in this case. According to Fish and Game records, three wolves had been legally trapped in the Nugget Creek basin area (a steep-sided, high-country drainage between Bullard and Thunder Mountains, on the south side of the glacier) the prior year. Due to proximity, they were likely members of the same pack, and one could have been the female's original mate. In his absence, a younger wolf may have become king by his own paw and sired the pups she was carrying. Researchers have recorded just such fluid dynamics in disrupted packs. The urge for a wolf family to produce pups runs strong, from a genetically imprinted point of view; a pack that misses a litter year risks decline, if not extinction. Romeo's size, too, supported the notion that he could have gained sudden dominance over smaller wolves and become the black female's mate of opportunity.

There were other possibilities. Romeo could have just as easily been not a stand-in mate, but simply the taxi-struck female's pup from the previous season, or maybe her sibling. And, while most likely he was indeed a member of that same pack, it's also conceivable he was an unrelated wolf that appeared in the months after her death, perhaps to fill a territorial vacuum after the surviving wolves scattered, as members of a disrupted pack may do. One male, a hundred-pound wolf fitted with a satellite collar by National Park Service biologist John Burch on a tributary of the upper Charley River in February 2011, traveled an astounding 1,500 miles in four months after his mate died—from north-central Alaska into Canada's Yukon Territory, as far northeast as the MacKenzie Delta, then west again into Alaska, to within twenty miles of Deadhorse and the sprawling oil fields at Prudhoe Bay. In the process, he crossed dozens of streams and rivers, including the powerful Yukon when it was running ice, the broad Porcupine River, and a rugged portion of the Brooks Range. No one knows what compelled that walkabout, but surely he could have found a mate or territory in fewer miles. Think of that wolf: a social, territorial, highly intelligent creature, traveling utterly alone through hard, unknown country. Wolves do this as a regular part of their hardwired species strategy, but it doesn't mean it's easy, exacting an inner toll that can never be quantified. While we have GPS points to track the lone male's meandering journey, and studies with which we can correlate or compare data, we can't chart the shape of his memories and experiences or accurately project his emotions through the lens of our own. But if a dog can sense the weight of profound loss in a way humans have long recognized, safe to say a wolf can at least equal that emotional complexity.

Musings regarding that complex inner, emotional landscape lead toward questions regarding comparative intelligence between dogs and wolves. In pure physical terms, domestic canines' brains (in proportion to body size) are 25 percent smaller than their wild ancestors'; that substantial figure alone points to some sort of diminished capacity. However, researchers conducting experiments in this field agree that comparing intelligence across species is a dicey business at best. The consensus among the Inupiaq elders I knew—people who had worked with sled dogs all of their lives; hunted, trapped, and observed wolves; and inherited experience-based lore about both, passed down through generations—was that the average wolf is far smarter than the average sled dog. By that they meant on the wolf's own terms, out in the country: finding and killing prey, avoiding traps, learning from experience, innovating and solving problems, and so on. On the other hand, any Inupiaq dog musher understood that a wolf pup or a wolf hybrid was "too wild" to learn to pull a sled or learn to cooperate with humans. Most dog-wolf mixes tended to be high-strung, difficult, and even dangerous, though their genetic input into a breed line was considered valuable. I recall one such wolf-dog in Noatak, a large, rangy animal belonging to my neighbor, an old traditional Inupiaq named Dwight Arnold. The hybrid waxed feral and jaw-snapping aggressive, unapproachable by anyone except Dwight, and was staked away from the other dogs in his team. Careful breeding and selection for several generations would be necessary to produce useful work dogs from such a cross. In short, wolves and dogs of the northwest Arctic region, so similar genetically, were viewed as quite different by the people who knew them best, especially in one key respect: their willingness and/ or ability to interact cooperatively with humans.

Scientists at work on the subject, comparing problem-solving abilities and learning patterns between hand-raised wolves and domestic dogs, concur that dogs rely on humans as partners in problem solving. Wolves, even those imprinted on people from an early age and affectionately bonded to their handlers, tend toward independent thought and action. Furthermore, wolves seem to possess a more sophisticated understanding of physical cause and effect, while dogs (especially herding breeds such as border collies and blue heelers like Chase) are much more able to pick up, somehow translate, and respond to nuances of human language. However, arriving at some sort of statistically meaningful comparison of overall intellectual ability between the two species is an elusive goal. The only experiments addressing the issue involve comparing bright dogs (most of the subjects seem to have been highly trained and intelligent individuals, from a human point of view) to captive wolves, environmentally and socially impoverished in comparison to their wild brethren, and quite possibly dumbed down further by nonselective breeding. As any astute breeder will tell you, all dogs are far from equal in both innate intelligence and willingness or capacity to learn; most would agree to the same sort of intellectual range that exists among humans. It's fair to assume that a similar variation occurs in wolves — though natural selection in the wild, which would presumably weed out the dunces from the gene pool, is absent in captivity, further contaminating any firm research conclusions based on captive-raised wolves. Then we have the further issue of parsing out the differences between genetically transmitted, ancestral knowledge, and active, adaptable cognition by the individual, and the degree to which the former constitutes intelligence, rather than what Victorians (including Darwin—himself a hard-core dog lover—who praised the moral and intellectual superiority of dogs over wolves) would have dismissed as brute instinct. All we can say with relative certainty is that the two species, though so similar in so many respects, possess overlapping but divergent intellectual abilities, each shaped by its unique environmental necessities. My own belief, based on experience and study, is that an average wild wolf is at least the equal of a brilliant dog in pure, sentient, problem-solving intelligence, and probably its superior. And Romeo certainly proved in his time among us to be, at the very least, one damn smart wolf.

Some watchers still believed Romeo must be a released dog-wolf hybrid. That would explain, they said, his inexplicable attraction to canines and his high-level tolerance of humans, and eliminate the confounding notion that a fully wild, adult wolf could exhibit that sort of—well, dammit, friendly behavior. However, a number of people with well over a century of combined wolf experience with hundreds of animals pointed to the inconsistencies that suggested an alternate history. Not only Joel Bennett, but my longtime friend and fellow writer/photographer Seth Kantner, who'd been born and raised in a dirt-floored homestead in the Brooks Range, where wolves ebbed and flowed past with the caribou, stood beside me on the lake on a visit south, watched the black wolf, and agreed this was a creature of the wild, plain and simple. My neighbor Tim Hall, who hailed from northwestern Canada and had seen his own share of wolves, said it best. As he and I paused to regard Romeo along the lake edge on a still, sun-dazzled March morning, Tim leaned against the handlebars of the big Ski-Doo snowmobile he used to set the skiing track on the lake. "Nope," he said, nodding toward the wolf, "that's the original machine."

In the absence of a scientific test comparing the dead female's

DNA with Romeo's for a possible link (and though such a test was discussed, none was ever attempted) all theories regarding the wolf's origins were just that. We'd never have a sure answer to any of our questions, and perhaps such mystery, added to a growing pile, suited the story best.

Regardless of where the black wolf had come from, we could all agree on one thing. There was nothing to match this spectacle any-where on the planet. No pack interaction, it was true, but still a wolf, right there, more accessible and dependable in his appearances than anyone had ever heard of. Even in those early days, and with the same easy grace with which he moved, Romeo became part of the Juneau scene, one of the wrinkles that defined us. To some, he was no more than a curiosity; but to the ever-growing crowd of watchers, he was a new neighbor and a natural, charisma-loaded mixer—the sort everyone wanted at their party. He was well on his way to be-coming the town's de facto mascot.

Paradoxically, now that the black wolf was no longer a secret, he somehow stayed one in the larger sense of the word. Sure, whatever ran in the *Empire* got picked up by the Anchorage and Fairbanks papers, and I spun the first installments of the unfolding tale in my *Alaska* magazine column. But no one tipped off CNN or the *Today* show. YouTube, Facebook, and Twitter didn't exist in those days. If they had, the phenomenon of Romeo the wolf might well have ex-ploded into viral mode with the help of a few smartphone videos. And, though up to a million cruise ship tourists funneled through Juneau annually, and more than a third of them ended up at the gla-cier on their Gilligan-style three-hour tour, these masses were a May-through-September phenomenon. The dark, storm-lashed rain forest winter was strictly for locals and their wolf. What happened in Juneau stayed in Juneau, at least for the time being.

SHOOT, SHOVEL, AND SHUT UP

April 2004

I woke from a hard sleep to a sound I knew too well: the crash of a large-caliber handgun, close enough that the thud of the muzzle blast shook the double-paned window and drawn, insulated blinds of our bedroom. Then another. Sherrie, earplugs in, stirred and murmured. The dogs' heads were up as I staggered for the window. I knew damn well what was going on. Some stupid bastard was letting fly with a hand cannon less than two hundred yards from our back door, from the beach near Skater's Cabin, a popular party spot where locals sometimes let their yee-haws loose, oblivious to the fact that the area was far less wilderness than it had been a dozen years before.

But suddenly, this was far more than a matter of home-owner outrage at the disruption and threat to family. At the first rolling crack, I'd been yanked into a new world where my first thought, more of an image than a word, was this: *The wolf!* I'd yanked on jeans, boots, and jacket before I realized the futility of running out into the darkness, now ringing with silence. Whoever had fired those shots was gone—probably jumped in his truck and roared off before my feet hit the floor. I dialed up the police dispatcher, who sounded decidedly uninterested in sending a unit out into the boonies to investigate a little Alaska-style fun. I slid back into bed beside my sleeping wife and lay awake until Sherrie's alarm kicked on, wondering what

I might find lying out on the ice in the gray light. Raising the blind, I reached for binoculars and discovered I didn't need them. There lay Romeo, curled up a half mile out, head up and alert, waiting for his first dog fix to appear. To this day, I don't know if those shots fired were mere drunken mayhem or an illegal, calculated attempt on the wolf's life. They weren't the first or last I'd hear at odd late hours, echoing across the lake.

From the earliest tales of The Last Frontier to last week's news item, wolves drift in and out of the shadows, their looming presence adding a dark-bitter spice that many Alaskans seem to relish — including (maybe most of all) those who complain the loudest. While most of the hand-wringing centers on their predation of game animals, the supposed menace of wolves as eaters of human flesh is inevitably trotted out as justification enough for killing wolves in general, and especially animals like Romeo whose territories brush against our own. In semi-urban areas, such as the outskirts of Anchorage or Fairbanks, state-supervised culling of such animals is performed only after a string of incidents and complaints (usually, attacks against pets or human encounters with bold, fearless wolves in a given area). However, plenty of chest thumpers don't hesitate to shoot first, and skip the part about questions later. Such killings are often illegal and unreported. Shoot, shovel, and shut up, the saying goes.

The perceived menace posed by Alaska killer wolves was amply dramatized in the 2011 survivalist-noir film *The Grey*. Liam Neeson plays a world-weary wolf biologist standing guard, rifle at the ready, to protect North Slope oil pipeline crews from the constant threat of all-out attacks. When the plane carrying Neeson and other workers crashes in the territory of a pack led by a black anti-Romeo digitized to nightmarish proportions and features, the puny, scruffy humans are hunted down relentlessly. A gripping tale to be sure, but one problem: the whole thing, start to finish, is a pack of Hollywood hooey. This film is also evidence that the fearsome wolf rooted in our collective subconscious, rather than fading into the past, is alive and well. In fact, several other recent mainstream films, including the *Twilight* series with its shape-shifting vampire/wolves and Peter Jackson's productions of the Tolkien Middle-earth sagas, replete with horrifically proportioned, howling, orc-ridden Wargs, seem custom-designed to perpetuate the myth of malevolent killer wolves to a new generation.

So, what about the stories of man-eaters: "Peter and the Wolf," "Little Red Riding Hood," wolves chasing down travelers on the Russian steppe, and so forth? By far the greatest number of predatory attacks in this and the last century have taken place in remote areas of India, Afghanistan, and Pakistan, where dwindling natural prey, human poverty, incursion on wolf habitat, and the tradition of leaving young children to tend livestock seem to have contributed to several hundred deaths in the past two centuries, though substantiated official records are generally lacking. Rudyard Kipling's *The Jungle Book,* with its central tale of the child Mowgli being adopted by a kindly pack (one of the few representations of sympathetic wolves in all human literature) apparently put a positive spin on a real-enough threat. Scattered cases of wolf predation on humans have also been recorded in Europe; most of these accounts are unverifiable, or wilt under serious investigation.

There is little doubt that wolves — avid, active scavengers — ate human dead during the waves of plague and wars that swept the continent, and horrified witnesses projected them as bloodthirsty man-eaters; the Old World werewolf legends may well have their roots there, as well. Conceivably, wolves that fed on bodies learned to associate humans with food, lost fear, and sought them more frequently as prey. However, concrete evidence of this progression is lacking.

As for North America, in 1944, a researcher named Young examined thirty cases of aggressive wolves on the continent before 1900, including six supposed human fatalities. In his introduction he stated, "Whether these stories are products of fertile imaginations, or are truth, is difficult to determine." In other words, he allowed that all six deaths — startlingly few, given the number of wolves and humans colliding all across the pioneering sprawl of America — may not have occurred at all. However, documented aggressive incidents and attacks by wild wolves on humans have undoubtedly taken place, and relatively recent reports focus on Alaska. In 2002, state biologist Mark McNay assembled a case study of eighty interactions between humans and wolves from 1970 to 2000, all but several in Alaska and Canada. Just sixteen of the eighty encounters involved nonrabid wolves biting people or grabbing at their clothing. No injuries were rated as life threatening, though several were considered serious. Four of the six serious bite cases were children, including a well-publicized and much-discussed attack in 2000 on a six-year-old boy at a logging camp in Icy Bay, Alaska. In fact, this incident was the impetus for McNay's report, he stated, in order to reexamine the danger of wolves to humans. The six-year-old was attacked while playing, bitten and dragged before a pet black Labrador and nearby adults intervened. The wolf, shot and killed, was proven by investigators to be a habituated, food-conditioned animal that had been known from the year before, and fed by camp workers in the weeks before the attack.

While McNay offered an incomplete analysis of the factors involved in wolf aggression toward humans, a careful reader can surmise what's implied and add to what is stated. Food conditioning clearly ranks at the top of the list. Habituation to human presence, though not a direct cause in itself, creates more potential for proximity, which could only increase the odds of something going wrong. Also, appearing vulnerable and/or small—lying down, being alone, or being a child—seems to add to the risk of attack. In more than a dozen of the perceived aggressive incidents (most of which stopped short of physical contact) wolves appeared to be defending themselves, pups, pack members, or kills from humans. In other instances, wolves seem to have mistaken people for other prey and retreated when they realized their mistake. Only a small fraction of the cases seemed to involve wild, unhabituated wolves making an unprovoked, serious attack, and few of those involved human injury of any kind.

Six of the total thirty-nine aggressive incidents, including the Icy Bay case, involved humans accompanied by dogs. While McNay stopped short of identifying domestic canines as a contributing factor or a trigger to wolf aggression against humans, he suggested the possibility of such a link—rooted, one might assume, in the enmity wolves of a given pack, defending territory, show toward all canine interlopers. Unknown wolves, coyotes, foxes, and domestic dogs are usually chased and killed on sight, and often eaten. If true, Romeo's countless peaceful interactions with people and dogs alike stand out as all the more remarkable.

Threats, whether real or perceived, and the odd bite aside, in the entire recorded history of Alaska, there has been just one confirmed fatal attack by nonrabid wild wolves on humans, and that occurred only recently. On March 8, 2010, a young, first-year teacher from Pennsylvania, Candice Berner, was killed two miles from the remote Alaska Peninsula village of Chignik Lake. Since there were no eyewitnesses, the exact circumstances will never be known. Berner was last seen around 4:30 P.M. at the village school after telling a co-worker she wanted to get some exercise. As she set out on the one narrow, curving, brush-lined roadway leading out of the Alutiiq Eskimo community of seventy-three residents, blowing snow hurled sideways on a west wind gusting past thirty-five miles an hour. She walked or jogged outward from the village, listening to music on her headphones, no more worried about her surroundings than any suburban jogger. An hour later, four villagers on snowmobiles found one of Berner's mittens and bloody drag marks on the road and discovered her torn and partially eaten body several dozen yards downhill, in a patch of willow brush, surrounded by animal tracks and signs of struggle. Three of the party went for help. Circling the area on his snowmobile, the remaining young man saw a wolf step out of the brush and fled. Berner's body was dragged some yards before her remains were recovered by an armed party and taken to the village. Alaska state troopers arrived the next morning to investigate a possible human crime scene (fingerprint dusting, fiber samples, rape swabs, and the rest). But given what they regarded as almost certain evidence of wild animal involvement, the state troopers turned the case over to Fish and Game, which conducted its own investigation. Though hampered by bad weather, department personnel in a helicopter tracked and killed two wolves, followed up by two pri-

vately contracted, expert aerial wolf hunters, who scoured the area
and managed to kill six more within a fifteen-mile radius of the village over the following three weeks.

News of the apparent attack blazed across the state; here was
proof of the danger, the antiwolf crowd said with grim, I-told-you-so
satisfaction. But many Alaskans, including some notable biologists
and wildlife experts, remained skeptical. Couldn't the killers have
been local dogs? After all, hundreds of Alaskans are assaulted by domestic canines each year, and such events, some fatal, are unfortu-
nately all too common in bush villages. I'd known a couple of kids
who had been severely injured by sled dogs, and had myself once
fought off a big husky mix that could easily have killed a smaller or
panicked individual. Perhaps Berner had encountered such an animal. Or had the wolves involved been fed by villagers, either by access to garbage or deliberately, and so learned to link humans with
food? Maybe she'd been murdered by a human and dumped out of
town, and wolves or dogs had fed on her already-dead body. Persistent rumors continued to circulate, fueled by the fact that a year after Berner's death, Fish and Game had yet to release their final report on the incident and remained tight-lipped (some would say
downright secretive) with any details. Finally the department's report was released, and I interviewed both State Trooper Dan Sadloske and Fish and Game area biologist Lem Butler, point men in their
respective investigations. Each was helpful, and candid. Though minor inconsistencies were apparent between the two reports, and
with earlier media releases, I found nothing to refute the official conclusion. Candice Berner had been killed by wolves, perhaps as few as
two or as many as four, judging from the tracks and later DNA analysis taken from the body. DNA from one of the last wolves killed was
a positive match with those samples. Berner had suffered numerous
bites, including fatal punctures to her neck, and portions of one but-
tock, shoulder, and arm had been eaten. If her body hadn't been recovered, it would likely have been consumed down to hair and bone
fragments, like any wolf kill.

There were a number of unique factors that helped explain why

Berner might have fallen victim. The weather had been poor, and in flat light and blowing snow, shapes can be difficult to recognize, distances distorted. She was attacked on a narrow, winding, brush-lined portion of the road. Wolf tracks in the willows suggested she hadn't been stalked; instead, wolves and human probably surprised each other as they met on a blind curve bordered by dense brush, just a few dozen yards apart. Statements from one of the villagers who discovered her body indicate Berner's tracks seem to have reversed direction back toward the village at that point. She may well have turned and run in panic, and the wolves, in hunting mode and anticipating usual prey (a moose calf, perhaps) locked on to a dark, fleeing shape. Berner's size—she was four feet ten inches tall—may have made her appear even more vulnerable. Flight response triggers pursuit and predatory behavior; perhaps if Berner had stood her ground and given the right physical message, the wolves would have stopped, gotten a good look, and either held off or retreated—which isn't to fault her understandable response or cast any blame her way.

But even given this synergy of factors, there is no final explanation for why this one encounter escalated into an all-out predatory attack, when the vast majority of wolf-human interactions—untold tens of thousands—have ended without a hint of lupine aggression. The one killed wolf positively linked by the DNA match was rated in excellent physical condition. Neither was there firm evidence of human habituation or food conditioning, though neither can be dismissed as a contributing factor. Biologist Butler's report notes that local dogs and cats had been eaten by wolves around Chignik in the past. Wolf tracks were found near the town's fenced but incompletely secured garbage dump, and he had observed a village dog dragging off a bag of trash. Surely wolves could have done the same and so begun to associate people with food.

There's only one other documented case implicating healthy, wild wolves in a North American human death. The animals involved, in Saskatchewan, near a remote geological exploration camp garbage dump in November 2005, seem to have been bold, habituated, food-conditioned wolves. The victim, a young geology student named

Kenton Carnegie, went for a walk after work and was attacked, killed, partially eaten, and cached (dragged off and covered) by one or more large carnivores. As the first-ever possible case of wild wolves killing humans in North America, Carnegie's death naturally drew intense scrutiny. Several highly respected biologists contended that the killer was most likely a black bear, while some, including Mark Mc-Nay, argued that the evidence implicated wolves. Still others, including researcher David Mech, suspended final judgment, which was the official conclusion. If wolves were indeed involved, that makes just two documented cases of human predation on the entire continent of North America in more than four centuries of wolf-human interactions. During that same period, many dozens of people have been killed by a variety of livestock and wild animals, including pigs, donkeys, deer, and llamas. Human deaths from domestic dogs in the United States alone average around thirty per year, and thousands are severely bitten by our supposed best friends.

In my own encounters with wolves, many of them under circumstances that should have rendered me especially vulnerable — including animals bounding toward me as I stood mired hip-deep in snow, or circling me in the dark — I've only once felt threatened, and that animal, a young female (and like a disproportionate number of the wolves I've met in my life, black), probably meant no harm. She and her pack were locked on to a cornered moose. She spotted my indistinct shape in the brush, struggling with a stuck snowmobile, and charged with what seemed predatory intent before skidding to a halt thirty feet away, regarding me wide-eyed and then running full tilt in the opposite direction. Aside from that wolf, and Romeo, of course, the rest of the nonfearful wolves that have reacted to me at close range — a couple of dozen or so — seemed cautiously curious, indifferent, or to be taking restrained exception to my presence.

Meanwhile, every trapped or wounded wolf I've seen has made submissive or fearful gestures, or tried its best to escape. Growling or snapping is a totally defensive reaction to being closely approached or physically prodded and signals not ferocity, but a desire to avoid conflict. Virtually every bit of titillating film footage featuring apparently vicious snarling and snapping among a pack is actually wolves gathered close over a kill, signaling others that they want to feed with no trouble.

By comparison with my wolf experiences, over the same three-plus decades I've been charged, chased, or aggressively approached by more than a dozen grizzlies and triple that number of moose; been rushed by several musk oxen; been growled at, jaw-snapped, and/or bluff-charged by a handful of black bears and a female polar bear; and had to grapple, hands and knife against antlers, with a wounded bull caribou that lowered its head and tried to gore me. I've personally known a double handful of brown/grizzly mauling victims (several of them my friends, one of them killed). But no one I've known, including homesteaders, trappers, and hunters with combined centuries of wilderness experience, has been so much as nipped by a wild, healthy wolf. Clarence Wood's old Inupiaq friend, Zach Hugo, from Anaktuvuk Pass, was attacked in 1943, at age fourteen, by a wolf he and his father presumed rabid, based on its behavior. Caribou skin clothing protected Zach, and he went on to live into old age and tell me the story over coffee one stormy April day, years ago.

Fearless wolves are often suspected of being rabid; the virus is almost absent in Southeast and South-central Alaska, though outbreaks do occur, especially in the Arctic and western reaches of the state, where the disease smolders and erupts every few years. A mammal struck by the fatal virus, which attacks and systematically destroys the brain, may seem oddly tame or fearless; it might stagger or drool and, in rare instances, become blindly aggressive. In addition to Zach Hugo's, several attacks in Alaska have been recorded, at least two resulting in death when individuals contracted the invariably fatal disease after having been bitten. However, such instances are more a minor footnote than an ongoing public health risk.

The hanging question isn't why Berner and Carnegie were attacked and killed, but why wolf attacks on humans on this continent, and pretty much everywhere except remote areas of south-central Asia, are as rare as they are. Wolves are opportunistic, adaptable predators. Why not choose humans — comparatively slow, small, and weak compared to most wild prey — on a regular basis? Surely, if North American wolves saw humans as potential food, thousands should have died at their fangs. Instead, just two. As for nonpredatory motives, wolves don't attack humans in defense of territory, like the monster wolves in *The Grey*. In fact, wolves around a den, even with pups present, are oddly unwilling to be aggressive toward encroaching people, though they may bark like dogs in alarm, howl, bluff-charge, and show anxiety before retreating (though they will attack bears). Why this reluctance? Through long coevolution and natural selection, perhaps we're ingrained in wolves' genetic memory as demigods or (quite rightly) a mortal threat to be avoided. Or maybe we're simply so strange, like nothing else in the landscape, that our alien presence invokes fear. So it is that wolves collectively seem at least as worried about us as we are about them, and our own fears have minuscule grounding in reality. You have to be exponentially unlucky — right up there with being struck dead by a piece of space junk — to be killed by a wolf.

One further question: After all these centuries of no human fatalities in North America, why these two, at the start of a new century? Is it just coincidence, or an inevitable by-product of increased human-wolf contact? Or are wolves, encountering less human persecution, losing their fear of us? Of course, the sample size is too small to allow for meaningful generalizations. Too, wolves across their North American range are subject to sport hunting, trapping, and predator control at high levels. Modern snowmobiles and ATVs allow unprecedented access to remote areas, and chasing wolves down with such machines is currently legal in Alaska. Meanwhile, sport hunting of lower-48 wolf populations, until recently protected under the Endangered Species Act (including in Montana, Idaho, Wyoming, Michigan, Minnesota, and Wisconsin), has exacted a heavy toll. By the principles of natural selection (bold, unafraid wolves must run an exponentially higher risk of human-inflicted death), they should be as wary of us as any wolves in history. Consider that roughly one in ten Alaska wolves is killed each year by humans — and that's just the recorded take. The actual figure may be double or triple that. I know that in the small Arctic native villages where I lived, a wolf hide bearing the required plastic Fish and Game recording seal was a rare sight, and two dozen or more were taken every year. Extrapolate that lack of registered take to similar communities in the region and across Alaska, and the total must pile into the hundreds each year. Thus, the persecution wolves currently face in Alaska should indeed be shaping their behavior toward increased avoidance of humans. However, there is no sign that contact between the two species is diminishing in The Great Land; and most of it goes badly for the wolves.

That Romeo avoided being shot that first winter, just for being close to so many humans, was a minor miracle. If hunger had trumped cross-species social impulses as anyone might have expected, he'd have been whacked in those first few weeks. Even if his early dog and human contacts were friendly or neutral, people knew the Alaska backstory and those darker tales of myth and legend. Unlike most wolves, Romeo presented an easy target for the most casual of killers: drive into the West Glacier Trail parking lot at the right moment and squeeze off a round, or throw out some poisoned bait in the nearby brush, or maybe set a cluster of snares on one of his trails. Too, the odds kept increasing that the wolf would wander into the wrong yard and be offed in imagined or fabricated self-defense. The sight of Romeo trotting across the lake may have been thrilling, but it also swept many of his watchers with tidal worry that ebbed and flowed but never quite ceased over the years that we knew him. For the most part, keeping alive was up to him, and to the fates that spin, measure, and cut every thread of life. We could no more safeguard him than we could have kept him secret. Though some master of philosophy and spiritualism might have been able to open a clenched hand and release the fear of that seemingly inevitable future, I never quite managed.

Matters weren't helped by the wolf's occasional wanderings. He, or another black wolf, or several that looked and acted one hell of a lot the same, started popping up here and there about the Mendenhall valley with increasing frequency: in Thunder Mountain neighborhoods, on the Mendenhall wetlands less than a mile from the airport, and even near Amalga Harbor, twenty-seven miles to the north (on Juneau's double-dead-end main highway, a fifty-odd-mile-long coastal artery known variously as Egan Drive, Glacier Highway, or The Road). Though Romeo's home base near the glacier was a no-hunting area, all he had to do was cross an imaginary line a quarter mile off the West Glacier Trail or wander up Montana Creek into free-fire zones. And, at times, he apparently went far beyond that. A prime, large hide like that beckoned as an impressive trophy, one plenty of self-styled sportsmen would jump at taking, legally or otherwise. Juneau's black wolf would have disappeared out of the country and reemerged on someone's den wall, teeth bared in a comic-book, glassy-eyed snarl, and few would have ever known his fate. But against all odds, the black wolf not only survived, but prospered.

Very seldom does a single animal become a social issue all to itself, but over his life, Romeo paradoxically divided and united a community: a living, breathing focal point for the broad, ongoing topic of wolves and people in Alaska. As with that larger issue, there weren't really two camps when it came to the black wolf. A truer model would be a continuum with a few ardent, prowolf advocates on one end, a small number of equally impassioned voices pulling toward the opposite extreme, and the vast majority falling along a sliding scale that covered every possible shade of reaction, up to and including indifference. But even those who knew little about this wolf, and never would glimpse him, would offer, if pressed, some sort of opinion regarding his presence. Regardless of the division, Juneauites who bore deep enmity toward the black wolf held back, either out of respect for fellow citizens or unwillingness to risk the ire of neighbors and community. Without that restraint, the wolf would have been unlikely to survive.

Considering the lay of the land, a wolf as a centerpiece civic issue made perfect sense. The Juneau Borough, totaling 3,255 square miles, stretches nearly one hundred miles south to north, and eastward across deep tidal fjords to include a number of sizeable islands (notably, nearby Douglas) plus a portion of huge, remote Admiralty Island, known for its numbers of outsized coastal brown bears. The actual road-serviced area ranges roughly fifty miles along a narrow coastal shelf caught between mountains and sea. In total area, Juneau ranks as the largest-in-area incorporated city not only in Alaska, but in the entire United States—Los Angeles, Chicago, and New York included. Thinking big was apparently a ploy by Juneau boosters in the 1890s gold rush era to keep as much incorporated land as possible (and as many future mining claims) within the city's jurisdiction and revenue base. The population density works out to just ten inhabitants per square mile, but even that sparse statistic doesn't give a true image. While some Juneauites live beyond hollering distance of neighbors, and a handful are wrapped in wilderness isolation, most of the thirty-some thousand residents cluster in a narrow, twenty-mile stretch along the coast and along loop or spur roads that dead-end up densely populated valleys.

Development is bounded on one side by avalanche-swept slopes too steep for building, and tidewater on the other. Most of Juneau's incorporated area consists of wild, uninhabited territory, cheek by jowl, in places, with fairly dense development. Even the most urban-seeming portions of the Capital City, including state office buildings and the main street row of tourist gift stores and eateries, lie within a mile or less of prime wildlife habitat—often much less. Black bears pad at night just yards from the state senate office building; killer whales stalk seals near beachfront houses. State capital or no, by deliberate thought or accident, Juneau is far more mingled with the wild than most cities its size, whether in Alaska or beyond. So sure, why not throw a wolf into the mix?

In fact, the appearance of Romeo wasn't the first time that the presence of wolves had stirred controversy in Juneau. In the spring and summer of 2001, a pack—two adults and a litter of pups—appeared on Douglas Island, which lies just across Gastineau Channel from downtown Juneau. Even at high tide, scarcely a half mile away, easy swimming distance for a wolf. No wolves had been seen on Douglas in decades, and they thrilled tourists and locals alike by making regular appearances on a rocky beach on the island's remote back side, showing a relaxed tolerance for viewers who watched them from boats and kayaks. That following winter, a local trapper snared, killed, and skinned seven (probably all) of the half-grown young. His actions were entirely legal and cheered by some local hunters who claimed the wolves would have decimated the island's deer population. But the resulting furor was decided not in human but lupine favor. Notwithstanding a great gnashing of teeth among the fervent antiwolf crowd, wolf trapping was banned on Douglas. Part of the forbearance shown Romeo was almost surely due to re-verberations from that civic battle, just two years before.

More than a dozen years earlier, a single, far less publicized and almost forgotten incident cast a shadow at least as large. On a late-winter day in 1988, Judith Cooper, a local dog musher, was taking a walk up the West Glacier Trail with three of her Siberian huskies. Not far up the trail, her dogs cued her to something ahead; then she heard an odd clanking. Just a few yards off the trail lay a black wolf, with three of its four paws caught in steel traps, its eyes glazed with pain. The pummeled, blood-spattered snow and the wolf's emaci-ated condition indicated the young male had been there for days. In-stead of retreating or hurrying past, Cooper moved closer. The wolf had wandered into an amateurish but obviously effective-enough trap spread: several deer forelegs hung from trees, surrounded by a cluster of Newhouse number four leg-hold traps chained to those same trees. The wolf had followed the West Glacier Trail down from the high country, making frequent scent posts as he went; Judith later saw these, along with his tracks. As he meandered downhill, his nose led him into trouble. The first steel jaws snapped high on a front wrist. Struggling to free himself, he'd stepped in two more traps and become hopelessly tangled. Wolves caught in such devices — un-changed in design for more than a century — have been known to wring off paws or chew through bone and sinew to free themselves; many have left toes behind, or lost feet to freezing. The young black wolf's struggles had torn and gouged hide and flesh around the trap jaws, and probably broken some bones. Twenty-three years later, Ju-dith, by then in her seventies, squinted back, remembering. "There was frozen blood everywhere. The wolf could barely move. He didn't snarl and wasn't aggressive at all. It was like looking into one of my own dogs' eyes," she told me.

Cooper didn't hesitate. She hurried back down the trail to her car, and returned with two men, one of them a local vet. Though they deployed a noose-mounted restraint pole while they worked to release the powerful trap jaws, they hardly needed it. "The wolf never struggled or snapped at us," Cooper said. "He seemed to understand we were helping." With the animal freed, Cooper and her companions backed off and waited, but the exhausted wolf didn't rise. Finally the three decided to go around the bend, then move up the trail, making as much racket as possible. It worked. Startled to its feet, the animal limped off into the trees. As a result of snapshots Judith Cooper took of the scene and her testimony regarding the potential danger to the dozens of domestic dogs that regularly used the trail, the Alaska Board of Game, spearheaded by Joel Bennett (then a member), prohibited trapping within a quarter mile of any trail in the Mendenhall Glacier Recreation Area—the same trails that, years later, Romeo would range on an almost daily basis. In saving that young black wolf's life, Cooper may well have saved Romeo's, years later, and who knows, perhaps in another sense, as well. It's entirely possible that injured wolf, limping off into the late-winter afternoon years before, lived to be part of the bloodline and pack that gave birth to the wolf we called Romeo.

THE SURVIVAL SWEEPSTAKES

November 2004

I sat on the snow-covered ice, peering into my camera's viewfinder as flakes sifted from a low sky. Gus curled next to me, patient as always. Twenty yards away, Romeo stood against the Big Rock, and I waited, finger on the shutter, for him to lift his muzzle and howl. The afternoon lay quiet, the ice so new, so thin that it creaked and bowed underfoot. Winter had drifted down from the high country, again, and with it the black wolf—returned for a second winter among us. Miracle enough that he had stayed the previous winter and into spring, even more that he would disappear one April evening—gone, as we knew he would be one day—and return months later. Of course we had worried ourselves sick that he'd been killed, but we'd also celebrated his possible survival, and perhaps a home with a new pack. There had been no way of knowing which was true, and either way, we had no choice but to let go as best we could. Now he was back, and for all the solidity of his dark shape against the snow, and the insistent lines of tracks, he seemed more apparition than ever. Our first season of the wolf may have been chance; now we knew he'd chosen this ground not once, but twice, deepening the mystery of this solitary wolf and his bond to this place.

Harry Robinson was the first to encounter Romeo that autumn of 2004 as he hiked the West Glacier Trail, on the shoulder of Mount

McGinnis. Thinking he heard a distant howl higher up the mountain, Harry replied several times, bad wolf accent and all. On his return down the trail, along the lakeshore, there was Romeo. "He saw us, his tail went up, and he came running right over," Harry remembers, brushing back the years. "There was no doubt he was happy to see Brittain [Harry's dog]. I'd like to think me, as well." In fact, his hiking partner, attorney Jan Van Dort, commented that the wolf seemed to greet Harry. Harry figured Romeo had followed Brittain's scent, and perhaps his own howls, down the West Glacier Trail. Harry isn't much for emotional displays, but even years later, his eyes soften at remembering.

At first, the wolf came and went, as if wrapping up business elsewhere. Sightings swelled as lake and wetlands froze, again transforming brushy morass into firm-footed arena. If any of us doubted this was the same animal, uncertainty evaporated as he bounded toward the dogs he favored, keening that same high whine of invitation. We marked, too, the same grizzled streak on his chin and left shoulder, and the tiny white vee on one jowl. Of course this was the same wolf, but not the same. Those of us who knew him saw the filled-out neck, chest, and haunches. As sleek as he'd been before, this year's winter coat had come in even glossier. He'd not only survived his summer hiatus, but flourished. And now, at least a three-year-old, less teenager than adult, he approached his prime: the explosive resiliency of youth combined with mature thickening of muscle and bone.

As for wisdom, that must have grown as well over the time since we'd last seen him, and would continue to increase as long as he breathed—as life span itself would depend on that ever-rising curve of knowledge and judgment. According to biologists, a ripe old age for a wild wolf is between seven and ten years, though most never live that long, and a few exceed that mark. A young, solitary wolf like Romeo stood at far higher risk. Having had fewer chances than many wolves to learn a territory and hunting tactics from senior pack members—which ridges to traverse, which niches of habitat held marmots or goats, what paths to take across alpine ice fields, the boundaries of neighboring packs—he had by necessity forged his own way. If the black wolf's choice of hanging near humans for half the year had seemed odd, its soundness had been proven by the feat of his survival. I'd argue beyond mere soundness toward brilliance, based on the unique, proactive decisions he made on an almost daily basis. Even within the boundaries of Denali National Park, where all human hunting and trapping is banned, one study found the average life of a wolf spans just three years, subject to the usual natural forces: accidents, disease, starvation, and fights with other packs — the latter the leading cause of death, at 25 percent annually, of the total Denali Park population. Despite less apparent protection — certainly lacking the defensive umbrella of a family to help fend off invading wolves, and a far narrower area excluding human hunting and trapping — the black wolf had already broken even.

Even more than the first winter, how well his gambit worked could depend on forces beyond his horizon. He'd moved beyond rumor, even to those who'd never seen him and never would. Attention fixed like a spotlight the instant he reappeared, and our own cycles of elation and angst began anew. Among the watchers sat those wielding the power to shape his fate — what little that meant to a wolf.

Though Romeo had returned, not all his friends waited to greet him. Dakotah, who had always been in the health you'd expect from her sleek, muscled form, had wakened us in the dark one early-summer morning, her brown eyes pleading. A few hours later, our vet diagnosed ileus, a dire bowel malady triggered by an unknown cause. She survived emergency surgery, and we breathed again when we knew she was awake and should be able to come home the next day. But she died alone that night, without us to comfort her. Why doesn't matter, even if we knew. Loss lies beyond cause or effect, a hard, hollow country all to itself. There was nothing to do but travel its expanse for a time, bearing the weight of grief — Sherrie, whose heart is too gentle for this world, most of all. The subdued dogs searched on and off for their lost companion. Years later, they still perked ears whenever they heard her name, and whined when they spied a light-colored Lab that could have been her rounding a bend in a trail. When Romeo approached us that winter, he seemed to be searching and wondering as well, scanning in all directions for our missing pack member. But the dog that helped give the wolf a name was gone, as if she'd never been. A few of us cried, and the world moved on. And through that world, a dark shape still moved, carving out a life at the edge of us.

Inexplicable as it had first seemed, Romeo's choice of a winter territory made perfect sense. Viewed from above, the lake served as the hub of a great wheel, with human-made and animal trails and natural corridors radiating outward in every direction. Wolves, even more than some creatures, seek the path of least resistance. Survival hinges on a brutal imperative: more energy must be gained than lost, across endless hard miles. To fail is to die. A hunting pack in tough going moves single file, commonly covering fifteen to thirty miles a day, with different animals taking turns in the taxing lead position. This isn't a matter of wanderlust, but necessity — covering the empty distance between meals. Research shows that wolves far more often fail in their hunts than succeed and, even when hungry, don't bother to study, let alone attack, the vast majority of animals they see, apparently recognizing that the price of a meal — precious calories burned in the chase and kill, as well as risk of injury — might be too steep. Though healthy adult moose, caribou, and deer may fall prey if caught at a disadvantage, the high percentage of animals seen but not even tested, let alone attacked, by hunting wolves (more than 90 percent in one study) bears testament to the fact that wolves take primarily the sick, weak, and injured. Without the benefit of scientific studies, Lewis and Clark seemed to understand the relationship, calling the prairie wolves they saw "shepherds of the buffalo"—caretakers that strengthened the herd, rather than scourges. A moose that stands its ground and can't be compelled to break into a run is virtually never taken down. But such culling requires nearly endless travel, often in hard conditions. Biologist David Mech quotes a Russian proverb that sums up the essence of lupine existence: A wolf lives by its feet.

So, why forge through chest-deep snow when a packed route offers three times faster travel for the same calories spent? A firm trail can be so alluring that some of my Inupiaq trapper friends often simply drove a snowmobile through likely country and made sets right off the back of their machines, square in their own mechanical footprint. Not much need for deception, beyond the trap itself, nestled in a depression covered by sifted snow, and surrounded by a scattering of meat shavings and rancid seal oil. I've backtracked over my own machine or ski trails many times over the years to find practically every wild thing that traveled the country, from wolverine to moose, taking advantage of my ribbon of firmer snow, and wolves among the most frequent followers of all. Besides offering easier going, trails lead to food—either to the creatures that made them, or to kills made by others that might be scavenged. By selecting Mendenhall Lake as the anchor of his territory, Romeo inherited a ready-made transportation network so perfectly suited to his use that he might as well have designed it. In terms of survival, these ready-shaped trails may well have been the most critical feature of the black wolf's chosen ground. In heavy snow country—and the upper Mendenhall valley was surely that—a single wolf would have been hard-pressed to break trail even in such a compressed area and keep a positive energy flow. Romeo probably traveled no less than an average wolf in his daily rambles, but he floated back and forth, mostly in short segments with easy going. Not only did he burn less energy, he required less food, which meant less time and physical stress hunting, and more time for rest and his social calendar. One more thought on the importance of those trails: they were, after all, probably what had led the black wolf here in the first place. But his remaining for months and then returning showed he must have found abundant prey along those trails.

It's true that the dietary—which is to say, evolutionary—fortunes of *Canis lupus* lie firmly intertwined with those of large, hoofed prey species—in Alaska, mostly moose, caribou, Sitka deer, mountain goats, and Dall sheep, depending on what's locally available. Formidable quarry each in their own right, these ungulates have shaped wolves, and vice versa, in a mutually adaptive arms race stretching across millennia. Some Alaska packs specialize in one species, to the extent that biologists speak of moose wolves or those that depend on caribou, while other families may rotate between two or three species, according to opportunity. My longtime friend Fish and Game area biologist Jim Dau also describes highly successful, generalist packs he and colleagues call sport-hunting packs. Despite that ungulate link, wolves as a species prove highly adaptable and opportunistic in finding the answer to the age-old question of what's for dinner; and some individuals take that quest to a whole new level.

An active, healthy wolf needs around six pounds of food a day; in times of opportunity, it's capable of devouring more than twenty pounds at one sitting (after which it sleeps, heavy-bellied, nearly comatose, for several hours —"meat drunk," my Eskimo friend Clarence calls it). A wolf can also make do without eating for a month or more if need be, and the often-high starvation rate of wolves in the wild proves that many take in far less than the minimum, let alone that optimal amount. Since wolf population numbers rise and fall in direct proportion to prey abundance, and wolves reproduce quickly, some, even in times of relative plenty, are bound to starve.

Let's work in round, generous numbers, and say a well-fed wolf the size of Romeo would require around two thousand pounds of digestible food a year. Add in something more than five hundred pounds to account for the indigestible stuff, and we have a wolf consuming well over a ton of live-weight food a year. In deer, that works out to a couple dozen animals, or several moose, depending on size. Wolves draw nutrition from the bulk of any animal they eat —meat, fluids, organs, fat, the entire hide, connective tissue, and marrow-filled bones small enough to crunch apart and/or swallow. They start with the delicacies —organs, blood, fat, and flesh —and work their way down. Contrary to persistent tales of wanton killing with only tongues or livers taken and the rest left to rot, wolves, if not disturbed, tend to visit a carcass many times, sometimes dropping by to check, or perhaps reminisce, months or even years after nothing edible remains. A freshly killed, apparently abandoned, hardly touched carcass is most likely a result of wolves being temporarily displaced by approaching humans, or the wolves waiting nearby, soon to return. Prey is too hard-won to squander. Instances of so-called surplus killing—when wolves, finding easy opportunity, indeed kill more than they can readily eat—are rare as they are vilified, and the wolves involved would probably still make use of the meat if not disturbed or out-competed by scavengers.

One can glean a great deal of information from a quick glance at a wolf's scats. Dark, runny stools indicate not sickness, but wolves that are feeding heavily off the rich, choicest parts of a fresh kill. Well-formed stools with some bone and hair mixed in means they've moved past that point but are still gaining plenty of useful nutrition. Scats composed almost totally of hair and bone are signs of the final stages of cleanup, or a hungry, perhaps desperate wolf gleaning whatever he can from an old kill. In the cold, near-desert of the Brooks Range, some of these bleached, half-fossilized turds may persevere for years, long after even bacteria have given up and moved on. Over the years, I've used these familiar relics, far up empty canyons or on the crests of windswept ridges, as trail markers, even thought of them as friends—something that made the country less lonely. And each and every one stands as a testament to the hard life of a wolf.

Call it luck or skill, Romeo had struck another jackpot in the upper Mendenhall valley—an oasis of relative plenty that hadn't existed just a half century earlier. Like more than 90 percent of Alaska's glaciers, the Mendenhall had been steadily receding for the past century; but in the late 1970s the retreat decayed into a rout. Since I first glimpsed the Mendenhall nearly thirty years ago, its craggy leading edge has galloped backward nearly a mile, exposing a tumult of fresh-gouged granite cut by several new waterfalls. The body of the glacier has shrunk several hundred vertical feet—untold billions of tons of ancient ice lost, far faster than it could be replaced.

Farther down-valley, and a few decades earlier, the ice river's retreat had bared a rubble-strewn, sandy bottomland drained by a network of ponds and sloughs into the ice-cold, silt-laden Mendenhall River: an austere-seeming patch of ground that provides an object lesson in the intimate tie between destruction and creation. Nurtured by the cloudy, rain-soaked climate of the upper valley and pockets of rich glacial silt, an outburst of pioneering plant life followed the fading ice—a shrub, moss, and grass community with cottonwood, alder, and Sitka spruce mixing in, which in turn has attracted burgeoning populations of small herbivores: snowshoe hares, beaver, porcupines, red squirrels, mice, and voles, plus a wide array of birds, hordes of insects, and microscopic life. Several streams feeding into the lake or river, some of which hadn't existed a century ago, now host salmon runs of one or more species—an annual tsunami of marine energy surging inland, enriching soils and stimulating life across the food web, from delicate mosses to great coastal brown bears.

For all that, traditional wolf-sized prey in the upper Mendenhall—hoofed mammals with which they coevolved—remains scarce. Except for a few recorded transients over the years, moose are absent, due to marginal forage and soft, deep snow. Even if a dozen of the big ungulates had yarded up for the winter along the lake fringes, it's tough to imagine a single wolf making a steady living from them. While lone wolves have been known to kill moose, the perilous, arduous task of taking down even a sick or injured adult usually requires the concerted work of at least two animals, and more often, a full pack's attention, sometimes over days.

The upper valley and surrounding country holds solid numbers of mountain goats. These surly animals pose tough targets for a lone wolf in summer, fall, and early winter, when they frequent near-vertical escape terrain. Goats become more vulnerable in times of deep snow when they settle below the timberline, and also in spring, when goats forage low after fresh greens, and young are born. However, they're neither plentiful nor available enough to qualify as a year-round, go-to species for a single, homebody wolf. The diminutive Sitka black-tailed deer that are a mainstay for most Alexander Archipelago wolves are rare around the glacier, though small pockets cling here and there, with better numbers nearer the coast, just a several-mile trot away. No doubt there were times when Romeo availed himself of that opportunity.

One more large prey possibility presented itself. On occasion, wolves deliberately seek bears — sometimes a cub or young brown/ grizzlies, but especially black bears — as food. A number of such predatory attacks have been recorded in Alaska and Canada, and there's at least one documented case of a pack digging out, killing, and eating a winter-denned bear. Though not predatory in nature, that wolf and grizzly brawl I witnessed thirty-some years ago reflected the general antipathy the species hold for each other. More recently, I witnessed the obvious fear wolves can trigger in black bears. One spring some years ago, in a distant inlet of Glacier Bay, photographer Mark Kelley and I sat perched on huge granite boulders, leaning into our cameras as two enormous, fight-scarred males jockeyed for turf and mating rights. Suddenly, though, a gray blur shot out of the trees, straight at the bears, and the two broke and ran, fleeing a wolf that might have weighed eighty pounds. The wolf was probably just running off the bears from a nearby den site or hunting area rather than launching a predatory attack, but the utter panic the bears displayed was unmistakable. Both brown/grizzly and black species occur in the upper Mendenhall, with the latter far more common; and younger animals, far less formidable than adults, could easily fall within the abilities of a wolf like Romeo now and then. But in such a limited area, the number of young bears was too small to provide a dependable food source.

All told, that was the sum of Romeo's prospective menu; all of the abundant, easily accessible items more coyote fare than lupine, it seemed, and standard fare scarce or problematic. What, then, was he eating? Following the black wolf's trails, I came across kill remains and teased apart dozens of scats. In them I found the bits of bone and hair that bore witness to the stuff from which this wolf was built.

Direct observation, along with analyses of not only scat, kills, and stomach contents, but of signature chemical traces found in DNA (which can be gathered nonlethally from tranquilized animals via hair or whisker samples), demonstrate that many Alaska wolves dedicate a surprising amount of energy — and gain a great deal in return — from nonhoofed sources. No huge shock that the Alexander Archipelago wolf subspecies of coastal Southeast Alaska and British Columbia joins other land-based carnivores in spending much time beachcombing for whatever the tides bring their way—washed-up carcasses of seals, whales, fish, and seabirds—and many of these coastal wolves regularly forage, as well, for clams and other shell-fish. The beachfront also functions as trail, often with good travel on flats or bear paths, the easy going every bit as attractive as the food to which it leads. Coastal wolves with salmon stream access also make heavy use of these fat-rich fish during those brief periods of bounty when runs may almost clog some creeks. From a wolf's per-spective, the choice makes no-brainer sense: high-value food, with minimal energy expenditure or chance of injury (though for health reasons, they need to avoid the tapeworm cysts that riddle many salmon—accomplished by focusing on the nutritious and parasite-free heads, skin, and eggs; how they know this is a mystery). Some fishing wolves are damn good at what they do; in one British Co-lumbia study, adults caught as many as twenty-seven pink salmon an hour, with a catch success rate of 49 percent. DNA research by for-mer Fish and Game biologist Dr. Dave Person on massive Prince of Wales Island, on the southeastern edge of Alaska, found the summer and fall diet of at least some local wolves worked out to 20 percent salmon—this despite the island's thriving deer population.

But even farther north, wolves that live near Alaska's convoluted, peninsular coast (which totals more miles than earth's circumference at the equator) follow suit. DNA analysis there shows similar strong traces of marine mammal species, and, in some cases, remarked one researcher, the sort of seafood levels one might expect to find in seals. Along the Katmai coast in southwestern Alaska, wolves some-times fish for salmon side by side with coastal brown bears. Even hundreds of miles inland, a DNA study shows heavy salmon con-sumption by a population of interior wolves that has access to fish, and, farther north still, in the upper Kobuk and Noatak valleys, I of-ten noted the density of wolf action along active salmon spawning streams, though those same wolves no doubt relied on caribou and moose as a staple. No surprise, then, that with four species of salmon available in his territory—pinks, chums, sockeye, and coho, in overlapping runs spanning early July into October—Romeo's scats were seasonally packed with scales, fins, and bones. He was just being a sensible wolf, taking advantage of easy calories.

While deer or goat hair seldom showed in Romeo's waste, it often bore the fur, feathers, and bone fragments of small prey—red squirrels, mink, waterfowl, plus mice and voles (which he must have eaten like popcorn), and most abundant by far, snowshoe hares and beaver. Twice over the years I saw him trot across the lake with a white hare dangling in his jaws, and often came across signs of the hunt: gnawed-off feet and clumps of fur on blood-tinged snow. One might think that wolves wouldn't be agile enough to tackle such nimble prey, or that hunting something so small wouldn't be energy efficient; but some wolves focus on hares (whether the smaller varying [snowshoe] or much larger, far-north-dwelling arctic hares) with great success. They patrol brushy areas where hare populations are locally dense, following the bunnies' own runways, which inevitably lead to their makers and offer better footing. The wolf may employ either of two tactics: trample through and flush out hares in panic-stricken bursts, or hunt carefully and catlike, relying on keen senses to detect a snow-camouflaged hare holding fast against cover. Either way, a sudden burst of speed and an agile pounce win a meal often enough. At the brushy mouth of a remote Brooks Range creek valley, Seth Kantner and I watched a diminutive gray wolf hunting hares in the willows; its overlapping tracks showed it had been doing so for days. Biologist Gordon Haber also documented one Denali pack whose principal food became varying hares during a population explosion, despite no tradition of this in the past—yet another example of wolves adapting to opportunity.

Romeo's hunting trails and leavings also traced his regular visits to the many beaver lodges and dams across the upper valley. Harry Robinson and photographer John Hyde each witnessed Romeo making successful kills. Though these burly, outsized aquatic rodents, some weighing in excess of fifty pounds, are tough, hard-to-kill customers, both men recall the overwhelming power of the wolf's assault. Hyde sat at the northwest corner of the lake in late spring when a medium-sized beaver hauled out on the sandy shore. He didn't even know the wolf was nearby until a black streak bounded from the brush and slammed in, teeth and paws first. "He didn't screw around," remembers Hyde. "He bit down hard, boom, at the back of the neck, gave a couple of hard shakes, and that beaver was dead." The wolf then picked up the thirty-pound animal as if it were a squirrel and trotted off to feast in seclusion. Like the rest of us, wolves don't much like being watched while they eat. They also cache leftovers in exclusive places for later snacks, a behavior echoed by domestic canines burying bones and toys.

Like a sizeable percentage of Southeast Alaska wolves, Romeo specialized in one particularly dangerous prey item. Though porcupines seem slow of both foot and wit, their quills present a deadly problem to would-be predators—and that's just the point, so to speak. While they can't throw quills, when threatened they tail-swat and whirl with startling quickness, brandishing their bristled backsides at attackers. The quills, all thirty thousand or so of them, are not only sticky sharp, they're covered with microbarbs that impale with the slightest pressure and work their way inward, migrating through muscle and piercing organs, sometimes causing crippling injuries and a lingering death. Most predators leave porcupines the hell alone and apparently pass on that avoidance to offspring; those that don't risk an exit from the gene pool. Get around those nasty spines, though, and you have a fat-laden and easily caught meal, living up to the old sourdough term *quill hog*. The trick is to make a quick killing bite to the skull or perhaps to the belly—both quill-free areas that the porcupine strives to protect. Then eat from the underside outward, leaving the flayed skin in one piece, quills face-down, with the end result resembling a spiky orange rind. While I'm not sure of his exact technique (I'd bet on a head-on bite, affording maximum avoidance of quills), Romeo certainly solved that prickly problem many times over the years. Porcupine husks lay scattered here and there throughout his domain, and I regularly found tiny, soft, not-yet-barbed replacement quills—they're actually specialized hairs—in his droppings. One early-spring evening I watched him reclining at the base of a small cottonwood, gazing up at an obviously concerned porcupine that perched in its scant branches. An expectant-looking eagle lounged at the tree's peak. The next morning, all were gone, but the waddling tracks of the porcupine, ending in a spatter of frozen blood a few dozen yards away, pointed to the outcome. The eagle had apparently carried away the spiny skin to pick over. Regardless of how the black wolf pulled off these specialized hunts, one wrong bite or misjudgment, even long after the porcupine was dead, could have spelled his end. Call it luck, but like a seasoned poker player, the wolf seemed to make his own — not only with hazardous prey, but all things.

Though wolves are best known as predators, Romeo, like all of his kind, was an adept and avid scavenger; there's no better meal than one that will neither run off nor fight back. Patrolling wolves are ever alert for a free lunch of any size, and they may go to surprising lengths to glean rather than kill. Gordon Haber monitored one Denali National Park pack that spent more than a week digging out two moose buried deep in an avalanche. Just detecting the carcasses beneath twenty feet of hard-packed snow was a feat to make a bloodhound proud. And, as anyone who's ever dug avalanche-packed snow might attest, the excavation was itself a major feat — all for two frozen-solid carcasses that would test the teeth of any wolf. Expending all that effort was apparently a more inviting prospect than searching out, chasing, and dragging down two live moose. That single example illustrates the scavenging drive of *Canis lupus*. Consider, too, that this drive is precisely what trappers depend on: wolves are most often lured into a trap by scented bait that promises food for the easy taking. While Romeo had no moose to scavenge, no doubt he found steady opportunity, from winter-killed goats and deer to nasty old salmon carcasses. In thin times, he probably branched out into omnivorous endeavors, as many wolves will (scat analyses sometimes show surprising quantities of nonanimal matter, including berries, various plant parts, and insects).

A persistent rumor had followed the wolf from the start — one that offered an explanation for not only his apparent tameness, but his presence in the first place. Some murmured worriedly, while others groused: *Someone's feeding that damn wolf.* If so, a potentially dangerous case of food conditioning in the making. And a 2004 analysis of several Romeo scats by Fish and Game biologist Neil Barten indeed proved he'd ingested measurable quantities of dog kibble. Case closed, it seemed. If not being deliberately fed (one morning, handfuls of dry dog food lay scattered in the Mendenhall Glacier visitor center parking lot), he must have been snitching from backyard bowls. Not good news, either from a wildlife management or wolf lover's perspective. A quick shuffle through documented cases of what might be called friendly wolf-human interactions, including those recorded by McNay, links many such instances of amicable behavior — ranging from play invitations to fearless, inquisitive encounters — to wolves somehow getting food from humans. Food conditioning tends to occur in exactly the places you'd expect: at wilderness area campgrounds, along remote highways, around logging camps, and so on. No matter if the feedings are deliberate or accidental. The more they're repeated, the more likely some, if not all, involved wolves will become food conditioned; that is, they learn to associate people with food and, as a result, become increasingly tolerant — in fact, may actively seek out human contact. This tolerance sometimes broadens out to include stealing and chewing nonfood items like backpacks and shoes, or investigating camping gear and people themselves. In a number of instances, likely including the Icy Bay attack of the boy and Kenton Carnegie's death, and possibly that of Candice Berner, this fearless behavior has been linked to aggression. Even low-level fearlessness is viewed as troublesome enough that the wolves involved are often killed. Thus, the old line "A fed bear is a dead bear" applies at least equally to *Canis lupus.* Romeo the wolf seemed at high risk for a similar fate; friendly, playful behavior and toy stealing could well be symptomatic of food conditioning rather than social nature. It was just a matter of time, some figured, before things escalated.

What to make of these claims? Romeo almost certainly took advantage of deer offal and freezer-burned halibut or salmon that careless residents habitually dumped along roadsides and in parking lots as a means of avoiding either an expensive, odiferous trip to the dump or bears in their trash. Perhaps, too, he filched dog food off of back porches now and then; and it's possible he was deliberately fed by folks who didn't know any better. I heard my own name, as well as Harry Robinson's and photographer John Hyde's, connected to such rumors. How else to explain such close contact between the wolf and certain individuals? Respected naturalist and retired Fish and Game biologist Bob Armstrong told me that he once found dog treats scattered around the bases of willows along the Dredge Lakes shore, though he saw no evidence that they were left for the wolf or that he had eaten any. One woman who lived near Dredge Lakes admitted to me, years later, that during a hard spell of winter weather, she and a friend had left a deer head and some frozen fish where Romeo could find them. That was the single admission, from dozens of people I questioned, of an attempt to deliberately feed the wolf. Meanwhile, I never once saw the wolf approaching people as if he expected food, nor anyone offering him any. Nor did I ever find anything except wild prey remains in his scat. Of course, I didn't have the luxury of a testing lab, which brings us to the matter of that dog kibble Fish and Game found in his droppings.

While he may indeed have been the original consumer, I'm sure that much of it was secondhand. With so many dogs in the area every day, it was bound to be littered with clumps of stool, especially when a month's worth of snow melted down and a month's worth of leavings emerged. Not uncommonly, I noted wolf tracks leading from one to the next patch of brown-stained snow, and the piles conspicuously absent, with no sign of human cleanup. John Hyde saw the same thing. "No doubt about it," he told me. "[The wolf] scrounged his share of shit, especially his first year or two." The technical name for fecal consumption is coprophagia—a fairly common practice among many species domestic and wild, including members of the dog family. My own observations dovetail with Hyde's. The wolf ate feces but seemed to outgrow the behavior, or maybe it came and went, a fallback in thin times, when every calorie counted.

Whether by design or coincidence, Romeo's highly generalized, small-prey strategy at the glacier scored huge in the survival
sweepstakes. First, the black wolf had gained exclusive, convenience-
store access to most of his hunting areas. He not only avoided direct
competition from others of his kind on his human-made trails, but
also found reduced exposure to deadly territorial fights—our collective, surrogate pack presence helping to deflect human-intoler-
ant wolves. He also cut actual hunting stress to a minimum. Unlike
moose, salmon and beaver don't kick in your ribs, require time-in-
tensive, exhausting hunts, or present massive, tooth-wearing bones
to gnaw—the latter, a serious issue. Aged wolves with worn and broken teeth are among the first to starve; Dr. David Mech recorded
a case of just such a wolf, apparently unable to feed from a frozen,
scavenged moose carcass, while his younger, stronger-toothed pack
mates survived.

The black wolf's food also came in readily handled portions—a
huge, energy-saving advantage. One well-regarded theory among
wolf biologists explains why wolves evolved into group hunters: not
as much to tackle big, high-value prey as to beat would-be scavengers to the punch. Browns/grizzlies frequently usurp wolf kills, and
smaller mammals such as foxes and wolverines pilfer as they can.
Birds are often the worst looters of all—in Alaska, chiefly ravens,
gulls, eagles, jays, and magpies. One study showed that ravens alone
can consume 60 percent of a single wolf's deer kill before it can eat
it all, great for the freeloaders, not so much for the wolf. Thus a pack
is able to keep more of its hard-won meat by virtue of being able to
consume it so much faster. A dozen wolves can polish off a moose
carcass—say, six hundred to a thousand pounds of edibles—in two
or three heavy feeds just hours apart, leaving only a scattering of
well-gnawed bones, tufts of hair, and a dark pile of rumen in a tram-
pled circle. I've come across many such recent, stripped-down kills,
where every bone that can be has been snapped for its thread of
marrow, and every scrap of bloodstained snow eaten—more a testament to necessary efficiency than voraciousness. Even if a solitary
wolf like Romeo did knock down a moose, he would probably lose

more than half his kill just to ravens and magpies, whether he ate as fast as he could, tried to guard it, or cached leftovers. By focusing on prey he could chomp down in a single sitting, combined with the other advantages he'd gained, Romeo the wolf kept his energy currency in his own pocket. If his ethos had inspired those in charge of cutting government waste, we'd be turning a surplus in a finger snap.

In the end, no one can say with certainty whether the black wolf received food from humans, and if he did, how often or how directly. No one who spent much time around the wolf believed he was steadily fed. His behavior seemed too subtle, too consistent, and too relaxed to be anything but a natural expression of who he was. For all the complex, close situations that streamed toward the wolf we called Romeo, there had been zero reports of aggression to humans, and scarcely a curled lip so far toward our dogs. But whether or not the wolf was in fact receiving food from people, a time of trouble lay just over the horizon.

Romeo and Jessie

WHAT'S IN A NAME?

February 2005

There went Tim and Maureen Hall's female border collie, Jessie, racing across the lake, and Romeo, all 120-plus pounds of him, bounding toward her at top speed. They met in an ecstatic pas de deux, like two long-parted lovers — Jessie wriggling and fawning as the wolf leaped and whirled, tail high, both of them carrying on in pure celebration of each other's company.

The fact was, they saw each other all the time. Jessie lived two doors down from us, and all she had to do was slip out of the yard and across fifty yards of woods onto the lake. Or the wolf would show up at the edge of the Halls' backyard and wait, tail curled across his toes, the way he once did for Dakotah. This unlikely pair, a thirty-pound sheep-herding dog and its antithesis — a huge, wild wolf that would (at least in theory) stalk and eat the sheep the other might safeguard — disappeared together for hours at a time, and at least once, overnight. No doubt Jessie and Romeo were a tight, yin and yang item.

Of course the wolf wanted to hang with dogs. By the second winter, he traded pleasantries with pretty much every mutt that was willing to come his way — the usual tail-wag, sniff, and play-invite thing, sometimes leading to elaborate hijinks that lasted until the dogs got distracted, humans butted in, or the wolf spied a more interesting opportunity and went dashing toward wherever that might be, including a mile across the lake. On a busy day, he might have as many as three dozen canine meet and greets, most only a minute or two long, but a few that lasted an hour or more. With a few rare and notable exceptions, the wolf just plain dug his domestic cousins — apparently more than the company of other wolves, more than a meal of fresh beaver, and more than pretty much anything else, far as we could tell. In a number of cases, that attraction extended past fun-loving affability to the sort of personal bond you might expect of an ultra-intelligent, family-oriented animal on his own, trying to fill a void — not for purely biological purpose, like reproducing, or seeking hunting and patrol partners (the better to kill with, or defend territory). The dog-wolf social interplay offered no apparent survival benefits, and often the contrary, judging from the energy and time he expended. But the degree to which they mattered to the wolf indicated some complex need, no less real than food or shelter. Hard not to label these ties with certain dogs as social contact for its own intrinsic value: friendship, as we understand the word. As with human relationships, these bonds came in all categories, from strong interest to outright adoration, sometimes for reasons others might find inexplicable.

Though once upon a time such ties were dismissed as the products of wishful imagination, myriad cases of interspecies friendship — including such improbable pairings as a cat and an iguana, a lion and a gazelle, and a dog and an elephant — are well documented, from YouTube to formal journalism and, increasingly, research. A number of accessible books on the subject come to mind. *Unlikely Friendships,* by *National Geographic* senior writer Jennifer Holland, and *The Emotional Lives of Animals,* by biologist Marc Bekoff, serve as examples of a rising wave focused on animal behaviorism: the recognition that animals of not only identical but different species, some wild, others domesticated, possess the ability to establish filial and affectionate bonds, sometimes at astoundingly complex levels. Consider Holland's example of a cat that led around and protected an elderly dog for years after it went blind (one of several such documented "seeing-eye" pairings between animals of different species, from a variety of sources). So, a wolf and dog, friends? From a dispassionate, left-brain point of view, far more difficult to dismiss than accept the notion. All that's left to debate is the nature and depth of what we don't know.

This much for sure: Romeo didn't settle on his favorites due to lack of choices. Dozens, even hundreds of dogs of all sizes and forms came his way in any given week, brought by us as if at his command. Juneau is a dog city as much as it is an outdoor town, and the two are a natural mix. Going for a brisk ski loop with buddies, or sledding with the whole family? Catching up with a friend over a long walk, or just out for a few minutes at lunch? The glacier was the perfect spot—gorgeous and sprawling, wild yet accessible—and of course the pooches came along, part of our own pack thing.

Once again, our own, species-specific shaping of the landscape and its rules played perfectly for the wolf. Not only was the Mendenhall Glacier Recreation Area ideally shaped for Romeo's hunting needs; unlike most surrounding city land, the recreation area allowed dogs off leash, a big attraction for those who wanted to give their guys some room to run free without risking a ticket or dirty looks. The end result a grand outdoor soufflé, well seasoned with dogs—mostly loose and under shaky voice control. All perfect for a lonely wolf hoping to pry away the creatures we thought ours, if not permanently, at least for some face time with what they once had been.

As affable as the black wolf was, and always open to making new buddies, he knew what he liked most—often, it seemed, at first sight and ever after. Dakotah and Jessie were just two of the dogs he adored, and who could say one more than another? He harbored at least a dozen such intense attractions over the years, and though he seemed totally smitten in the presence of any one, he could switch to another without any apparent inner contradiction—more a Don Juan than a Romeo (though still curiously lacking that let's-make-pups component that would have wrung some hardwired biological sense out of the whole thing). As curious as the pull to Dakotah or Jessie may have seemed, it did make some sense. Both dogs were, after all, cute and sociable females that seemed as smitten with the wolf as he with them. You could argue they filled the role of surrogate mates, anyhow.

Now, consider the case of our friend Anita's big, black neutered male Newfoundland-Lab mix, Sugar. The dog was a total galoot — big-headed, goofy-eyed, slobber-jawed, given to hysterical fits of barking, and so incorrigible he seemed a sitcom prop: the sort of dog that bowls over little kids to steal their toys, rolls in rancid bear crap and chomps porcupines for fun, and nearly poisons himself to death by gobbling coagulated oil paint that couldn't possibly have tasted anywhere close to okay. I know, because I witnessed all the above. But wait — it gets worse. We're talking about a dog that serially humped an enormous stuffed-bear toy Anita dubbed Teddy Precious, in an obscene daily ritual best left to imagination. Anita had rescued Sugar as a gangly adolescent; no doubt he'd been ditched by someone who finally threw up his hands. Even kindhearted Anita, who loved him dearly (and in return was lavished with kisses often redolent of rotten salmon carcasses), agreed that the Big Shug must have been last in line for brains and been slipped a pair of dice instead. So, what does a galumphing nitwit of a dog have to offer the übercanid? A continuance of our good question, but here an already odd story shifts even stranger.

Sugar held one great passion beyond ingesting all things foul and making whoopie with Teddy Precious: chasing objects and bringing them back, over and over, to be flung again — sticks, toys, balls, whatever. He would have fetched in his sleep if he could have figured a way to keep one side of his pea brain awake. Much of Anita's bonding time with Shug, and by default with her border collie mix, Jonti, amounted to long walks and fetches out on the lake, right out the back door of the apartment we rented her. Anita and Sugar both needed the exercise, and dog and human were nuts about each other, one more case illustrating the point about inexplicable attraction. All in all, it was a perfect arrangement.

We'd taken Anita to see the wolf the previous year, within days of our very first sighting. It wasn't long after that she and her dogs were walking up the lake one cold afternoon, dogs coursing back and forth, the crunch of footsteps echoing in the silence between Sugar's earsplitting yelps for another throw, strained through Anita's own diminished hearing and her winter hat, that she realized she wasn't alone. She turned, and there was the wolf, trotting along behind them, whining his high-pitched come-hither serenade. Of course, she just about jumped out of her boots, as anyone would, especially out alone. But the wolf, grinning and tail waving, radiated body language that reassured her; and she and her dogs had already been introduced to the wolf by us. When she turned to face it, the wolf stopped; when she turned her back and walked, it kept pace about thirty feet behind her. Meanwhile, Sugar continued on his endless go-and-get mission, oblivious to the stranger; as long as the wolf didn't hijack his saliva-matted tennis ball, all things were good. Jonti, who had a tendency toward antisocial lip-curling—no offense taken by the wolf—ended up on a leash, just in case.

And so an odd, several-times-a-week quartet formed: book-ish, not-so-outdoorsy, forty-something Anita with her two dogs out front, and a big black wolf trotting along a dozen yards behind, whine-whine-whining, apparently thrilled to be going somewhere, anywhere with Sugar, who couldn't possibly have cared less. I don't think I ever saw that damn dog notice, let alone react to Romeo. He might as well have been invisible. For her part, Anita seldom looked at the wolf either and never locked eyes; her movements, too, stayed measured and predictable—a message I'm sure the wolf understood in the spirit in which it was offered. He must have appreciated the break from all the staring and jabbering he endured on an almost daily basis. Anita accepted the wolf as she did Sugar, without con-ditions; and, unlike just about everyone else the wolf encountered, she sought nothing in return. She never carried a camera, invited others along, chatted up her forays, or made any overture to the wolf. Sometimes I watched from afar for a few minutes with binoculars; other times I ran into our friend and her gang out on the lake, traded pleasantries, snapped a picture or two, and skied on. Cast in the slanted winter light, their circular pilgrimage in the glacier's cathedral presence, ever-shadowed by the dark wolf, seemed a living, breathing Salvador Dalí canvas, fraught with symbol and dream.

Anita and her dogs never sought the wolf; he found them and followed, cementing the relationship as one of his choosing. One afternoon Gus and I were sitting out past the Big Rock, chatting with two burly commercial fishermen and their Labs as the wolf stood fifty yards away, sizing up the social opening and ready to engage. A half mile down the lake, figures emerged onto the ice near Skater's Cabin: Anita and her boys. The wolf's head snapped around, and he was off and running toward them as if wire-drawn; he knew exactly who the hell that was. As the two fishermen watched open-mouthed, Anita and crew moved past to the north, Romeo trotting along as always, a few paces behind. "Well," one of the guys muttered, "she's got a lot of nerve, running off with the wolf like that." Pointing out the obvious — that Anita didn't have a whole lot to say about the arrangement — was, I decided, a waste of breath.

Though this odd canine couple posed a number of head-scratching contrasts, one clear difference lay in the matter of scale. Sugar wasn't known as the Big Shug for nothing. He stood a hair under ninety pounds in his muscular prime, stretched over a long, lean, big-boned frame built for running. With a more sedate lifestyle, he could have easily filled out another fifteen and still been buff. Next to Romeo, though, he dwindled to junior status. For that matter, so did all other dogs, even those few that outweighed him. The length of the wolf's legs, the density of his winter coat, and his chiseled head and chest made him loom far larger than his actual size. And no matter the pooch, I never saw a paw print in the snow that looked anything but puny next to his. Shug's big, floppy foot spanned little more than Romeo's palm.

There were other dogs and their humans, all with their own tales of platonic dalliance with the wolf; some I knew as friends or simply by face, and others I never glimpsed. Most wolf acolytes guarded their privacy, sometimes in elaborate fashion. Everyone who entertained such trysts thought their own experiences unique, and they were absolutely right — except for the stage-whispered fact that there was a queue of others doing pretty much the same thing, carving out private audiences at secret meeting places and times, all over the valley and beyond; some with dogs, a few without.

For me, one of the most memorable of these ties to the wolf existed between my friend Joel Bennett and his wife, Louisa. Several years preceding Romeo's first appearance, she had been diagnosed with breast cancer. In between harrowing bouts of surgery, chemotherapy, and radiation, she still made regular pilgrimages out to see the wolf, alongside Joel and sometimes me, shuffling along on skis or on foot, a beatific smile spread across her face. Louisa, beautiful in body and spirit, wracked by pain and sickness, never once complained. As Joel would later say, seeing the wolf helped keep her alive and filled with hope. And like Sherrie, Joel, and I, Louisa saw her love of Alaska personified in the graceful shape of Romeo, silhouetted against the mountain-framed glacier.

Beyond all others, though, Harry Robinson and his black Lab mix, Brittain, set an entirely different standard for social contact with the wolf. Close as it had begun, the connection between Harry, Brittain, and the wolf only deepened that second winter. Attraction and shared experience became interwoven, stretched across the frame of time. The three began to cover more ground together, wandering the forested slopes ever higher along the West Glacier Trail as well as Dredge, and along the base of Thunder Mountain, man and dog following, in weather foul and fair, wherever the black wolf led. Increasingly, they were a pack according to social function: they patrolled territory, and they rested and played — the latter in a way that included Harry. "He'd sometimes brush past me and bonk me on the leg with his nose," he remembers. "He loved to make snow angels or snow wolves or whatever you want to call them, and roll clumps of snow with his paws and push them, like he was building a snowman, and he'd look at me sometimes with that big wolf grin, as if to say, 'Look what I just did.'" On these forays, the wolf sometimes shifted into hunting mode; he'd disappear on purposeful loops, scouring for prey, and rejoin Harry and Brittain. And so these daily meetings between man, dog, and wolf—three beings of three species united in a manner more astonishing than explicable—became cemented in habit. The wolf often waited at the edge of the West Glacier Trail parking lot and bounded into view at the sound of Harry's engine. If the wolf didn't show, Harry couldn't avoid twinges of disappointment and sometimes worry. On the rare occasions when he and his dog couldn't make it, he was sure the wolf felt let down—certainly over his canine companion, and, he was certain, on his account as well. The three had set out together down a singular trail, and miles lay ahead, passing through light and shadow.

As for me, I continued the course Sherrie and I had decided on by the middle of the first winter. Though I saw the wolf practically every day, sometimes several times, and though he often waited a hundred yards from the house, I hung back and generally discouraged the point-blank contact that easily could have been mine, with either tireless Sugar or gentle Gus as intermediaries. And yet Romeo clearly knew me, and I him, a mutually relaxed and sociable connection. If he spotted me, with or without a dog, he'd often come trotting my way to trade friendly yawns and bows and allow me to approach if I so chose—something he wouldn't do if I had anyone besides Sherrie along. Sometimes he'd lope along for a time in parallel as I skied, the dogs running along behind, and we'd rest on the ice a stone's throw apart. I'm sure he never guessed how tempted I was to close that distance, but when he moved too close, I called the dogs to me and waved a ski pole. If we were up some empty Brooks Range valley, it might have been different; but here we were. As much as I wished, I couldn't squint the houses and people away.

Meanwhile, Juneau as a whole had continued to settle into a broader version of the same familiarity. There was, people realized, a wolf not just passing through, but living around us, an individual you could recognize and come to know, in some sense of the word: not *a* wolf, but *the* wolf. Romeo. The name had slid into such common use that even people who had never seen him adopted it, and everyone knew who that was, much to the chagrin of some wildlife managers and traditionalists, who believed naming any wild creature — especially something large, uncuddly, and carnivorous — was a foolhardy exercise in anthropomorphic fantasy.

The name issue struck a special sore spot among some local Alaska Department of Fish and Game and Forest Service officials. In the words of Pete Griffin, district ranger (head administrator) of the Juneau district at that time, "Naming an animal creates an illusion of a relationship that doesn't exist." Pete, remember, was a guy who thought having the wolf around was "pretty cool," so it wasn't about the animal itself, but the naming and all it stood for. The logic goes like this: by giving a wild creature a name, people unavoidably attach humanlike traits as well and come to believe, somehow, that some sort of reciprocal bond exists — friendship, or at least mutual understanding. This belief leads to overfamiliarity, close-range habituation, and conflict. Sooner or later someone gets hurt or killed. And if it ends up being a human victim, the animal inevitably follows. The carry-away lesson most biologists and managers point to is that human-wildlife relationships sooner or later come to no good.

The policy about naming, while clear and commonsense enough, isn't uniform among management agencies in Alaska or elsewhere, nor even within the Forest Service. For example, at the Anan Creek Wildlife Observatory, about two hundred miles south of Juneau, administered by the Ketchikan ranger district, dozens of bears, both black and brown/grizzly, show up every summer to feast on the creek's pink salmon run. As soon as a new bear can be reliably identified by local staff, it's given a name, often whimsical, that suits the animal's appearance or personality — about the same way junior high kids give each other nicknames, about as personal and unscientific as it gets. Same thing goes at McNeil River and Brooks Falls in southwestern Alaska — the first under State of Alaska supervision, the latter controlled by the National Park Service. Three different agencies rely on the same system for a simple reason: names are easier to recall and less likely to confuse than numbers, and everyone knows right away who Shorty or Alice is, how that bear behaves, where it hangs out. While one could argue those names are simply administrative tools, serving the purpose of science and management, there's obviously a deeper connection. Practically everyone at Brooks Falls twenty years ago knew who Diver was, and the same for Mrs. White at McNeil, and dozens of other animals, shared back and forth between staff, tour guides, and thousands of enthralled visitors, along with stories of those bears — each one a named individual known by appearance, habits, and personality. Some of the humans with the closest ties were not naïve tourists, but agency field staff who knew the animals best and, in most cases, christened them. As for names leading to trouble, those three viewing areas have remained models of safety over hundreds of thousands of human-animal interactions; and specific examples of animal names leading to management issues in Alaska or elsewhere are, at best, hard to come by. In truth, the to-name-or-not debate seems more a red herring than a genuine problem. Some folks mumble in their beards that it just ain't fittin', others ask, why not, and what's the harm if now and then an animal gets a name? Why not recognize certain wild creatures as unique individuals? The wolf sure as hell was that, and much more, in the minds of many.

The don't-name ethos carries an underlying message: *Keep your distance* — not just physical, but emotional. A wolf, like any wild creature, is technically a faceless resource, and there are those who would much rather keep it that way for a variety of reasons, not the least of which are the potential headaches posed by managing a recognized, popular individual — especially if "managing" means removing or killing, or allowing that animal to be subject to legal hunting or trapping.

At the far end of the attitudinal spectrum — common among self-styled sportsmen — lurks a deep-seated, knee-jerk disdain for those who would attempt to recognize and engage a wild creature as a sentient being. Palling around with a wolf, like Harry was doing, verges on cultural taboo in that crowd, where such behavior is considered not just misguided, but deeply offensive and a danger to the modern sport-hunting tradition—a strange disconnect, considering that traditional hunter-gatherer societies insisted on a deep spiritual bond with the creatures they sought, gave them respectful, meaning-laden names, and generally saw them as equals, if not beings with supernatural powers; in the terminology of Austrian theologian Martin Buber, an I-Thou relationship. Mainstream modern sport hunting, as represented in hook-and-bullet television and magazines, insists on a link Buber would have labeled as I-It—objectification rather than engagement, pursuing and killing faceless creatures as a given, legal right, for our own entertainment or profit, or just on a whim. California bear advocate Timothy Treadwell, who pushed the social envelope by giving cutesy names like Booble and Cupcake to Alaska coastal brown bears and hanging around with them for years, until he and a female companion were killed by one, became a magnet for ridicule among the hunting crowd, both before and after his death. If Treadwell had been a trophy hunter and had been mauled to death clutching a lever-action .45/70 as he stalked Ol' Baldy, he would have instead been mourned by the mockers, the same folks that would think it fine to give names to "rogue" bears, wolves, or whatever and establish individual relationships built on grudging admiration as long as the animal is inevitably hunted down and killed. But what was going on with this black wolf was something else entirely, something dangerously not right—and it all started with that damn name.

So let's back up and say the black wolf was never called anything beyond that simple adjective and noun or, in common research practice, was tagged with a neutral identifier—W-14A or whatever. Would that have changed anything that had so far happened, shifted his fate, or altered how we perceived him? The wolf arrived without a name, and his personality and actions over time led to it, not the other way around. And how many wild wolves have been named, in all our history? A double handful in dark notoriety, to be sure, but none in fond recognition, at least not while alive. "What's in a name?" Shakespeare's Juliet mused. "That which we call a rose by any other name would smell as sweet." Perhaps the same could be said for her lover's wild namesake, centuries later and worlds apart.

Romeo and Brittain

THE NEW NORMAL

March 2005

Romeo lay alone on the ice near the river mouth, stretched out in the afternoon sun. As I skied past a hundred yards away, he lifted his head to regard me, yawned, and squinted against the glare, but didn't rise. *Oh, just you,* he seemed to say, and settled back for another one-eye-open wolf nap. I paused, nodded in wordless gratitude — for both his familiar indifference and his presence — and double-poled on toward the glacier. Our second winter of the wolf had all but passed. The soul-numbing dark of January had given way to the ever-lengthening days of almost-spring, and all had gone far better than most of us had ever dared hope. To be sure, some carping persisted, but it had settled to background noise. Everyone, Romeo included, seemed to be setting a new standard for a large, wild, free-ranging carnivore peacefully interacting with humans and their domestic creatures — day in and day out, over weeks, months, and beyond. And not within the confines of some wilderness park with regulations and uniforms imposing order, but in semi-urban Alaska — as unrestricted as such an interchange could possibly be. Yet, over thousands of encounters, some of them in backyards and parking lots, interlaced with episodes of shaky human and canine behavior, there had still been no game-changing acts on either side — none of the menacing incidents, slaughtered pets, or worse some had predicted and, at least as surprisingly, no dead wolf.

As he'd become more settled and relaxed around us, and vice versa, getting rid of him would have been easier than ever; and his life had always hung by a strand. Most Juneauites seemed to have bought into the outlandish notion that this good-big-wolf-out-the-back-door arrangement was the new normal and those that didn't share that view continued to exercise remarkable, even admirable, forbearance. Of course, it was all too good to last.

A twenty-year-old local named Rick Huteson was walking in Dredge one mid-March day with friends and his two dogs, one of them a two-year-old beagle named Tank. According to Huteson, Tank, who was off leash, bolted and ran off into the woods, hot on the trail of something—in other words, normal beagle behavior. Huteson said he raced after his dog, trying to call him back. "It was only a matter of seconds before I heard a deep growl right in front of me and lost sight of Tank," Huteson told a *Juneau Empire* reporter. "A few seconds later, I saw the wolf running from me and I knew that Tank was in his mouth." Huteson and his friends were unable to find the dog, dead or alive. He reported the incident to Fish and Game and the next day renewed the search, accompanied by Fish and Game area biologist Neil Barten. As part of standard field protocol, Barten carried a 12-gauge shotgun slung over his shoulder, loaded with rubber bullets, with some slug shells in his pocket, just in case—enough firepower in the latter to knock down a charging grizzly.

Barten and Huteson scoured the brushy area. The spring snow was difficult—so crusty it scarcely bore marks from the day before, and laced with older, intermingled tracks, distorted by repeated melts and thaws: wolf, dogs, humans, and various small animals, from hares to squirrels. In places, water lay beneath the crust; the ice on some sloughs was starting to rot. Despite Huteson having been there just the day before, Barten couldn't find clear tracks or other signs corroborating the young man's story. They did locate a patch of blood soaked into icy snow, but not that much and hard to say how fresh. But no hanks of dog hair, chunks of bone, or a telltale collar.

Huteson's account, too, seemed less than certain and hazy in some details. One thing Barten did note: Huteson had a predator call in his possession, which he inadvertently pulled from his pocket as Barten watched. People use such devices for one reason only: to mimic the squeals of an injured hare, for the purpose of drawing a carnivore in close. "I asked him why he had it," said Barten, "and he fumbled around and told me he only blew it in his yard. That put a whole new color on everything." Barten offered a possible scenario in which Huteson had been attempting to lure in the wolf and had been successful. Coming on the run, all set for an easy meal, Romeo had seen a hare-sized, similarly colored animal darting through the brush, and his predatory instinct had kicked in. After all, the area was one of Romeo's favored hunting grounds, crisscrossed with bunny runways. Under those circumstances, and considering Huteson didn't have control of his dog, Barten felt he could hardly hold the wolf responsible. Besides, they didn't have solid evidence that Romeo had even killed the beagle; the blood could have been from a hare, or Tank could have even fallen prey to a bald eagle. (As if to underscore that possibility, a Juneau friend of mine reported an eagle dropped part of a dog carcass of unknown origin in her yard just days after I wrote this, years after the actual incident.)

Huteson asked Barten to hunt down the wolf and shoot it, and the biologist refused. Years later, Barten still feels he made the correct decision. "I saw no justification for killing the wolf," he said. "It's not as if he'd showed up the day before and killed the beagle the following day. We had a very large sample set of peaceful interactions between the wolf and dogs." A follow-up scouting of the area by Harry Robinson came up empty as well. He also found the bloody snow but no trace of the beagle, and did find tracks that could have been Tank's leading out onto some precarious rotting ice. As a final bit of circumstantial counterevidence, just a couple of hours after Tank vanished, an acquaintance of Sherrie's and her dog ran into Romeo on the northwest corner of the lake, and he seemed to be the same wolf that had never harmed a dog, nor had ever acted as if he might.

If the beagle's disappearance had been a criminal investigation, here's how the case to that point would have stacked up: no body and no positive evidence of a killing; no firm proof placing the suspect at the scene of the presumed crime; no history of the suspect's prior bad behavior in countless similar circumstances — in fact, the contrary; and the entire case hinging on the problematic testimony of a single witness. In short, no sensible district attorney would have found cause to file charges.

However, the details about the predator call, like Barten's view of the situation and those observations by others, never made it into the paper or passed into the realm of common knowledge. Instead, Juneau residents several days later met a feature article over their morning coffee: LAKE WOLF APPARENTLY KILLS BEAGLE, with the subhead DOG'S OWNER WANTS WOLF KILLED OR MOVED. Though the following piece was basically accurate and restrained in its conclusions, enough damage was done by the cause-effect headline and by what hadn't been included in the story. The piece also featured an unchallenged version of events from Huteson, who was quoted as saying, "Had there been signs and frequent warnings about the location of this wolf, and the danger it posed to humans, I would not have put my dogs or myself in danger." In short, Huteson claimed negligence on the part of authorities, though he admitted seeing the wolf the previous year and told Barten that he knew the wolf was around.

Rather than Barten (who was conspicuously absent from the *Empire* piece), Matt Robus, then Alaska Department of Fish and Game's director of wildlife conservation, defended the state's position. The press involvement of a senior department administrator, one rung below the departmental commissioner, was highly unusual in a decidedly local matter regarding a single animal. Years later, Robus would tell me his taking the reporter's call was incidental rather than planned (he wasn't even Barten's direct superior), and he had full confidence in Barten to say and do the right things on his own. But this was a touchy matter, and Robus, a longtime Juneau resident, knew it.

Beyond strong local sentiment in favor of Romeo, the department was catching heat for its controversial aerial wolf control programs in other areas of the state, which had recently been restarted.

While there was no such program in Southeast, the last thing Fish and Game needed was additional bad press, especially involving a unique, high-profile animal that might give a poster-child face to a broader, unconnected issue. The previous furor over state-supervised wolf killing under Governor Walter Hickel in the early 1990s had resulted in a widespread Alaska tourism boycott and the state's wolf-killing program being suspended. Caught between the larger issue and local realpolitik, the department needed to play its cards carefully. Meanwhile, a small but vocal Juneau anti-Romeo crowd had been stirred into action by the incident. Huteson's mother filed an angry and lengthy written protest with Fish and Game and posted one-page flyers around town, including in the Dredge area. A vehement letter by her to the *Juneau Empire* fumed, "What are we waiting for, another observation of a pet being carried off, or God forbid, Little Johnny carried away by a wild wolf? . . . I would hate to think Fish and Game is more interested in protecting the wolf for a tourist attraction then [sic] protecting the people who live here." Of course, the department had hardly been protecting the wolf any more than any other and, in fact, had not lifted a finger to do so. In addition, the added traffic at the lake was decidedly local, with few or no tourists mixed in; nor was there any record to suggest humans had ever required safeguarding from this animal. But no matter how inaccurate or overblown the rhetoric, the message had been broadcast, and damage done. *This could be the end of him,* I breathed to Sherrie. She nodded back, fully knowing what was at stake.

The black wolf had been effectively branded as a threat to people, and Fish and Game, the state agency charged with addressing such concerns (by default if not mandate), had been challenged to do something about it — in a manner the department could scarcely ignore. Not only had Robus not contradicted or qualified the uncertain evidence surrounding the beagle's death; he agreed that it seemed to have indeed been killed by the wolf. If the department didn't act in some fashion and someone did get hurt, Fish and Game (not to mention their federal partners in management, the U.S. Forest Service) could be subject to nasty, potentially landmark lawsuits.

The department biologists had four choices: do what they had been doing all along, which was maintain a lightly monitored, hands-off stance; relocate the wolf; attempt to condition him to avoid contact with humans and their dogs; or take lethal action. Due to that possible legal exposure, the do-nothing course was out. And while killing the wolf had to be somewhere on the back of the table, it was a nuclear option, with guaranteed toxic fallout.

Relocation, on the other hand, presented a nonlethal, viable alternative. This involved a team of biologists shooting the wolf with a tranquilizer dart, securing and stabilizing him, and transporting him to a suitable release point, far enough away to make his return unlikely — say, on the far side of the Lynn Canal fjord, somewhere south of Taku Inlet, or along the upper Chilkat valley, ninety miles to the north. Darting is approved capture protocol, and the state had relocated a number of wolves from the Fortymile River on the upper Yukon hundreds of miles south to the Kenai Peninsula a few years before, in an experimental program. Who could bitch about that? Wolf safe, people safe, story over.

Tranquilizer darting, however, can be a tricky business. The drug is powerful, administering it in correct dosage via a shoulder-fired weapon is touchy, and numbers of tranquilized wildlife, from polar bears to moose, die from stress, adverse drug reactions, and being injured by the darts themselves. Generally this mortality rate hovers around one percent, but occasionally it's much, much higher. Animals sometimes die during transport, as well, for a variety of reasons; in fact, several wolves from that Fortymile-to-Kenai relocation did exactly that.

Even if the wolf were successfully moved and released, dropping him off in an unfamiliar area, in bottomless spring snow, might amount to a death sentence — if not by starvation, then at the jaws of an established pack defending its territory against a weakened, hopelessly outnumbered, and disoriented interloper. And the wolf's movements and fate would most likely be recorded by a satellite tracking collar that would be bolted on after capture, the better to trace the wanderings of a known individual, for both study and management purposes—a two- to three-pound burden that some biologists believe can only make life more difficult. Consider such an added weight to an animal that depends on speed and flotation over snow for survival—the equivalent of a marathoner lugging several pounds of rocks in (quite literally) the race of his life. To further complicate matters, tracking data, especially in such a high-interest case, is often available to the public, and killing the wolf accidentally, or even the appearance of perhaps having done so indirectly, could balloon into a public relations nightmare. Robus summed up the dilemma in a nutshell: "Lots of people want to keep the wolf here. They think it is a fantastic opportunity to enjoy wildlife. If we try to remove or kill the animal, we will get more criticism than the current situation. This is a no-win situation for us."

The last option, attempting to train the wolf to be more wary of humans through a principle known as adverse operant conditioning, made perfect, low-risk management sense. In layman's terms, it's simple enough: send out biologists with a dog; when the wolf gets close, fire nonlethal hazing rounds at him—stuff that would sting or startle him, but do no lasting physical harm. After a few episodes, he'd theoretically connect people and dogs to the unpleasant experiences he'd had and keep his distance. The department had three types of hazing devices at its disposal: so-called rubber bullets (not always rubber, but projectiles designed to be nonlethal), bean bags, and cracker shells. All have been used extensively to repel or condition large problem wildlife. Rubber bullets, shot from a pistol, shotgun, or special-purpose firearm, have the most range and impact. But they're far from benign; such projectiles fired by riot police around the world have resulted in scores of human deaths and thousands of maiming injuries, and anything that would damage or kill a person could easily do the same to a wolf. Despite having fired very few rubber bullets at wolves (due to their normally elusive, nonconfrontational nature), Fish and Game biologist McNay recorded one wolf death caused by such a projectile, in the Canadian high Arctic. Bean bag rounds, a tiny pillow of pellets fired from a 12-gauge shotgun, offer far less chance of injury; but they're also inaccurate, with an effective range of less than thirty yards. The last choice, cracker shells, aka pyrotechnic rounds, are shotgun-propelled explosive devices that rely on the startle effect rather than impact.

The *Empire* article stated that the deterrent of choice would be a rubber bullet, though Matt Robus told me years later this detail was a case of misreporting. It wasn't his place to make such an order, and Barten would have consulted with his direct supervisor or been free to decide on his own. Barten affirmed in an interview that he used a bean bag round for the first hazing attempt, which happened to be witnessed by photographer John Hyde. "And I missed," Barten added wryly. "However, it seemed to have the desired effect. . . . [The wolf] was obviously frightened by the gun shot. I don't know that it even noticed the bean bag as it landed well in front of it. However, upon running off, he got into the cover of the forest and howled for a bit . . . and wasn't seen very often for the next several weeks." And though Barten patrolled the lake several more times as a follow-up, he said he never fired at the wolf again for a simple reason: he never got the chance. Whether Romeo had been successfully conditioned to avoid dogs and humans, or just Barten, was a matter open to debate, especially given that the wolf soon resumed regular contact with many of his friends, Brittain and Harry included.

Of course, a number of Romeo followers were upset by the hazing, which they felt was uncalled for. They worried, too, that driving the wolf elsewhere, to less-protected areas, would only place him in greater danger. Harry maintained that Romeo had indeed been struck with a rubber bullet and was limping as a result (and the wolf did favor his left front leg on and off the rest of that spring, though the injury could have been the result of a slip, a porcupine quill, or even a leg-hold trap he'd escaped). I, like many who knew the wolf, had mixed feelings myself. Making Romeo more cautious around our kind might well aid his survival, and if we weren't being selfish, his life was the bottom line. Whether by bean bag or rubber bullet, hazing was a restrained official response to an incident that could have easily ended up far worse.

Ahead lay at least a month of heavy wolf-human interaction on the lake and in Dredge—plenty of time for things to go wrong, and for some irate antiwolfers waiting for an excuse to insist on drastic action or to even take matters in their own hands. And what if Romeo had just decided that some dogs—maybe certain small ones that acted or looked a certain way, or had strayed away a certain distance from people—were now a blue plate special? What if one dog's disappearance were followed by another? A second such event on the heels of the first might well doom the black wolf, and the seasonal clock was ticking.

Within days of Tank the beagle's disappearance, a young veterinary technician named Bill was walking his twelve-week-old Akita puppy along the northeast edge of the lake. Relatively new to both Juneau and Alaska, he was a big Romeo fan and so of course was thrilled when the black wolf appeared out of the brush and began to gently play with the twenty-five-pound pup. But suddenly the wolf seized the Akita by the neck and bounded off into the willows. Bill's frantic calls for his puppy were met by echoing silence. Shocked disbelief gave way to waves of grief and remorse; he'd stood there and allowed the dog he loved to be taken. How could he have been so thoughtless and foolish to risk its life in the first place? What now? What could he do? He realized that if he reported the incident, he would have not one, but two hard deaths on his conscience; the wolf would almost certainly be killed in response. Though the thought of following the wolf's trail into the brush, alone and without a weapon, swept him with fear, he plunged into the off-trail maze before him. Before he had gone thirty yards, his puppy came scampering toward him, whining. It must have somehow escaped! He swept the young Akita into his arms and ran far out onto the lake before pausing to assess its injuries, bound to be major—and a nose-to-tail exam under his practiced, frantic hands couldn't detect a single laceration or bruise. Not a scratch. He scanned the tree line; the lakeshore lay silent in the twilight. The black wolf had vanished, leaving Bill both profoundly grateful and wondering what the hell. A year later, he'd be gone from Alaska, taking with him the sort of experience he'd see in his sleep the rest of his life.

What the hell indeed. How had the Akita pup managed to escape the not merely figurative, but literal jaws of death? Clearly, the wolf had let him go. But why? And was this a predatory incident inexplicably gone touchy-feely, like those nature television sequences of a cheetah expending a huge burst of energy to capture a gazelle, only to release it; or a hunting killer whale gently nudging a seal pup ashore, unharmed? Of course, even the most experienced researcher can no more than guess as to what crosses the mind of any wolf. My own hypothesis, shared by others, is as plausible as any: Romeo was puppy-napping—acting not as predator, but caretaker. All wolves in a pack, remember, are solicitous of the pups born to their family, and actively share rearing duties. Some pack members other than the parents seem to take special interest and display incredible devotion and patience in caring for the pack's genetic future. Romeo, a wolf of undeniably social and gentle temperament, was a perfect candidate for playing the role of an uncle wolf, and the dogs of Juneau had become his pack. Overwhelmed by the instinctive desire to tend the pup, he had carefully picked up the Akita (a breed with more than passing lupine resemblance and behavior) in those bone-crushing jaws and toted it off. When the pup wanted to return toward Bill's calls, he understood its distress and let it go. I can't think of another plausible explanation for why the wolf would have picked up that young dog so gently, carried it away, and then released it.

But that story, like so many others about the wolf, never drifted outside a relatively closed circle; or if it did, in a game of telephone with details lost or transposed, in some cases so skewed that the wolf killed another dog. As for Tank the beagle, I think it's entirely possible, even probable, that Romeo did kill it under the circumstances Barten suspected, though Harry Robinson and others argued, with good reason, that such a killing was unlikely, circumstantial at best, and totally out of character. Or perhaps Romeo had tried to pick up the beagle, and it had either panicked or turned aggressive and triggered a response from the wolf. Or maybe the dog had indeed fallen through the ice. We'll never fully know what transpired in those two encounters. Even those who knew the wolf best peered toward him like astronomers viewing a distant star, on the far edge of our galaxy.

The spring of 2005 continued. A rainy spell and a thaw interceded at the right time, keeping most people and their dogs off the lake for several weeks. Two feet of solid ice remained beneath the slush and water, and the wolf still trotted back and forth. A few diehards slogged around in knee boots. Dredge, too, collapsed into a half-thawed, flooded mess. Romeo appeared in the usual places less and less often; then one day, he was gone. Maybe he'd finally found a mate up in the hills and started his own pack. March faded into a warm, early-spring April, and there were no tracks on the dark, rotting ice. I still often sat outside at dusk, listening for a familiar howl echoing off the ridges, and patrolled the lakeshore, searching for a sign. And though I should have known better, I couldn't help but hope.

9

THE MIRACLE WOLF

March 2006

The black wolf stood at the lake's west edge at twilight, his form mirrored in the water's surface as he scanned the Dredge Lakes shore, a half mile away. He and the surrounding landscape stood silent, bathed in the glow that spilled through a veil of mist, casting a palette too subtle for any camera to record. A raven's cry echoed against the mountain as I stood alone, waiting for the world to exhale. At last the wolf stepped forward—not into the water, but onto it—and as I watched, he trotted across the lake, each step raising a silver-white plume and the spreading vee of a wake to mark his passing. At the far side, the wolf paused, a shadow among shadows, and merged into the night.

Though the wolf's evening stroll on the lake seemed an event of biblical proportions, a simple explanation lay several inches below the water's surface. A weeklong winter thaw, accompanied by torrential rains, had flooded the lake, dissolving snow but not the two feet of hard ice beneath it. But even if you knew the key to the wolf's deus ex machina, the scene was a spectacle to behold, and a reminder of the near miracle of his survival over three winters, now, among us.

Like any wild wolf, Romeo had run a gauntlet of natural threats since birth: starvation, hostile wolves, disease, injury. One slip, one piece of bad luck, and he'd have been gone. While his choice of a territory near and among humans had clearly worked in his favor, he'd also traded one set of advantages for an opposing cluster of threats, paradoxically from the same species that afforded him safety. No matter if most Juneauites wished him no ill; his death could hinge on the act of a single individual. Whether deliberate or careless, malevolent or thoughtless, lawful or not, the result would have been the same. No one will ever know the number of bullets, literal and figurative, the black wolf dodged over his time, but the few we knew of hinted at a veritable barrage.

While trapping as a way of earning a full-time living is fading away, Juneau, like most Alaska towns, includes an active enclave of recreational trappers. The best among them are skilled, persistent individuals who claim they're not just connecting to a vital frontier tradition, but contributing a community service by controlling pests and predators. They go quietly about their business and keep within their own circle. Properly placed snares or traps, either with a urine scent lure or fragrant food bait, are indeed the most effective way to catch and kill wolves, especially in rugged, forested terrain. The fate of the Douglas Island wolves and others, including those that may have been from Romeo's pack, attests to the local efficiency of both trappers and methods. Contrary to lore, most wolves are quite susceptible to traps; consider that the steel-jawed leg-hold trap, essentially the same in design over more than a century, played a vital role in their eradication in the lower 48. Though such trapping (with the exception of small-diameter sets for hares) was prohibited in all of Dredge Lakes, and within a quarter mile of established trails or roads both within the Mendenhall Glacier Recreation Area and on adjoining Juneau borough lands, enforcement was lax. Several times over the years, Harry Robinson and other hikers found evidence of illegal sets near the glacier and along other area trails — not all intended for the wolf, but some that could at least cause serious injury, all the same. However, reports to authorities were met with inaction. Enforcement officers probably saw a full-blown investigation for at best a wrist-slap ticket on some local hobbyist as effort poorly spent.

Filling that vacuum, some folks took to disarming or removing traps on their own.

While there was never sure evidence that Romeo ever ran afoul of such a device, wolf watchers at least twice noted the sort of pronounced limp and lower leg injury that well could have resulted from a trap or snare (wolves escaping sets is common, due to their raw strength). In the winter of 2005–2006, the wolf had disappeared for nearly two weeks; not even Harry knew where he was. When Romeo finally materialized, ribs against hide and more bedraggled than anyone had ever seen him, people who knew the wolf breathed a relieved, collective sigh — hardly the first, or the last. Maybe he'd been caught in an untended set for days before finally pulling free; we'd never know for sure. Even if the black wolf never felt the snap of a leg-hold trap or the tightening noose of a cable snare, there's little doubt he repeatedly encountered such hazards over the years and stepped around them. Through a combination of luck and that ever-broadening experience, he somehow managed to avoid the fate met by untold thousands of his kind.

Like trapping, large game hunting wasn't permitted in much of the recreation area. Bearing firearms, however, was legal; and while packing a gun never occurred to the vast majority of glacier visitors, a few availed themselves in the name of self-preservation. What constitutes a threat is, of course, a highly subjective matter. I've known lifelong Alaskans who considered any grizzly or wolf within sight to be a looming menace, and others who shooed bears off their porches as if they were outsized squirrels, and never felt the least twinge of danger from any wolf. One seventy-something Romeo viewer I encountered several times — clearly not of the latter camp — wore a holstered .44 Magnum stainless revolver on his Carhartt-clad hip on walks with his young grandchildren to view and take point-and-shoot pictures of the wolf. In my one brief conversation with him, in which I pointed out the questionable necessity of that sidearm and the danger it posed to other people on the lake if indeed he fired, he made it clear he owned the God-given right to protect his family as he saw fit.

I skied off, knowing he was beyond convincing that he could have tied a pork chop to his head and lain down and been in no danger. And anyhow, if he felt that great a risk to himself or those kids, he should have been somewhere else, and surely not deliberately approaching the animal that worried him. All too well I could imagine Romeo loping right toward that guy, on his way to visit a dog pal on the far shore, and ending up in a ruined, bloody heap over nothing.

Hunting for hares and waterfowl was allowed in certain small, remote areas of Dredge (not coincidentally, game-rich locales frequented by the wolf) and many of the hunters were local neighborhood kids, walking or riding bikes from their homes. Hard for an inexperienced, young buck out on a hunt not to yank the trigger at pretty much anything that moved, from mink to beaver, let alone a target as man-making as a wolf. One autumn day, Harry and Brittain had an object lesson in the dangers Romeo (not to mention the rest of us) faced from such budding sportsmen. Walking off-trail in Dredge one autumn twilight, hoping to hook up with Romeo, they found themselves instead on the wrong end of a poorly aimed 12-gauge slug, which thudded into a tree above Brittain. When Harry called out, a teenager appeared out of the brush, flustered and apologetic, while his friend broke and ran. Sorry, they'd thought that dark shape was the wolf. Doubtless there were other incidents. From my house and yard, I often heard single shots at odd hours emanating from Dredge or the surrounding slopes, and often I wondered if one of those would be the last sound Romeo would ever hear. And who knew what might go on in the adjoining upper Montana Creek valley, the high muskeg-draped forests of Spaulding Meadows, and beyond to the Herbert River, areas the wolf almost certainly traveled, where hunting and trapping in season were perfectly legal?

What, too, about backyard encounters—some guy opens his back door, and there's the wolf nose to nose with the family pet, and maybe his kids nearby? One of my neighbors, a crusty, lifelong Juneauite, informed me with a sardonic leer that the first time the wolf stepped on his property—a scant hundred yards from one of Romeo's favored trails—would be the last. Another local from a nearby subdivision, a woman who walked and skied with her young children near Skater's Cabin, told me she didn't want a wolf anywhere near her children—though she still went out on the lake, by far her best bet to ensure that proximity. The obvious message: something ought to change, and it sure as hell wasn't her. Such attitudes reflected more than a status quo from Romeo's early days; attitudinal lines that had been drawn seemed to be spreading ever farther apart. Folks who didn't like the idea of a wolf in the first place now pointed to the beagle incident, far from forgotten, as proof positive that Romeo constituted a danger to the community that shouldn't be tolerated, while his supporters maintained that we lived in Alaska after all, and people, not the wolf, were to blame for whatever had happened, or might.

You didn't need to be anywhere near the glacier or the wolf to sense the enmity simmering. At my photography booth at the annual Thanksgiving craft fair, a man smirked to his sons in a stage voice I was obviously meant to hear, "Hey, boys, doesn't that wolf in those pictures look like that one we skinned out this spring?" And as I stood in a checkout line at Fred's one winter afternoon, I overheard one rugged-looking, rangy guy confiding to another that a buddy had "taken care of" that damn black wolf; no one would be seeing *him* again any time soon, *heh-heh-heh.* However, Romeo, apparently unaware of his own demise, continued to trot across the lake on his daily business. Of course he was lucky, but far more than that. The black wolf was hardly a passive presence, subject to our whims. He moved among and around us, a formidable melding of intelligence, power, razor-honed reflex, and sensory input, constantly interpreting, reacting, and making decisions on which his life depended. He obviously had learned to read nuances of human posture and scent, and to fade into the shadows when danger whispered.

But even if he dodged humans of ill will time and again, dogs, the very creatures the wolf had come to adore, had ironically become the greatest threat to his existence. Any scuffle, even involving some out-of-control, poorly mannered, aggressive, or fear-reactive mutt, might trigger a deadly response—not from canines, of course, but their keepers. And such bad encounters, while rare, were inevitable, as they had been since the first days—no surprise, considering the sheer number of dog-wolf contacts on any given day, and the cluelessness, carelessness, or, in rare instances, the calculated intentions of some owners. Now and then dogs still approached the wolf with teeth bared and hackles raised, not knowing they were bringing a knife (and a dull one at that) to a gunfight. The wolf continued to dodge snarky dogs with grace and seemingly endless patience. Every now and then, though, Romeo would signal enough already, as when he shoulder-slammed a huge, persistently belligerent Malamute, then stood over him in a dominating wolf pose without making a further move, though he could have easily gone for a killing throat hold. I once saw him hook his snout under the chin of an overweight golden retriever—one of a trio that sometimes pursued him with more than playful zeal—and send the surprised dog somersaulting hard onto its back with a toss of his head. Another confrontation involved a male wire-haired pointing griffon that lake regulars knew to be sometimes aggressive toward dogs. Harry and others watched the griffon talking dog smack to the wolf and getting smacked down and pinned instead; though again, the dog was uninjured in the exchange. By the time the owner reported the incident to Fish and Game, however, the wolf had become the attacker, and the griffon an innocent bystander—one more black mark added to the wolf's record under questionable circumstances.

The centerpiece of one-sided aggression, though, involved two adult German shepherd dogs that launched an unprovoked surprise attack and ripped open a gash on the black wolf's back that third winter, an event witnessed by John Hyde. Romeo knew the dogs, and I'd observed them interacting with him without incident on several occasions over at least two years. But this time was different, who knows why. "They ran up to him, no warning, and literally tore hunks of hair and a piece of hide off of him," said Hyde, who picked up some of the loose fur and a chunk of skin. The injured wolf stood his ground, teeth bared, and the shepherds backed down as their owner scrambled to reel them in. The resulting wound on Romeo's back, and the reddish-blond, sun-bleached hair around it, was viewed by Fish and Game biologists and their veterinarian (who weren't aware of the attack) as possible signs that the wolf had contracted lice from domestic canines and now might spread it to other wolves in a potentially deadly and devastating epidemic — one more reason to consider taking action on the wolf. Such an outbreak had occurred on the Kenai Peninsula, south of Anchorage, a decade before, resulting in the decimation of local wolves. But over the course of weeks, Romeo's wound slowly healed; instead of spreading bodywide, as lice would have, the ratty-looking spot shrank, then disappeared, and Fish and Game once again held off.

There was another random, constant danger hanging over Romeo. Wolves, like bears, infrequently but steadily fall victim to vehicles wherever habitat is cut by roads; both are active in low light conditions, travel widely, are hard to see, and are prone to bolt at an angle to dodge a suddenly approaching threat — a proposition that may take them across an oncoming car's path. Locally, the threat was real enough; the reminder stood in that glass case at the Mendenhall Glacier visitor center: the black wolf struck by the cab on Glacier Spur Road, around the time Romeo had first appeared. Glacier Spur, and several other almost-highways where drivers often drive much faster than they should, bisected wooded areas where the wolf wandered. Then there was Egan Drive (aka Glacier Highway, or The Road), Juneau's heavily traveled main highway along the peopled coast, with skeins of drivers going sixty-plus, and of course, the grid of neighborhood lanes, avenues, and streets that crisscrossed the Mendenhall valley. We knew from sightings that Romeo traversed those major roads and plenty of others on a semiregular basis; he (or a lupine doppelganger) popped up here and there across the Mendenhall valley, and sometimes twenty or more miles to the north or south. No doubt the wolf was streetwise, in the literal sense. A guy I know happened to spy Romeo along Back Loop Road, north of the Montana Creek bridge, standing by the roadside. He pulled over to watch as the wolf, like some well-trained schoolkid, looked twice in each direction before trotting briskly across the blacktop and into the trees. That sort of caution would serve him well. Harry witnessed one driver, on the narrow, snow-bermed road between the West Glacier Trail and Skater's Cabin, take aim at the wolf and accelerate in an obvious attempt to run him down. Romeo leaped over the snowbank and out of harm's way—another narrow escape in a seemingly charmed life.

But one bright summer day in 2006, all that luck and grace came to an end. Part of me had known it had always been just a matter of time, but foreknowledge in such matters offers more curse than comfort. A woman out berry picking found a male black wolf carcass on the south end of town, bullet-riddled, throat cut, and dumped by a roadside turnout like a two-bit punk in some gangland execution. I sat listening, phone clenched in my fingers, staring out across the rippled surface of the lake toward the glacier, seeing nothing.

He'd been killed several times over. The slit throat, plus the carcass being ditched where it was bound to be discovered, seemed a pointed message. State wildlife biologist Neil Barten conducted a necropsy. The photos showed a large, black, young, and very dead male wolf. Just by those facts, it had to be Romeo, though I had trouble recognizing the face I thought I knew. This head was narrower, muzzle thinner. And a white blaze on his chest seemed different—larger and higher up. Well, a wolf in short, ratty summer coat could look totally different from a winter animal, and markings, even a wolf's color, can change with time. Death, too, transforms features. I didn't want to believe it was Romeo, but I didn't have a better explanation. Sherrie, I, and hundreds of others went about our business half-dazed and gut-punched, knowing it was over.

Investigation of the case fell under the jurisdiction of the State Wildlife Troopers. The killing had been illegal on two counts: shooting a game animal out of season, and wasting the carcass without salvaging the hide (which, given the time of year, was worthless, either as a trophy or for sale). But without any witness or lead, the odds of finding the killer seemed minuscule. Even if they wanted to, the

State Wildlife Troopers were stretched too thin to spend much time on the case. A request for phoned-in tips was the best they could do.

My longtime filmmaker friend Joel Bennett, who'd always held a protective interest toward wolves in general and Romeo in particular, dragged me into action. "Let's get to the bottom of this," he said. Though far from hopeful, I went along with him to meet the woman who'd first found the dead wolf. She led us to the spot, but beyond an arc of flattened grass on the steep, brushy hillside, there wasn't much to see — no shell casing you could match to a certain gun or exotic-brand, traceable cigarette butts like in the movies. Footprints and blood had washed away in the rain. Joel and I knocked on a few doors along that stretch of road and made calls; a commercial fisher named Paula Terrell, who lived in the area and had first alerted us to the killing, pitched in and made inquiries. Some folks had glimpsed a black wolf at dusk, trotting through the neighborhood two days before. Suspects? Well, a small, totally circumstantial handful: folks who were known to have a mean or wolf-hating streak, others who kept chickens they might have worried about, whatever offered a hint of motive. I felt like what I was, a second-rate gumshoe bumbling along a stone-cold trail. Joel was more determined. He, Lynn Schooler, and several others pooled in for a reward for information leading to a prosecution. "All right," I said, and added to the pot, then volunteered to make a poster. We started off offering $3,000. Several days later, Sherrie and Joel had plastered dozens of western-style reward announcements on bulletin boards all over town. Some were immediately ripped down; others became discussion forums. On one, someone scrawled *Shoot all wolves.* Below it, someone printed in ink, *How about shooting you instead?*

My phone kept ringing — a steady flow of people who didn't have information but were anywhere between shaken and enraged. Some were hunters, others glow-in-the-dark greenies, but all united around a dead wolf, shot in our town. Though at first we hadn't been looking for contributions, the reward swelled as Juneauites chipped in amounts ranging from $10 to $100, then jumped to $9,000 as a local dog-mushing tour owner pitched in $5,000 of his own — in part out of insult because he'd been pointed to as a potential suspect, and also because he was a Romeo supporter. Then we were over $11,000 and counting, so fast that we didn't bother to change the posters.

Meanwhile, I kept studying the necropsy photos, comparing them to the hundreds of images I'd taken of Romeo over the years. My certainty wavered. Several people who knew Romeo close up weighed in with differing opinions: it surely was him, or it wasn't. Harry Robinson was convinced it was not the same wolf, and yet, no one had seen him alive since the dead wolf had been discovered. I kept getting stuck on the same point: What are the odds of two different black, male wolves being killed inside Juneau city limits?

A month and more passed. Whatever thread of hope we'd held was frayed to a single strand when the first quiet report came in, perfectly tuned to the turn of leaves, and the salmon run in Steep Creek: someone had glimpsed a black wolf crossing the road near the visitor center. And soon after, Harry reported that he, Brittain, and the wolf found each other, and all was as it had ever been. Romeo had once again risen from the dead. In late August, the remaining mystery dissolved in equally miraculous fashion. Acting on an anonymous tip, the State Wildlife Troopers charged two men in the shooting of the other wolf. They'd been overheard bragging in a Douglas Island bar. The animal wasn't killed in Juneau after all, but near the mouth of the Taku River, a dozen miles south by boat. The men admitted to troopers they'd shot it when it had appeared along the shore, loaded it in their skiff, and cut its throat when the wolf, which they'd mistaken for dead, had stirred. They brought it back to town, then dumped the carcass by the road when they realized (so they said) that they'd shot it out of season and didn't want to risk getting caught with their illegal take. In the end, one man pled guilty to a misdemeanor and received a minor fine; the other went to trial, where a jury of his peers found him not guilty on the basis of his claim that he wasn't aware that wolf season was closed, despite the fact that ignorance of the law is technically not a valid defense. The whole business just went to show how little the life of a wolf was valued in Alaska; and Romeo, though still alive, was just another.

As for the $11,000 reward: no one stepped forward to claim it, a fact that speaks to the character of some unnamed soul, who could have been any of us. And Romeo? As I sat writing on a frost-dusted morning in November of 2006, I looked out across the lake toward a dark shape flowing across the ice in that familiar straight-backed, loose-footed trot and felt a burst of gratitude for a place and its people. While the glacier wolf didn't belong to any of us, he'd become part of who we were.

$9000 REWARD

For Information Leading to criminal prosecution of those responsible for illegal killing and dumping of a black wolf on Thane Road around Sunday, July 16. Call 321-5427. Donations to the fund accepted!

Harry and Romeo

10

THE WOLF WHISPERER

January 2007

Whatever the traditional Chinese calendar claimed, anyone whose life had twined into Romeo's would remember 2007 as the year of the wolf—a time of deep-drifted storm and swelling tension, and beneath it all, the sense that the raveled trails of the story, once soft and new-broken, had set hard, with no going back. We who shared space with the black wolf for four consecutive winters struggled with an ever more strident local reality; wills flexed, paths diverged, and divisions formed, not only between the wolf's enemies, but among his allies as well. Meanwhile, beyond the wrangles and our own glowing, warm dens, Romeo dealt with the work of living that only a wolf can know. The rest was not his business.

I stood at an upstairs window, jaw clenched as I stared out over the white sprawl of the lake on a sunlit, late-January midday. Near the Big Rock, a scant half mile from our back door, a small crowd milled—maybe twenty people and half as many dogs. Of course I knew why; the reason stood out, darker than any shadow against the snow, holding audience as always with his canine courtiers. But unlike years past, this was less spontaneous dog party than organized affair, and it had been going on for more than an hour—not only this day, but the past several, and on and off over the past two weeks. I tweaked my binoculars and sure enough, at the center of the action a guy with a long, straight-backed stride and a big-bodied black Lab mix merged into focus: Harry Robinson and his dog, Brittain. Whenever the wolf moved out from the group, or cast glances across the lake, as if preparing to leave, Harry approached near touching distance and stood by as Brittain and Romeo nuzzled and wrestled, and cameras pointed. When the wolf relaxed and trotted closer to the crowd, Harry, the ringmaster of this dog-and-wolf show, faded back, and left center stage to the black wolf and his playmates.

Harry Robinson, normally quiet if not downright secretive in his twilit wolf rambles for three years, had suddenly pulled a 180, placing both himself and Romeo in a hard-to-ignore spotlight. By choosing an arena just a couple hundred yards from the West Glacier Trail parking lot, during banker's hours and on a more or less regular schedule, he'd ushered in an era of up-close wolf access to anyone who could walk a hundred yards — sometimes without even changing from street shoes. Sure, folks who put in the effort and hours had long since watched the wolf many times from a distance, and perhaps thrilled at a closer encounter or two; but Romeo's social ease around our kind was still relative. Despite his general affability, he'd always remained standoffish, even skittish, around most strangers, especially those who stared and marched straight toward him and didn't have the right dog, or none at all. To the average viewer, he remained an enigmatic, intimidating presence, most often seen at a distance. Now Harry and Brittain, the ultimate tag-team wolf magnets and reassuring guides, pulled him in tight and held him within thirty or forty yards, and sometimes much closer. What the hell was he up to, and why?

That was just the first act in a surreal two-ring circus. Within a few minutes of Harry's early-afternoon departure, another knot of dogs and humans formed around the wolf along the opposite side of the lake, near the river mouth. Some people simply marched across the lake from one spot to the next, as if the wolf were Tiger Woods at the Masters. There, photographer John Hyde's shift picked right up where Harry's left off — by early January of 2007, practically an everyday event. With steady persistence and the help of a neighbor's two good-natured chocolate Labs (apparently on permanent loan) Hyde had conditioned Romeo over the past two years to accept his presence at breathtakingly close distances, sometimes so tight you could barely glimpse air between them. He didn't have to seek the wolf; it came to visit the dogs, and by extension, him. Hyde, being a superb professional wildlife photographer, understood the opportunity that he had before him and shot like there might be no tomorrow, which, on any given day, could have been true. While he followed wherever the wolf might lead, he purposely frequented locations with well-lit, knockout backdrops; and the Dredge beach near the river mouth on a sunny, snow-laden afternoon was quite literally picture-perfect in every direction. Even better, the area was one of Romeo's favored hangouts. But out in plain sight, where the unbroken scenic vistas lay, Hyde couldn't avoid attracting hangers-on. Operating as he was on public land, he couldn't shoo away anyone who wanted to follow and glean whatever opportunities or wolf juju they could. Much to his irritation, John ended up some days being shadowed by a gallery of photographers and watchers, sifting in and out of his compositions and distracting wolf and dogs. "I didn't want to share the wolf with anyone," he told me years later. "I wanted him all to myself."

Between them, Harry and Hyde had carved out as much face time with Romeo as the rest of Juneau put together. In addition to those regular public audiences, Harry was still going out at least once a day, early or late, to see the wolf alone, more than doubling Hyde's total contact hours. As one who'd stood within the wolf's aura and been smitten, I knew the pull that both men felt. I didn't blame them for that, but a glance out the window was all it took to know things weren't right. Regardless of opposing intent—one obviously trying to display the wolf to others, the other hoping not to—the end result of what some came to call The Harry and Hyde Show was the same: Romeo was exposed to more regular, up-close human contact than ever before, including folks who had little clue about how to behave around a wolf. At the same time, he was being inadvertently conditioned to accept a wide variety of strangers at point-blank range. A worrier could hardly begin to count the ways things could go wrong.

Romeo's life hung like a cornice of spring snow; the air beneath a raven's wing might be enough to bring it crashing down.

The foreboding was ratcheted up further by the political backstory. In December 2006, Sarah Palin had taken office as Alaska's governor and straightaway put her stamp on wildlife management: every moose a conservative and every wolf a liberal, and too many of the latter around. Although outside of Alaska, Sarah has frequently been blamed or praised for wolf control, the issue roiled The Great Land long before she was born. She merely served as the latest catalyst in an ongoing civil disagreement (and surely in terms of words and emotion, a war) that had long divided Alaskans in two roughly even-numbered camps. Two previous ballot initiative votes had put temporary halts to predator control, but each time the legislature had reinstated the program, and since 2002 it had steadily intensified under Governor Frank Murkowski. When Palin came on the scene, several areas the size of midwestern states were already open to aerial wolf shooting by private pilots and gunners with special permits. Palin appointees to the Alaska Department of Fish and Game and to the state Board of Game, connected to right-wing sport-hunting, out-of-state groups such as Sportsmen for Fish and Wildlife and Safari Club International, plus the in-state organization, the Alaska Outdoor Council, pushed for still more control areas and measures aimed at reducing predators, all under the scientifically shaky assumption that such tinkering with large-scale, complex ecosystems would automatically result in more moose, caribou, and deer for human hunters. And if not, so what? Fewer wolves could only be a good thing. The legislature's Intensive Management statute stipulated that wildlife be managed for human benefit, which they interpreted to mean maintaining maximum numbers of trophy and meat animals in a given area (maximum sustained yield). Most mainstream wildlife biologists agree that such management strains habitat and nearly assures perpetual boom-and-bust cycles and endless predator control, as wolves and bears take the rap for inevitable declines. Also, weren't wolves and bears also valuable, commercially and intrinsically? I once heard a highly respected senior Fish and Game biologist mutter that maximum sustained yield amounted to "smoke and mirrors"—an unattainable goal imposed by nonscientists who understood nothing about ecosystem dynamics. But state biologists who questioned the plan quickly learned to keep their opinions to themselves. Contrary to the principles of scientific discourse, a behind-the-scenes but very real gag order on the issue stifled dissent within the department. Both in and beyond Alaska, the always divisive issue waxed bitterer than ever, rendered all the more so by the scale and intensity of the program, unmatched since Alaska's territorial days, when wolves were exterminated by full-time federal hunters at taxpayer expense, including a bounty for each wolf killed.

Palin's rise to national attention would only throw more gas on the bonfire. Joel Bennett and I were caught up in it, too, as cosponsors of a statewide ballot initiative to curb the use of private pilots and gunners to kill wolves, and to require that predator control in a given area must be supported by local research that showed wolves were indeed causing low game populations (poor habitat quality and hard winters, rather than predation, are frequently the prime forcing mechanisms for low moose, caribou, and deer numbers). As a fail-safe, Fish and Game's commissioner would still be free to declare biological emergencies that could trigger localized predator control, conducted by department biologists. It seemed a modest-enough proposal, though of course we, the figureheads for the initiative, were cast as wolf worshipers and shills for Outside radicals—never mind my years traveling alongside Inupiaq wolf hunters up north. Sherrie and I and dozens of others across the subcontinental vastness of the state had stood on street corners from Ketchikan to Kotzebue, collecting tens of thousands of signatures to place the measure on the ballot. All we wanted was what many well-regarded wildlife biologists called for: a wolf management program built on area-specific scientific data, not politically driven angst and generalized pseudolore. Like others on the front lines, I gained enemies and lost friends across the state and got used to being cursed by people I'd never met; and though I'd hardly planned standing alone as the public face of such an issue, there I was. I'd expected Joel, seasoned by the previous two ballot measures and by long service on the Alaska Board of Game, to be the point man, but he had more important matters to face. His wife, Louisa, long struggling with breast cancer, was dying. He needed to attend to her, which included long absences to the hospital in Seattle, and caretaking at home. Of course, I understood his necessary absence.

This latest campaign in Alaska's long-standing war over wolves had been raging since 2005, and there was still nearly a year to go until the vote in 2008 — one that, unlike the two previous initiatives, would fall a few percentage points short, due to a variety of overlapping factors, not the least of which was ballot language (chosen by the state) so tricky that many voters marked the wrong box. No doubt, the politics of predator control were shifting toward the right — and whether the shift was temporary or not was anyone's guess. Looking back, I couldn't help but think of things I should have said or done that might have made a difference in the campaign.

A few weeks later, on a beautiful late-spring day, our friend Louisa died at home. Two days before, Sherrie and I had stopped by to bid farewell at the idyllic seaside home that she and Joel shared. The windows were open, and rufous hummingbirds flitted past the feeders as friends chatted; one by one, we went to take her hand. She was drifting in and out, beyond pain, eyes closed, smiling at our voices; and I remembered her just a few months before, pausing to lean on her ski poles at an opening along the campground trail, looking out on the lake toward the glacier, hoping to see Romeo one last time. Joel would commission a hand-built cedar bench installed on that spot, for passers-by to rest and watch as she had. On the back of that bench, cast in bronze, an inlay of Romeo reclines, howling — we hoped toward a place where Louisa could hear.

Though no systematic wolf culling was planned at that time for the Southeast region, Juneau, as state capital, was home to both the governor's mansion and Fish and Game's central offices; the top-down concentric ripples couldn't help but wash against Romeo's world. Local antiwolfers could only have been emboldened by the kill-and-grill crowd's party-line rhetoric: wolf control wasn't just about sensible resource stewardship, but saving wildlife and safeguarding our families, too. All in all, it was a bad time to be Alaska's best-known, most accessible wolf—and his affable nature only irked, even enraged, those who had no use for any of his species, especially not one that contradicted their own menacing version. Romeo, as unwitting poster figure for positive lupine-human relations, stood the ever-increasing risk of getting blasted for setting a too-good example.

And there I sat, caught up in a petty tiff, wondering what to say to either Harry or John. I understood the overarching motives of both men: Harry, to spend time with the wolf as his friend, while Hyde pursued a, if not *the*, professional photographic opportunity of a lifetime. While Hyde of course did what he could to protect the wolf while he was there, Harry saw it as his mission. All that separated me from them was personal philosophy and matter of degree. To all three of us, I'm sure the wolf felt closer to family than wild creature; and on top of that, Romeo was a living, breathing reminder of all I hoped and had failed to save, and of the ghosts from my past.

Considering the shared connection, you'd think it would have been easy to ski over for a friendly chat and straighten things out. But things between us three were far more complicated. Strangely enough, Harry and I, though among the first to meet the wolf in 2003, hadn't yet met in person. We'd spoken on the phone no more than four times, all during 2006, comparing impressions on the case of Romeo's body double and trading other wolf-specific information. And while I'd known John for years, we seldom talked; when we did in those days, it was cordial chitchat, never about the black wolf. Harry and Hyde rarely had much to do with each other, either. All three of us saw one another out on the lake over months and years, yet seldom acknowledged even the fact of each other's existence, as if we were suitors competing for the hand of the same exotic beauty, simultaneously bound and repelled by the force of that connection. Given our attachment and focus, such a comparison was apt enough. By ignoring one another, we each affirmed our own rightful position, while refusing to acknowledge that of our rivals. If we, the three peo-

ple who knew Romeo best, couldn't unite in defense of his best interests, who could or would?

Sure, I was angry — anywhere between irked and livid, depending on the day. Harry and Hyde were each spending way too much
time around the wolf for his own good, no two ways around it. However, that was just one of my opinions, and I held another that directly contradicted it. Just because Sherrie, I, and Anita had chosen to pull back both our dogs and ourselves, and some watchers
had always kept their distance, didn't necessarily mean others were
wrong for not following suit. Over and again I had to remind myself
that this wasn't my wolf or anyone else's. And never mind us — what
did the wolf want? Romeo, who waited day in and out for each of
these men and their dogs, and hung with them for hours at a time,
could have voted with his feet whenever he chose and melted into
the landscape, momentarily or forever. Claiming that either Harry or
John was somehow duping him was to sell short Romeo's own formidable intelligence, not to mention that already-proven, almost magical talent for turning strange situations to his own advantage. You
could easily make the case that rather than being used, he'd somehow conned those guys into providing what he most pined for: close,
regular contact with friendly canines, regular enough that he could
form a lasting, packlike bond. Romeo was making his own choices,
and we had to respect the instincts and judgment that had so far
served him so well.

But with this increased, almost ritualistic close contact, now
merged into public spectacle, weren't Harry and Hyde practically
cowriting a manual for everything not to do around wildlife: inter-
fering with the wolf's natural behaviors; habituating him to close
and prolonged human contact, which made him more vulnerable to
those with bad intent; stressing him out by their proximity; monop-
olizing a public resource; creating a bad example for others to follow;
and hurting his chances of survival by sucking up time he should
have spent hunting or resting? That was the commonsense analysis
most professional wildlife managers and enforcement officers would

(and did) espouse; and in most situations, that evaluation would be spot-on.

However, the ground-truth reality of this wolf, like everything else about him, was far more complex. Romeo, by then at least six years old, was in tremendous shape: glossy coat, clear eyes, unworn teeth, deep chest, and a smooth gait—all in all as handsome and healthy a wolf as ever trotted the earth. I had little doubt he tipped the scales well past 120, maybe even as high as 130 pounds in times of plenty—an exceptional example of the species, by any standard. If anything, spending all that time with those two and their dogs seemed to be a positive tonic. And folks who believed (as most of those who knew the wolf did) that the wrong human, whether wielding a gun, trap, vehicle, out-of-control dog, or poor judgment, posed by far the largest threat to his survival also realized the risk dropped to near zero in the right company. Simply put, no one was going to illegally shoot or trap the wolf with witnesses at hand. While hundreds of other Juneauites, consciously or not, contributed to the general wolf watch, and I probably had the most sightings, due to the commanding view from my house and its proximity to Romeo's territory, Harry and Hyde were the two individuals in the trenches most often by far. From a pragmatic angle, it'd be hard to find better guardians than those two: capable outdoorsmen who were comfortable and even-keeled around Romeo, knowledgeable of his mannerisms and habits, not shy to advise or correct viewers, and most important of all, present for long hours, day in and out. Neither the Forest Service, Wildlife Troopers, nor Fish and Game had the manpower, let alone the least inclination, to do what these men did on their own. Whether you saw the motives of each as pure or self-serving, or some blend of the two, the end result—what really mattered, if what you truly cared about was Romeo—was the same. As for my own jealousy (after all, I knew damn well it could have been me out there, hanging around each day within touching distance of a wild animal I loved like no other), I had to open my hand and let it go. Though I knew all that, I still was riled about those crowd scenes.

Too many people with too little experience and not enough common sense were getting too close for anyone's good, and no one could hope to control all the variables.

As it turned out, an altruistic motive lay behind Harry's public wolf-viewing sessions; he'd had requests from other Romeo aficionados, asking to see the wolf with him as guide. Naturally, Harry hoped more people seeing the wolf for the sociable creature he was would strengthen or forge their desire to protect him, and help in passing the word in all directions. Too, he seemed to embrace the name a local pilot applied to him, after spotting Harry, Brittain, and the wolf hiking together above the timberline on McGinnis: the Wolf Whisperer. Harry explained to anyone who asked that Romeo had accepted him as a friend, and vice versa — not as a brag, but calmly stated, level-eyed truth.

Friendship: an odd, and many would say naïve word to describe the relationship between any human and a wild beast, especially one that might devour one's children. The naming issue by itself lay bad enough in the eyes of wildlife managers, self-labeled sportsmen, and a general assortment of naysayers, for all that it implied. That the wolf had forged affectionate, personal bonds with certain dogs had to be conceded as observable fact. But outright friendship with a human seemed to insist on yet another, controversial (to some, hackle-raising) level of interspecies connection. Of course, friendship can be a one-way, nonreciprocal flow of positive thoughts and deeds from one being to another; just because we acted as the wolf's friends, didn't mean he was ours. But what about that ultimate bond, a human and a wild wolf, true bonded friends, each taking pleasure in the other's company? John Hyde, when I asked him years later, shrugged and shook his head. "Nah, it was all about the dogs. The wolf recognized me, and was used to me, and didn't mind me, but that was it." Then he paused and added, "He was one hell of an animal. . . . I can't even begin to describe the connection." Watching his eyes, I glimpsed something more, in the silence between words.

Harry Robinson has a different story to tell — one that seems straight out of some Pixar fantasy. As Harry told it then, and still does now, he and the wolf indeed became friends, in all ways that a bonded dog and human might be, and more. In his words, "Brittain was his pseudomate/love of his life, and I was more his trusted friend/alpha male role model. He began to depend upon me for guidance and security." Regardless of how self-assured and anchored the voice, that was a lot to believe; and I'm still not quite sure of the edge between what I do and don't. But anyone who really watched Harry and the wolf out on the ice couldn't help but notice the connection between them in those crowd situations — more than tolerance, more than acceptance, something closer to trust. And understanding, too — similar, outwardly, to the transactions of glance, posture, and utterance that connect human and dog: body language and gestures, eye contact, short vocalizations. I wouldn't call the wolf trained, and Harry agrees; the word implies a subservience that didn't exist. Instead, information flowed in both directions, in a way that made perfect sense. If dog is 99.98 percent wolf, then the reverse is true as well — and communication methods that worked between humans and one species should serve the sensory interface of the other. Granted, the gulf between Pekingese and *Canis lupus*, though measured in microns along a double helix, still yawns huge; a wolf remains centuries of selective breeding distant from a dog and can't become one merely by being treated as such, even if captive-born and imprinted by constant handling and interaction.

But neither was this an ordinary wolf, nor Harry an ordinary human; nor was their history together anything near ordinary. Since 2003, he and Brittain had been meeting the wolf on an almost daily basis, sometimes more than once a day, and often for hours at a time. They roamed together, rested, and played — tens, then hundreds, finally thousands of hours in all seasons and weather, over a growing sweep of years. Like any of us who'd met the wolf, the bond began with wolf to dog but, to an extent that must have surprised even Harry, ended up including him as well. "As time progressed," Harry said, "Romeo and I developed a personal relationship that was quite independent from the one he had with Brittain. Usually in the mornings, he would run to greet Brittain first and then come over and greet me separately." The hello amounted to a grinning approach, a gently waving, high-held tail, affable yawns, and play bows. Romeo had long passed simply accepting Harry. He engaged him: made and held eye contact, brushed against his leg as they passed on the trail, played with him, sometimes delivered a nose bonk on the back of his thigh. Harry said that he never reached out to touch or pet the wolf, though he might have many times; neither did he ever feed him, as some who never met Harry claimed — apparently supposing that was the only way anyone could lure and hold a wild, predatory beast that close. A social relationship between human and wolf, companionship for its own sake, couldn't be; though clearly, just such a bond must have formed not once, but many times in our collective past. How else did we end up with the shaped children of wolves lying at our feet?

"He would obey a number of my commands, although he would usually carefully consider them beforehand," Harry said. "He'd observe a situation and reason it through. . . . [But] he definitely knew what the word *no!* meant." Though claims of voice control over a wild, never-captive predator strain credibility, several times as I watched those crowd scenes through binoculars I saw Harry gesture or murmur unheard syllables to the wolf, and the wolf respond. Fish and Game area biologist Ryan Scott once sent Harry an email thanking him for intervening in and diffusing a physical confrontation with a large husky mix, in which the wolf apparently followed Harry's direction to back off.

Whatever Harry did with others watching, his most profound moments with the wolf came in their times alone — off in the wild, out of sight of others. Most often, especially during times of snow, cold, and short days, the three would trace game trails and visit rendezvous spots lower down, in the rolling spruce-hemlock forest above the West Glacier Trail or in hidden thickets in the Dredge Lakes, both areas the core of the black wolf's territory. In summer, when sightings of the wolf were so rare that most people assumed he wasn't around, their secret rambles often began in the pale, gathering light of 3 A.M. and reached far onto the alpine shoulders of

Mount McGinnis, so high they looked down on the glacier's furrowed expanse. Wolf and dog would range uphill and down, following their noses and scent-marking, pausing for play sessions, the wolf occasionally breaking off on his own, and returning. More than once the wolf led them, Harry said, to a crevasse-riddled crossing toward Bullard Mountain, less than a half mile from the glacier's face—and looked back, disappointed, before continuing alone, when man and dog did not follow through the deadly ice maze toward the fine hunting on the far side. Sometimes, too, Romeo brought out that tattered tennis ball (maybe one of ours from that first winter) or the plastic foam buoy he had stashed in the brush, and initiated games of fetch.

However unbelievable the tale to this point, it waxes more so. As Harry tells it, Romeo once sensed something ahead on one of their walks, bristled, then lunged forward, growling, as a locally known brown bear and grown cub appeared around a bend in the trail, a few dozen feet away. As the wolf charged in defense of his pack, the bear turned tail, and Romeo completed the rout. On another occasion, Romeo engaged in the same behavior to drive off what Harry suspected was an unseen black bear.

Again, what to believe? There are no eyewitnesses to corroborate most of Harry's accounts. However, his conversations with me in the years since have been marked by a consistency of detail and the sort of level-gazed assurance that are difficult to dismiss. He's pointed to me the exact places where certain events occurred—a rock outcropping, a mossy glade, a barely visible game trail—and led me to bits of physical evidence such as a scattering of goat bones from a kill site where he watched Romeo feed, and a certain spruce tree with drooping, springy limbs that the wolf loved to leap for, grab in his jaws, and tug against (indeed scarred by apparent tooth marks), all of which further cement his versions of events. What few witnesses there are—notably ex–Alaska state senator Kim Elton, who occasionally tagged along with Harry and in fact took pictures of Romeo reclining, gnawing on the ribs of that aforementioned goat kill—offer support rather than contradiction. Joel Bennett and attorney Jan Van Dort, too, tagged along with Harry a number of times and con-

firmed the close, interspecies connection between this man, a wild
wolf, and his dog.

What about precedents for this sort of relationship—an apex
predator and a man, friends? Dozens of well-documented tales of lifelong bonds of friendship between captive or rescued wild carnivores
and humans exist, from the real Grizzly Adams and his namesake
companion, Benjamin Franklin, strolling the streets of nineteenth-
century San Francisco to the contemporary story of Costa Rican fish-
erman Chito Shedden frolicking in a pond with a doting thousand-
pound saltwater crocodile he named Pocho. These and other stories
support the emotional capacity of certain individual "man-eating"
predators in unique circumstances to develop affectionate, lifelong
relationships with humans. But no matter how gilded, bars cast an
inescapable shadow. Even if a once-captive creature makes a full
transition into the wild—as in the celebrated 1970s case of Christian
the lion and Englishmen John Rendall and Ace Bourke, whose ecstatic reunion in Africa, years after Christian's release, is memorialized on film—the unavoidable circumstances of captivity and a fully
dependent relationship, including feeding, create a context quite different from that linking Harry to Romeo, a born-wild, free-wander-
ing animal that had always hunted on his own and showed no sign
of associating him with food. Again, Harry flatly denies ever having
fed the wolf, though he always carried a pocketful of dog jerky treats
for Brittain. "I once accidentally dropped a strip out of my pocket,"
he said, "and [Romeo] gave it a quick sniff and left it. He obviously
had better things to eat." On the other hand, the wolf was happy to
snatch up a shearling mitt someone had lost, toss it around, and rip
it to pieces.

Food conditioning—already discussed, frowned upon by wildlife
managers for obvious, valid reasons—can create at least the appearance of friendship between humans and wild predators, and such instances are fairly common. In one extreme example from contemporary Alaska, a man named Charlie Vandergaw fed dozens of bears,
both black and brown/grizzly, at his remote homestead over a period
of years and achieved a remarkable rapport with a number of indi-

vidual animals before being prosecuted by the state. Judging from the outtakes of his six-episode reality TV show, at least some of the bears ended up in it for more than the food; the human-ursine interaction seemed to go beyond caloric interest, to obvious social interaction for its own sake, and even affection. Using high-value treats for positive behavior reinforcement is standard procedure for animal trainers working with captive wildlife, including predators such as killer whales and grizzlies, with whom they have a close social bond many keepers would insist to be friendship, and with good reason; there's obviously more to the food conditioning issue than meets the eye. But managers point to such apparent friendships as false, anthropomorphic interpretations and rightly claim that such feeding leads straight to too-close interaction and potential animal-human aggression.

With no human feeding involved, sociable interactions between people and free-ranging predators are not only possible, but not as rare as you might think. I can recall at least a dozen times over the years when, for reasons unknown, an animal made some sort of social overture—that Brooks Range wolf picking up a stick and shaking it at me in a play invitation; a young brown bear on a wide grass flat sauntering over to plunk down twenty feet away and make relaxed, friendly gestures; a short-tailed weasel who turned the tables on food conditioning and brought me a fresh-killed vole as an offering, bounding over to lay it near my feet; a fox that kept me company on a woodcutting expedition; Romeo trotting over to say hello, as he did so many times. A Google or YouTube search will bring up dozens of positive social interchanges between humans and wild carnivores from lions to sharks. My personal favorite is another backward feeding episode: *National Geographic* photographer Paul Nicklen being offered penguins, one after another, by an enormous female leopard seal. But these moments are usually brief; few, if any, are sustained for days or months, let alone years.

Timothy Treadwell surely managed to establish amicable, individual relationships with a number of bears in western Alaska's Katmai National Park over thirteen years; but Joel Bennett, who filmed him repeatedly in the field, and himself became close friends with Treadwell, stops short of declaring that remarkable rapport with certain bears to be friendship. "Who knows?" he said, spreading his hands to the sky.

One clear case involves the more than quarter-century friendship between a wild dolphin named JoJo and naturalist Dean Bernal, in the British West Indies. Their shared affection, captured in video and still photography, is unmistakable; and though feeding is no doubt part of their relationship, it's clearly not the driving factor. Bernal, who's been JoJo's official warden for decades, has nursed him through a number of life-threatening injuries; they roam and hunt lobster together, JoJo following his skiff; the dolphin and he swirl in tender underwater ballets. Their case serves as exemplar, indicating such relationships are indeed possible. Wild dolphin and human, fine. *Flipper* and SeaWorld, not to mention dozens of anecdotes of contact between these two seemingly akin species, going back into ancient history, prepared us for that one. But what about a wild wolf?

Plenty of remarkable, sociable interactions between never-captive wolves and humans do indeed exist. Excluding Romeo, I'd experienced several myself, up north, and woods-wise friends have told me of their own; but they're all fleeting experiences, not relationships. When it comes to boots-on-the-ground, prolonged contact, well-respected wolf biologists like David Mech and Gordon Haber repeatedly gained high degrees of habituated tolerance from members of wild, free-ranging packs they studied, and occasionally had wild wolves initiate social behavior with them; but they followed a no-interaction model as part of good research practice — the exact opposite of Harry Robinson. Harry, of course, was no scientist and didn't pretend to be. He had no hypotheses to test and compiled no data; he didn't even keep a simple logbook or journal and almost never carried a camera. His agenda was simple: he wanted to be a friend to Romeo, whom he saw as desperately lonely. "I did it for the wolf," he said. "He depended on us."

What further persuades me to accept Harry's story overall is the lens of my own experience. Though I watched the wolf from a distance on an almost daily basis from late autumn through mid-spring, sometimes as many as a dozen times in any given day, I limited close, self-initiated contact to no more than a half-dozen times a year and usually less than an hour. I figured the wolf already had too many humans in his face, and the best thing I could do was set a good example and keep my distance. The times I broke down were simple failings of will. In any case, if I had dogs along, they weren't allowed to approach the wolf any longer. Despite that slim social reward, and no good reason for our cold shoulder from his point of view, Romeo would still come loping across the lake to greet us as if we were among his favorites, and trot along with us for a time. He knew exactly who we were and, judging from his reactions, remembered a fond past, now several years gone—Dakotah, tennis balls, and all. I have since been able to confirm the acute memory power and drive of a wolf to maintain cross-species bonding in my interactions with Isis, a captive-born, imprinted wolf at the Kroschel Wildlife Center in Haines, Alaska. I first held her when she was four weeks old and interacted with her—intensively, but just several times. Now age four, she clearly shows she remembers me by her excited, submissive greetings (this past summer, singling me out of a crowd of tourists at the park), despite months between visits. Incidentally, she also fetched the very first time I threw a toy, apparently a hardwired, rather than learned behavior, since Steve Kroschel told me not he nor anyone else had to that point engaged her that way.

If I was alone and moved gradually, Romeo would allow me to approach within a few yards with no sign of unease. Generalized tolerance or friendliness toward known dogs was one thing; but if I stopped and sat down, he'd often close the distance and display his usual sociable body language (bows and unstressed yawns, relaxed eye contact, and sometimes wolf grins) even if I didn't have a dog with me. He had a markedly different response to most strangers. I'd offered to help out photographer Mark Kelley, a good friend who had so far been unsuccessful in getting a decent shot of the wolf. We spotted Romeo lying over near the river mouth, and I told Mark to stay back and wait for my signal. I skied to within a hundred yards, sat on a boulder on the shore, and Romeo stretched, yawned, and trotted over to say hello, and lay down maybe twenty yards away. Once he settled in, I waved, and Mark meandered toward us from a third of a mile out, making no eye contact as I'd advised him. But he hadn't covered half that distance before Romeo took notice, abruptly rose, and trotted off into the willows. Mark would eventually get his shot, after he had put in enough time.

Sometimes, for reasons known only to himself, Romeo would take up with a little-known human. My neighbor Kim Turley, by his own admission, had few doings with the wolf, beyond occasional sightings. However, something extraordinary occurred between them one April day. Turley and his wife, Barbara, dedicated outdoors people and the cofounders of the Juneau Alpine Club, had run the ski loop out on the lake for nine mornings in a row. Each day, they saw Romeo lying in one of his usual waiting places. But on the tenth day, Romeo rose and trotted along behind them, following, in Kim's words, "as if he were our dog, just a few feet behind. He just seemed lonely and wanted the company." The couple and wolf trotted the entire four-mile circle together; Romeo stopped only as they left the lake. "I've never had an experience like that in my life," Turley murmured. When I think of Kim, and what I know passed between the wolf and me over the years, Harry's quiet claims seem not only plausible, but likely.

Of all my times with the wolf, some much more action packed and dramatic, this is the one that keeps coming back. One warm April afternoon, Romeo, Gus, and I dozed together out on the ice near the river mouth, me with my head on my pack, skis off; Gus with his head on my thigh; Romeo with his muzzle resting between his outstretched front paws. It was one of those still days when you could hear snowdrifts collapsing in hisses, the sun so dazzling off the white-crusted ice that we seemed suspended on a cloud, bathed in light radiating from below. Now and then the wolf would slit open an eye to check around, then settle back for another short snooze, and I'd do the same. Maybe twenty feet separated us, but in trusting enough to shut his eyes and sleep with me so near, he might as well have put his head alongside Gus's on my leg. There we lay, three different species bound by a complex, often bitter history, taking simple comfort in the others' presence, the sun's warmth, and the passing of another winter. That afternoon remains with me, one of those clear, still moments that grace the edge of dreams. When Gus and I finally rose, Romeo did the same, yawned and stretched, then lay back down and watched us glide away, toward the alien world from which we'd come. I recall looking back as he dwindled to a dark point against the snow, as if for the last time. I watched hard, hoping to remember.

The Afghans

PUGS AND POMERANIANS

February–April 2007

With all the politically charged background and human drama per-
colating, the last thing the wolf needed was a spate of negative dog
encounters. Call it bad luck or foregone conclusion, that's exactly
where the winter of 2006–2007 led. The season began well enough,
with the pattern we'd come to expect: increasing sightings from late
summer through the autumn, and almost daily, serial dog interactions out on the lake once the ice set, plus sporadic, sometimes startling cameos outside Romeo's core territory. His return from the
dead that summer had no doubt galvanized his base and gained new
supporters. His apparent loss had reminded us of what we had, and
the collective response had focused and knitted tighter the community that embraced him. All the space his story had garnered in
newsprint, radio, and conversation had stirred interest among those
who had yet to see the wolf. No wonder more people came to the
lake than ever: to discover what the fuss was about, or connect again
with what they already had felt. And on top of all that, the Harry and
Hyde show was playing at a lake near you. The hydra-headed management issue confronting us all was rooted in a simple matter of ra-
tio: triple the viewers, and still just one wolf—increasingly and inevitably relaxed and tolerant, and so ever more accessible. No matter,
either, that the vast majority wanted to do right. A varying combina-

tion of factors—inexperience and a sense of false familiarity among many, often bordering on crowd mentality (where whatever you're doing must be okay because everyone else is doing it)—led toward bad judgment and, in some cases, flat-out disregard. Plus the same old hard-core crowd wanted Romeo dead, on general principles. You didn't have to be John Fogerty to see a bad moon rising.

Scarcely into the winter, a pair of bizarre, bookend incidents highlighted how near we'd drifted to the edge. I was direct witness to one and missed the other by a matter of seconds. I'd taken to watching the watchers more than the wolf, whenever I could. By then, there was scarcely any separation between the clutter of everyday life and keeping an eye out for Romeo and his followers. In the middle of writing, shoveling the deck, or making dinner, a wrinkle of motion out on the lake would catch my eye, and I'd hit my inner pause button to peer into my spotting scope or binoculars, sometimes for a minute, often much more. Maybe it would be the wolf alone, or the wolf with some of his regular dog buddies and viewers—no big deal. Any newcomers, canine and human, drew extra scrutiny. If something didn't look right (maybe an overeager neophyte pushing the wolf too hard, or a crowd scene developing), I might throw on ski gear and pole over for a closer look. I knew I wasn't a cop, and my first choice, always, was to let everyone mind their own business. But if someone was putting Romeo in a tight spot, accidentally or otherwise, I felt bound to nudge things toward the better if I could. Just by skiing past with a dog or two loping behind me, I could often entice the wolf to break off from an iffy situation and follow along for a bit. If someone was clearly up to no good—egging on a reactive dog toward the wolf, for example, or in one instance, trying to dive-bomb him with a radio-controlled plane—I'd approach, often wearing a khaki jacket that looked like it might be enforcement agency issue, pull out a long lens, point it toward the action, and snap away. That was usually enough to diffuse the party. Or I drew closer, struck up a casual conversation, and worked around to suggesting that the wolf might need a bit more space. Whether people smiled and nodded or got huffy (and a few surely did), pretty much everyone backed off. A couple of times, both at twilight, I slid between a freaked-out dog-walker and a suddenly too-close-for-comfort, intent and whining wolf and escorted the visitors off the ice. I couldn't blame some woman with a kid and a Lab puppy for panicking, even if the wolf was just being sociable, and especially during the late-February into March mating season, when he was noticeably more aggressive about trying to herd dogs away from parking lots, back out onto the ice — even if his advances never warmed past that. Whether Romeo actually responded to my *no* command, or just to tone and body language (a couple of times, I extended a ski pole between him and a dog, once almost tapping him on the nose), he no doubt got the message and backed off a few yards. Meanwhile, I combined my daily workouts with a chance to at least tip my hat past the hubbub toward the wolf I loved. *Badges?* I took to murmuring toward him and to no one in particular. *We don't need no stinkin' badges.*

As for actual enforcement, this was the Forest Service's turf. They could have handed out fines at $150 a pop for wildlife harassment to anyone who either approached the wolf too closely or didn't stop their dogs from doing the same; and considering that many of the potential violations took place out in the open, visible from a road, trailhead, or parking lot, you'd think the law might have been more active. But from the start, the Forest Service had opted for a low-profile presence when it came to Romeo, and the one officer patrolling the glacier area had yet to write a single citation involving the wolf, going back to his first appearances in 2003. As District Ranger Pete Griffin later explained to me, they didn't have the manpower or inclination to engage in preventative enforcement of what they saw as a nonproblem. Anyhow, most of the activity occurred in the tourist off-season, on the western lobe of the lake, out of sight of the visitor center, and apparently out of mind.

Meanwhile, dealing with either Harry's or Hyde's gallery was a touchy matter. Even if I didn't approve of the entire scene, I respected the ability of each man to handle both himself and hangers-on near the wolf. Generally, I'd observe on and off from afar, or skirt by for a glance on my way around the lake. Once, though, to make a point, I trotted out Anita's goofball mutt Sugar on the beach behind our house when Harry's audience was out in force, and chucked a few tennis balls to egg the Big Shug into his manic, slobber-and-fetch routine. Sure enough, Romeo peeled off and came bounding from a half mile away, deserting his entourage to leap in apparent joy, and flash a wide wolf grin at the old dog pal he hadn't seen in ages. The party up the ice quickly dissolved.

One mild, sunny Saturday halfway through January, a swirl of activity near the Big Rock warranted a ski-by. The usual crew was on station: Harry and Brittain at the fore, several guys with sizeable camera gear, and an elderly couple with a pair of Afghans—slim, high-shouldered sight hounds originally bred on the central Asia steppe to chase down swift wild prey, which must have sometimes included wolves. Romeo and Brittain mouth-wrestling and play-jostling would serve as opening act and recurring theme, interspersed with the wolf trotting back and forth, sniffing and posturing with dogs, or lying nearby, studying the action. Then the older woman would set the two Afghans (themselves a bit over the hill) off leash, and they'd gallop creakily down the ice in the bright, blue-white day, with Romeo keeping easy stride a few paces back, wolf and dogs both enjoying the companionship and the chance to run against each other, just for the hey of it—hardly a situation, one might surmise, that the shapers of the breed envisioned. Then a rest period, more Romeo and Brittain tussling, some more group sniff-arounds, and maybe another dash with the Afghans.

The format of this particular get-together was normal enough, if you could call it that. As always, there were a couple of first-timers who had heard about the show, and others who just happened to be on the scene, so a few new dogs and humans were stirred into the mix. But this particular mild, sunny weekend day, cars kept pulling up, and more adults and kids and dogs piled out along the snowy shore, some of them obviously green, and too many, too spread out for Harry to manage. Most of the two dozen or more folks and half-dozen extra dogs had no idea who Harry was, anyhow. I pulled up with Gus at a hundred yards, unslung my camera, and started pointing and framing—not hoping to move anyone away (with so many people, everyone was past noticing another camera), but to capture the crazy carnival atmosphere swirling around the wolf, one of the more surreal interfaces between humans and wildlife that I'd ever witnessed. Romeo trotted back and forth, whining, tongue lolling, drawn into the same strange daze as everyone else. No doubt warm and a bit overstimulated, he finally trotted out onto the ice and lay down about seventy yards from me and Gus. After minutes of inaction, and the crowd getting restless and some edging closer, Harry strode out with Brittain, apparently to reassure Romeo and guide him away from the mob. Behind him, a three-year-old toddler wearing a bright red jester's cap and snowsuit picked that moment to flop down near his parents and throw a five-star tantrum, thrashing and belting out a high-pitched wounded-animal shriek. The wolf's head snapped erect as he stared, locked on to that small, blood-red spot squirming and squealing on the snow, hardly recognizable as a human shape. *Oh shit,* I hissed to myself. No one else seemed to realize Romeo's prey stimulus button had been pushed, and how much we were asking of him. Harry, with the crunch of snow echoing in his ears, and figuring the wolf was just focused on him, must not have heard the kid and surely didn't see him. Neither did he see the roly-poly, tan-gray pug that had broken off from the crowd to trot after him and Brittain, straight toward the wolf. As it passed Harry and saw the wolf, the dog lost its footing and skidded. Romeo tensed, mane up, eyes fixed on that small, incoming creature. With Harry just several paces away, he dashed forward, snatched the hapless pug, and loped for the Dredge Lakes shore with it crosswise in his mouth. Almost simultaneously, Harry, who himself slipped and fell, shouted "No!" and the wolf abruptly dropped the little dog onto the ice and kept going.

I watched the whole sequence through my viewfinder, not even aware I had the shutter button held down. The pug's owner, a local physician and Romeo supporter, scrambled out to retrieve his dazed pet. Other than an understandable fit of trembling and some bruises, it seemed little worse for wear, despite being dangled from jaws capable of exerting more than a thousand pounds of pressure per square inch. With the wolf gone, the crowd sifted off, and it was just another winter day on the lake.

All that was crazy enough, but damned if just a few days later Romeo didn't snatch a second pug, an event so similar it could have been a replay of the first — this time within a few feet of John Hyde and his followers, along the Dredge Lakes shore. Again, the wolf had apparently responded to a single sharp shout (this time from Hyde) and released the animal posthaste. I skied up seconds after Romeo had vanished into the willows; the pug, though quivering and saliva-coated, six feet from me, was once more unharmed. "That's your fault!" Hyde yelled toward the owner, a local hobby photographer who had encouraged the little dog to approach the wolf, so he could get a picture. The guy seemed totally unaware of just what lay at stake. "No big deal, that's just my wife's dog anyhow," I heard him wisecrack to the several nonplussed photographers standing there. And sure enough, he got his shot — Romeo carrying off his dog — and landed it on the front page of the state's largest paper, the *Anchorage Daily News,* underscored by the somewhat misleading caption: "Juneau Predator." Never mind the fine print with the outcome; most people apparently never read that far.

Set off by that image and word of mouth about both incidents, rumor spread that the wolf was on a dog-devouring rampage. Fist-banging letters to the *Empire* further fanned the rhetorical flames that once more licked through town: *Do something, only a matter of time before he grabs someone . . . shoot the wolf . . . relocate the wolf . . . leave him the hell alone . . .* and so on. Lost in the hoopla were the simple details that both tiny dogs had emerged without shedding a drop of blood; that the wolf had apparently responded to human direction not once, but twice; and that the root cause, both times, had been questionable behavior not by his species, but ours. Not to mention, both had occurred within the boundaries of the nation's largest national forest, in by far the wildest of the fifty states. Where else on this planet was a wolf supposed to live?

If human behavior and motives were puzzling in these matters, the wolf's were no less so. You could interpret those bizarre twin incidents as aborted predatory attempts; but if so, what triggered them? Since Tank the beagle's disappearance, nearly two years before, Romeo had enjoyed thousands of close, sociable contacts with hundreds of canines (though far fewer with dogs under twenty pounds). Maybe both pugs and Tank were indeed cases of mistaken identity, and if Romeo didn't quite recognize them as dogs, you can hardly blame him. It could be that something unique about a pug's movement, appearance, or coloration had triggered the reaction; or perhaps that particular breed being involved twice, in two mirror-image incidents, was freakish coincidence. Considering that the dogs were both released unharmed, and the wolf's history of friendly intentions, you have to wonder if he was playing or maybe puppy-napping—a precedent set with the young Akita, two years before. However, when I recall the first pug grab, including Romeo's intense body language, the speed and force with which he pounced (frozen in one of my pictures), I find it hard to completely dismiss the predatory interpretation, perhaps set in motion by the stimulus of that screaming little kid in the snow and transferred over to the dog. As far as not killing or even hurting that pug, he didn't have to—at least not just then. The dog was hanging helpless in his jaws. Plenty of accounts confirm that wolves are often content to merely subdue, rather than kill, prey before eating it. The wolf may have not bothered with a fatal bite at that point because it wasn't necessary. But who's to say he wouldn't have released each dog without human intervention, as he had with the Akita puppy? In fact, maybe shouts had nothing to do with the wolf's actions, and he was simply involved in some game that ended in catch-and-release. In the strange case of the double pugs, about all we can do is shrug and flip a coin. The circumstantial evidence for friendly versus predatory motive on the wolf's part balances out damn near dead even, with no sure verdict possible.

Faced with the general uproar, Fish and Game was forced to come up with some sort of response, and once again, it was restraint. The department had every justification it needed for relocation, if so inclined. The trend toward trouble was obvious; perhaps it was time to step in for the good of wolf and humans alike. Still, Fish and Game was no doubt wary of public reaction; and besides, nothing had really happened. The department biologists seemed as baffled and mesmerized as the rest of us. Area Biologist Ryan Scott, accompanied by a dog to bait the wolf in, conducted a couple of hazing missions to the lake, with observational follow-ups. He opted for multiple-report pyrotechnic shotgun rounds designed to startle the wolf (similar in sound to a string of air-bursting firecrackers) and noted, "The immediate results . . . were that the wolf departed the area quickly, and my perception is that the animal's interactions with people and dogs were fewer for 2–3 weeks." In an incensed letter to the *Empire,* our friend Anita suggested a slightly different hazing approach: "Adverse conditioning is definitely the answer to solving the wolf problem at the Mendenhall Glacier. A few well-placed rubber bullets or bean bags should send the right message to the lamebrains who deliberately encourage their dogs to approach the wolf and the photographers who crowd and relentlessly seek him in pursuit of their own selfish interests. It's only fair they should be the ones — not Romeo — to be on the receiving end of a little behavior modification, because these people caused the problem in the first place."

It seemed as if Ryan's hazing shots and Anita's equally stinging words had broken a strange spell; though of course, the shift was due to a broader, collective shame that came from within for those with a conscience, and from a lack of opportunity for the care-nots. The wolf indeed seemed to draw back for a time, and the shows and crowds ceased as abruptly as they'd begun. And, while Harry and Hyde continued to fare out on an almost daily basis, they kept a distinctly lower profile. Harry took to setting a public example by walking Brittain on a leash (which he removed once out of sight) and taking an active role in encouraging others to do the same. Forest Service enforcement also suddenly raised its presence and handed out a spate of warnings, followed by an expensive ticket or two, to shocked and incensed dog owners who wondered why them and why now, while others agreed that it was about time. All boded well for a quiet spring on the lake, but the vortex of conflict merely shifted elsewhere.

As far back as 2004, a black wolf had been sighted some distance from the glacier, in the coastal area from Amalga Harbor to Eagle Beach, a rural neighborhood that encompassed several dozen homes. Most lay less than a half mile from The Road but abutting two vast, wild, life-rich river valleys leading inland—the Herbert and Eagle—and rimmed to the west by an equally untrammeled seascape. Both rivers bulged each summer into late fall with salmon; beaver, mink, otters, and waterfowl ranged through backwater ponds. Of course there were bears of both species, and wolves, at least one of them black—perhaps Romeo, or not. In any case, a black male wolf in the area seemed driven by a strong social attraction to local dogs—a compelling coincidence, to say the least. He made regular rounds of houses where certain dogs lived, and often howled to call them outside. It had to be Romeo, some Amalga area residents insisted, and common-enough sense supported that conclusion. Others swore that the playful wolf was a different animal from the one at the glacier, a noticeably smaller guy some locals called Junior. They pointed to the distances involved and to the undeniable fact that the wolf couldn't be in two places at once; at times, sightings on the lake and near Amalga were noted on the same day, and sometimes damn near simultaneously. While true that the driving distance between Amalga and the Mendenhall Glacier totaled more than twenty-five miles, a far more direct, wolf-friendly route existed: a human-made trail network that stretched from upper Montana Creek, near the heart of Romeo's home territory, over a low divide into the Herbert River valley near Windfall Lake, and to eventually within a half mile of tidewater. The route traced roughly a dozen miles, a comfortable two-hour wolf trot under good conditions—all through prime country affording the small animals, occasional deer and mountain goat, carrion, and salmon (whether frozen, half-rotted, or in season) upon which the black wolf depended. Far more strange if Romeo, like any other wolf, hadn't used that route and adjacent hunting grounds, beckoning away to the north. "I know for a fact he went out that way on a regular basis," John Hyde told me, years later. "At certain times, especially in spring when the snow got hard, he had a beaten trail." John also added that he positively identified Romeo near Amalga, through snapshots taken by a local resident. But Hyde also encountered at least two other lone black wolves in the area over the same time period: a somewhat smaller male, and a female, each identified by its urinating style—leg-lifting versus squatting. Nene Wolfe (an itinerant veterinarian, with an incidentally perfect name in this context) also confirmed a close sighting of a smallish, shy, black-gray female wolf she was positive was not Romeo, on a winter beach walk near the mouth of the Herbert River.

Writer and seasoned outdoorsman Lynn Schooler, an Amalga resident himself and among the first to see Romeo out on the lake in late 2003, told me he was "a hundred percent sure" the tolerant black male wolf he and other neighbors saw around Amalga in 2006–2007 was a different, smaller animal. "I think there were several wolves operating around Amalga that winter," he said. "It was the worst winter in Juneau history for snow, and everything got pushed to the coast. I think the wolves followed the deer to tidewater."

Positively identifying a given animal can be a tricky business; several times over the years, I spied a distant black wolf out on Mendenhall Lake that seemed to not be Romeo (apparently smaller, or perhaps a different shade, or moving differently), only to discover, upon getting closer, that my eyes had been fooled by vagaries of light or perspective. That said, Hyde's, Nene Wolfe's, and Schooler's identifications, supported by their detailed observations and their expertise, along with corroborating evidence from others, support the assertion that more than one wolf frequented the Amalga area, and one of them was almost certainly Romeo. I had my own corroboration of at least two black wolves in the general area, as well. On a late winter afternoon, I watched Romeo lounging at the northwest corner of the lake; at exactly that same time—a bit after 4 P.M.—photographer Mark Kelley encountered friends on Spaulding Meadows, an alpine area several miles distant, in the direction of Amalga, who had just seen a black wolf. Obviously, Romeo couldn't have been in two places at once.

The identity of the Amalga wolf (or wolves) would have been nothing more than topic for a spirited conversation over an Alaskan Brewing Winter Ale or two, if not for the vehemence of several lupophobic locals. The residents in question—a vocal subminority of the Amalga community—didn't like the idea of any wolf hanging around. Amalga wasn't some designated wilderness or recreation area, they said, but a place where families lived. Never mind that bears wandered near houses in season and occasionally engaged in nuisance activity. This was different. A wolf was lurking: playing with dogs, scattering unsecured garbage, howling, trying to get near dogs, and . . . and . . . well, they sputtered, that was about it so far, but it could get worse, fast. The biologists listened and nodded; management of problem wildlife was part of their job. But there was no basis for action unless something actually happened. And then it did.

Denise Chase, herself a Fish and Game employee, and her partner, Bob Frampton, had two highly unusual dogs. Korc and Bobber were lundehunds—a breed so rare it was just recognized by the AKC in 2008, with less than four hundred registered in the entire United States. These small, independent canines—feral, foxlike, and dainty, with six toes and an amazing proclivity for climbing (originally island cliffs off the Norwegian coast, in pursuit of nesting puffins)—were allowed by Bob and Denise to range in the forests surrounding their waterfront cabin, a quarter mile from the nearest road on the southern lobe of Amalga Harbor. The two half sisters were inseparable; Korc was highly protective of Bobber.

So, when Bobber came limping home alone one snowy March day, Denise Chase was alarmed—even more when she discovered deep wounds piercing the dog's shoulders, as if seized from above. Tracing the dog's trail through deep, fresh snow, she found evidence of an attack. "You could read the story in the snow," she remembered. Korc's and Bobber's tracks were crossed by those of a single wolf, which then climbed a hill and came out in front of the two dogs. At that point, there were signs of a struggle, along with a clump or two of dog hair. Only one set of dog tracks continued from that point, and the wolf's trail wound off into the timber. "One dog just disappeared," murmured Chase, the emotion still thick in her throat five years later.

By the time Fish and Game area biologist Ryan Scott investigated the scene, enough new snow had fallen to blur the trails and make the going still more difficult; he was unable to find any sure sign of a kill, or even that a wolf was positively involved. Meanwhile, Bobber needed eighteen stitches to close deep punctures the vet determined were made by the bite of "a very large canine." Chase believes the wolf first attacked Bobber, and Korc was overpowered as she tried to defend her companion, and carried off. By sticking to personal observations, and being cautious in his on-the-record conclusions, Scott was just doing his job as a scientist. Most Amalga residents who knew of the incident, though, were certain a wolf killed the dog. The question remained: Which one? The morning of the attack, a black wolf was spotted playing with the two black Labs at a house several miles away. Was it Romeo, Junior, or neither? "We're not sure [Romeo] killed Korc," said Chase. "We never saw him or any other wolf near our house, only tracks now and then, and three times, like once a year, wolf droppings. . . . We never blamed Romeo. I let my dogs run free. I knew they would encounter wildlife. I just never thought something like this would happen."

Chase and Frampton were forbearing; they and most of their neighbors (including Schooler and Fish and Game) kept the incident so low-key that it didn't even show up in the *Empire,* and even those with ears to the ground didn't hear much. The couple came under immediate pressure from a local minority to push for removal of *the* wolf. At least one longtime Out The Road resident vowed to take things into his own hands if he had to. Chase and Frampton quietly resisted, and once more Fish and Game took a notably cautious approach. Ryan Scott set out a motion-activated trail camera near Chase and Frampton's cabin and asked the couple to report any fresh tracks or sightings. But in the ensuing weeks, there were no signs of a wolf near their home, and as snow piled deeper and deeper, wolf reports in the area dwindled. Whatever had killed Korc the lunde-hund had slipped away. The Amalga wolf issue faded into the background for the time being, though antiwolf angst among that same small cluster of residents continued to simmer. Things weren't settled by a long shot, they muttered.

Back at the lake, life for the wolf in the wake of the twin pug incidents was quiet — muffled, it seemed, by the feet of snow that continued to swirl from the sky at that record pace and pile up in head-high drifts. As one might expect, Romeo stuck close to his core territory, conserving energy on main trails. He appeared thinner than I could recall since his first winter; hare trails were as scarce as their makers, and beaver lodges lay buried deep. But spring was in the air. March faded into the lengthening days of April, and on sunny afternoons, water began to drip, then trickle and pool. I'd just snapped into my ski bindings on such a day when I encountered a neighbor named Debbie and a friend of hers headed off the ice, eyes wide. "You won't believe what I just saw," she exclaimed, and pushed a point-and-shoot camera toward me. There on the viewing screen was an image of Romeo bounding away with a small, brown, longhaired dog dangling in his jaws. "Where?" I asked, and she pointed toward the river mouth.

I skied over as fast as I could, but the wolf was gone. There were too many tracks in the crusted snow to sort out or hope to follow, and no one was there. I got the story later, from Debbie. A woman had been walking her dogs on one of the trails leading out of Dredge Lakes near the river mouth. She paused to wait for a Pomeranian that had lagged a few dozen yards behind her. The wolf rocketed out of the brush, snatched the dog just above the waist, and disappeared. From what I could see, zoomed in on the image on a computer screen, the dog seemed utterly limp and lifeless. Unlike with the pugs, there was no one nearby to shout *no;* and unlike the Akita puppy, the little dog didn't return, bouncing out of the willows. And as there had not been with Tank the beagle, there were both eyewitnesses and photographic proof. The Pomeranian was never seen again, though Harry Robinson said he and others found prints of a small, solo dog in Dredge Lakes, and that he heard through the grapevine that the dog had indeed been found wandering near the glacier and was adopted into a new home. Pretty to think so. Everyone who knew this latest story, and cared at all about the wolf, tensed.

However, the thunderclap never came. Thanks to the current news cycle or who knew what, the story, sans image, was relegated to a mere several-line mention on the second page of the *Empire.* There were no quotes from a distraught owner or outraged citizens, no plan of action from deeply concerned biologists, no angry public letters. It was as if all of Juneau gave a collective shrug and finally murmured, as one: *Well, it's Alaska, and we know there's a wolf around. What do you expect?* As for Romeo, not too hard to figure a possible motive. Winter had been long and hard, and here came this little, obviously limping creature all by itself—literally, fair game—right through one of his usual hunting spots. And maybe that was that. Or not. In the too-numerous-to-count dog-wolf interactions over the next few weeks, all was as it had been. I glanced out the window one early morning that spring, and there was Jessie, the rabbitlike border collie from two houses down, a thin-boned creature that weighed just a scant few pounds more than the larger pug, cavorting on the lake with Romeo. The snow melted, spring came, and the black wolf lived on.

Wolf grin

12

FRIENDS OF ROMEO

April 2008

The lake flexed with spring's rising flood, a patchwork of standing water and failing ice, riddled with sun-rot. Where the glacier's furrowed edge met the lake, currents bored dark, ever-widening holes; the past autumn's calved icebergs, caught in place, began to creak free. I watched from afar as Romeo stood on the westernmost point of the Dredge Lakes beach, gazing toward the opposite shore. He gathered and leaped over a moat of shore melt, onto a pan of solid ice, and picked his way, testing with nail, nose, and eye, at times almost crawling to spread his weight, once backtracking around a spot he must have judged uncertain. Angling toward Tern Island, just north of the Big Rock, the wolf read his way across the lake via the one avenue where passage was still possible, drawing on all he'd learned of ice, and on the echoes of what his forebears knew. As a matter of survival, any Southeast Alaska wolf must navigate water, whether liquid, frozen, or a mixture of both: mountain rivers etched with canyons, waterfalls, and glacial sluices fierce enough to drown a bear, and current-torn fjords that themselves must sometimes be swum. A wolf unable to traverse such obstacles is hemmed in to almost-sure starvation in too narrow a slice of country. But a wolf too bold is no less doomed in a land where a slip of foot or judgment forgives nothing.

At last Romeo hit an expanse of sure going and broke into a smooth, distance-dissolving wolf trot that carried him across the lake. Then, with a few last splash-haloed bounds, the black wolf disappeared into the timber rising toward the West Glacier Trail. A matter of days, and winter would collapse; the lake's cold, gray-green face would shift awake once more, murmuring in the wind. There wouldn't be many more crossings for the wolf.

Call it spring of 2008; which year doesn't matter now, if it ever did. Time swirls, expands, and contracts as the mystics and physicists confirm, even as our clocks and calendars insist otherwise. So it was the next stretch of Romeo's life seemed merged into one — a good sign, one might guess, marking less drama and an overall easing of the emotions that had always crackled about him. Most Juneauites did indeed step back, as if finally grasping how we, both together and as individuals, might better live with this wolf, accept him as full-partnered neighbor. The set-piece rhetoric from both sides swelled at times but always faded again; all seemed well enough from a filtered distance. But in truth, Romeo was no safer then than ever: his life, both among us and beyond, an endless crossing over unsure ice. We asked ourselves, and sometimes each other, if he would one day simply vanish into the land, or if we would discover how and where his end came. And if we could choose to know or not, which would we rather?

By winter 2007–2008 Romeo was no longer hewn of new sinew and synapse; the once deep-black guard hairs were now streaked with lighter, reddish and gray strands, and white peppered his muzzle. He rose from naps with slower, longer stretches and sometimes stiff first steps, but his teeth — one of the critical measures of a wolf's overall condition, and absolutely vital to his being — showed as unworn as a three-year-old's when he gave one of his wide, social yawns. His movements in play and travel, though creakier, still flowed with lupine grace; he'd so far avoided the sort of crippling injuries that shorten many a wolf's time. Approaching at least six years of age (perhaps as old as seven), he stood in his full prime, a half head higher and at least ten pounds more than an average Alaska male wolf, and as well-sculpted an example of *Canis lupus* as ever breathed. If indeed of the smaller Alexander Archipelago strain, he verged on towering paragon.

Even more formidable than his supercanine physiology was his inner maturing: the gangly exuberance of youth shaped on the lathe of years into a penetrating, sentient intelligence—steeped in wisdom, informed by hardwired instinct. With level-gazed amber eyes, he looked out on his chosen territory and those who crossed it, understanding both as well as any wolf that had spent his life on a single piece of ground. Woven into memory, a cognitive map of trails and routes, and the scent posts, rendezvous points, and pockets of prey to which they led, plus the features and dangers along each way; the catalog of individual dogs and humans, and their comings and goings—all strained through a sensory array beyond our ken. Romeo's survival had far exceeded chance. Running a Darwinian gauntlet that demanded constant adaptation and complex responses, with scant margin for error, he had accomplished what few large, wild predators ever had, or will: he lived near, even among, thousands of humans over most of his life—not just a shadowed presence or camp follower, but as an independent, socially interactive creature whose territory overlapped our own—without the benefit of a large-scale preserve. Through his time among us, he remained his own gatekeeper, his comings and goings defining the ever-shifting boundary between worlds, rendering our own surveys and markers meaningless. And though the core of the Mendenhall Glacier Recreation Area of course did offer protection by rule, actual enforcement presence (even after it picked up) focused on little more than discouraging dog interactions during peak daylight hours. The wolf's safety, even on that shard of terrain at the core of his territory, continued to be far from certain, and anywhere else, downright tenuous.

Consider that one of Romeo's routes north up the Montana Creek drainage led across the target end of a rural, sparsely monitored, yet steadily busy shooting range, and onward through a bow-hunting target area to a road's-end turnaround where twenty-something partiers whooped around pallet bonfires, people dumped mattresses

and tires, and the Juneau cops seldom patrolled. Beyond that, and on
either side of Montana Creek Road, stretched boggy muskeg country and wooded hillside slopes roamed by a steady smattering of
armed locals, many of whom would welcome a wolf, any wolf (especially this wolf), in their crosshairs or traps. How did Romeo know
to switch between approaching and trusting humans at the lake to
dodging would-be killers just a few minutes later and less than two
miles away? He understood the difference and acted accordingly
from his earliest days, with a power approaching prescience; his
mere continued existence served as testament to that. And the Montana Creek corridor, though probably the most perilous, was just one
of several worrisome spots.

Case in point: matters near Amalga were far from settled. Evidence tying Romeo to Korc the lundehund's death had proved vague
at best, and wolf reports in the area had tapered. However, by the autumn of 2007, they had picked up enough to inspire a fresh spatter
of complaints from that same sharp-voiced minority. The most vehement of the bunch, an elderly Out The Road resident, made good
his threat from months before. Tired of waiting for Fish and Game,
and unbeknownst to them, the old man took matters into his own
hands by setting out poisoned baits. As an old-school, wolf-loathing
Alaskan, he figured he was engaged in community service, shield-
ing the entire neighborhood from certain threat. Attempting to poison wildlife in Alaska is strictly forbidden under any circumstances,
with good reason. But that didn't deter the old man. Some of the baits
he set out did disappear, and no doubt a number of creatures died,
wracked with spasms — probably a mink or two, some ravens, and at
least one bald eagle whose carcass was discovered nearby, and who
knows, maybe a bear or wolf that staggered off. In a perversely ironic
turn, one of the creatures the neighbor did apparently manage to poison was the lone surviving lundehund, Bobber, whose companion's
fate had at least partially inspired the old man's actions. Denise Chase
suspects the little dog didn't wander as far as the man's yard from her
own, but scavenged part of a strychnine-dosed animal that had traveled some distance before succumbing. Though veterinary diagno-

sis and action saved her life, Bobber lived with crippling, permanent nerve damage. Stung by remorse, the man ceased his campaign.

One animal that didn't end up dead was Romeo—fresh evidence of either the wolf's almost magical ability to dodge deadly threats, or an indicator that he might not have been the trouble wolf in Amalga, after all. But though the poison plot passed, repeated complaints to Fish and Game from Out The Road continued into November. A black wolf had been hanging around, digging into trash, and scavenging human leavings, which raised the red flag possibility of food conditioning, with all its ties to aggressive behavior. The department had an obligation to intercede in such matters, in the interest of public safety. They quietly began exploring their options. Scott and other Fish and Game biologists including former area biologist Neil Barten, and Doug Larsen, director of wildlife conservation at the time, realized the wolf they were targeting could well be Romeo and, in fact, suspected as much. Without firm evidence of a second male black wolf that played with dogs, they weren't ready to accept the multiwolf theory. As Juneau residents (Larsen born and raised here), they knew full well the toxic backwash they and the department would attract if they captured and relocated Romeo, whether he survived or not. That last information would be conveyed by a satellite collar with which they'd decided to fit him—to identify him beyond doubt, trace his movements, and (as a bonus) provide data for study. The biologists had repeated complaints in a limited-enough area that they felt they had reason to intercede, and a real chance of success. They took a collective breath and prepared to act.

No self-respecting wolf would enter a large box or culvert trap of the kind commonly used for bears, and in that sort of dense-timbered, rough country, visibility was too limited to count on firing a successful tranquilizer dart. Cable snares were also out of the question: too much chance of causing fatal damage. The only real hope for live capture was deploying a spread of four-inch-diameter leg-hold traps with scent or bait for attraction, just like a fur trapper might use, though the steel jaws would be padded to reduce the odds of injury. In winter snow, wolves, like most wildlife, tend to stick to

already-broken trails. In order to hold any hope of capture, Scott first
had to locate specific, high-traffic areas for sets; snow (with frequent
freshening, and the deeper, the better on either side of the broken
trail) would hold evidence of whatever passed, draw the wolf toward
the spread, and help conceal the traps. If a wolf did get caught, Fish
and Game could then safely tranquilize and transport it.

Before deploying any traps, though — to be set by a contracted,
expert trapper — the biologists had to determine the course of action that would follow a capture. Due to the wolf's possible exposure
to domestic canine diseases and parasites, they'd have to quarantine
him for a few weeks in an isolated enclosure to avoid the risk of in-
fecting other wildlife, including wolves. Depending on the results,
he might be euthanized or else cleared for transport and release in a
suitable area. Then there was the matter of finding such a place — a
large chunk of reasonably wolf-friendly terrain far enough from Juneau (not to mention other communities) to minimize the odds of
his return to the same habits somewhere else. Even in a landscape as
immense and thinly populated as Southeast Alaska, they had fewer
available options than you'd suppose. Given the ability of any wolf to
cover serious ground, and many wolves' documented homing ten-
dencies when moved, a hundred miles might not be enough. But
even a Southeast wolf will rarely swim two miles of open water; so
the far side of Lynn Canal from Juneau came to mind, or south on
the mainland — the farther, and across as many fjords as possible, the
better.

Also on the short list was somewhere in the remote, mountain-
ous country north and west of Haines, along the Canadian border. In
the same area, up the Chilkat valley, lay a secluded wildlife viewing
park owned and operated by my friend Steve Kroschel. (Incidentally,
Steve's captive animals have appeared in many television features
and films, including National Geographic specials and the well-
regarded Disney classic *Never Cry Wolf*.) Kroschel was approached
by Fish and Game to ask if he'd be willing to serve as temporary host.
Veterinarian Nene Wolfe, the same woman who encountered that

little black female near Amalga, also later confirmed that she'd been asked by the department if she would agree to monitor a quarantined wolf. Both inquiries were hypothetical, in that they were never followed up by an actual request. All communications and meetings were conducted inside the department, without notice or fanfare. While Fish and Game wasn't being willfully covert, neither was it attempting to include the public in its planning, for completely understandable reasons. Factors for keeping the location of a potential live trap area secret included promoting the safety of the public and wildlife; protecting the privacy of those who had lodged the complaint; and reducing the chances of vigilante meddling.

But as the biologists debated their course of action, the Amalga wolf, whether Romeo or not, rendered the point moot by turning sporadic and unpredictable in his Out The Road appearances—so much so that Fish and Game abandoned the notion of live trapping and, with it, any final decision on where they might move him.

Harry Robinson, however, offers a different version of Fish and Game's deliberations. On the basis of inside information he claimed was leaked to him, he pronounced emphatically, "[Fish and Game] absolutely had made up its mind to relocate Romeo. It was a done deal, and they were proceeding forward." He approached Juneau Alpine Club founder and respected outdoorsman Kim Turley—the same guy who had been mesmerized by the wolf following him and his wife on that morning run the winter before—to form Friends of Romeo, a group without meetings, dues, elections, bylaws, or formal roster. Word was spread by mouth, posted bulletins, and an email list. Anyone, anywhere who felt a bond to the wolf was included, just by saying so. The group's primary goal was to forge broad-based public advocacy for the wolf, aimed primarily at Fish and Game, the agency that held the power to determine his fate. Though it was all a fine idea in principle, and of course I shared the general sentiment, I kept my distance, wary of having my name pinned to statements that weren't mine. Instead, I called Neil Barten on my own, who assured me that there was no specific plan to trap Romeo near the glacier. He

omitted telling me of the discarded plan for whatever wolf was raising complaints from Out The Road — not out of deception, but because I failed to ask that direct question.

Three Friends of Romeo bulletins were broadcast by email, public posting, and limited door-to-door distribution in the winter of
2008. The first, dated January 7, stated, "Reliable sources have re-
vealed that the ADF&G has decided to dart and relocate him far
from Juneau," and also stated, "The current plan calls for . . . relocation in the spring, when the ice (and the viewing public) have left the
Mendenhall area." The second, dated February 1, escalated the call
to arms with the headline ROMEO'S LIFE IS IN DANGER and con-
tained bold-print phrases such as "a death sentence for Romeo." One
key part read, "Alaskan wolf relocation studies show that wolves have
less than a 10% chance of surviving a relocation. ADF&G of course
knows this, so for all practical purposes they intend to kill Romeo."
To be sure, this was an alarming statement. But when I delved into
the matter, I could find no Alaska research data on wolf relocation
survival rates. Several lower-48 studies suggest varying rates of survival for translocated wolves, ranging from nearly identical to resident control groups to significantly greater mortality. Wolves were
indeed successfully darted and moved from the Fortymile area in
east-central Alaska to the Kenai Peninsula during the mid-1990s,
though that success was qualified by those aforementioned deaths
of several wolves during transport. Still, examination of published
research and personal communication with experienced research
biologists suggest an overall survival percentage far higher than 10
percent. For a snapshot of the high end, consider the incredibly successful reintroduction of wolves into Montana's Yellowstone National Park two decades ago, where relocated wolves that had obviously been unharmed by tranquilizing and transport flourished and
multiplied. Nonetheless, relocation under less than ideal circumstances must often present added, sometimes insurmountable, risks.

Both Friends of Romeo bulletins supported the case for urgency;
unequivocally refuted Romeo's involvement in any of the Amalga
incidents or any other wrongdoing (in fact, flatly claimed that Ro-

meo never had been known to visit the Amalga area); characterized Fish and Game as "misinformed"; implicated unnamed department employees recently arrived from California as a major source of the complaints; and called for supporters of the black wolf to raise their voices in his defense, with contact information included for Barten, Larsen, and then state senator Kim Elton. As a result of this campaign, the department received dozens of emails and other contacts from Romeo supporters, both in Juneau and from around the world.

Neil Barten, who had several phone conversations and email exchanges with Harry and met with him in what he hoped was an air-clearing exchange before the second bulletin came out, offered this perspective, several years later: "I was pretty disenchanted with [Friends of Romeo] at that time. . . . I would have to say that some of their concerns were not reasonable or well founded, and much of their information was not reliable. . . . I felt that the group was trying to vilify the department in spite of our best efforts to be honest and open with them." He, like Larsen and Scott, confirmed to me years later that Fish and Game indeed had plans to relocate whatever wolf they might be able to trap near Amalga — an animal Friends of Romeo insisted couldn't possibly be their black wolf, even as their bulletins leaked between-the-lines concern that indeed it might be.

As for darting and removing the wolf from the vicinity of Mendenhall Lake (where its identity would be virtually certain, and witnesses to a capture would be quite possible, even likely), Doug Larsen told me in a retrospective, 2012 interview, "We never went there. Given the circumstances, we didn't think that was anywhere close to appropriate; . . . there were too many negatives to even consider it as an option. However, if we had decided to do something, we'd have owned it." He continued, "We as a department recognized the uniqueness of the situation. . . . It was a pretty remarkable period of time for this community." As a final thought, he added, "There was never any indication that the wolf was being aggressive around people. That would have been an entirely different deal." Larsen didn't need to spell out the swift and probably lethal action that "deal" would have entailed.

Harry, years later, hasn't budged from his allegations. He insists that the decision to specifically capture and move not just any black wolf, but Romeo—whether near Amalga or at Mendenhall Lake—had been set into motion, and that the Friends of Romeo bulletins, and the wave of public reaction they generated, stopped Fish and Game in midstep. In measured counterpoint, Area Biologist Ryan Scott responds, "As with any wildlife management decisions I am accountable to the public. . . . Management of the black wolf was not any different. All the decisions I made regarding the wolf were going to be critiqued and had to be founded in sound wildlife management principles and department policies for addressing public and wildlife safety concerns. The public involvement did not influence my management decisions per se, but it did ensure that any action was well thought out and defensible."

Whether Harry's version of Fish and Game's intentions was entirely accurate or a reaction to a contingency plan, and whether the resulting pressure swayed the department, the overall effect of the Friends of Romeo bulletin barrage could only have weighed in the black wolf's favor, and so it did. A second face-to-face meeting in February between Barten and Scott and a Friends of Romeo representative—mild-mannered cofounder Kim Turley—smoothed over the imbroglio. The third and last Friends of Romeo bulletin, dated February 28, struck a positive, collaborative, even conciliatory tone. Besides thanking everyone who'd expressed interest, it noted that the department had suspended any plans for relocating the wolf, and that Fish and Game had gone on record as being "open and eager" for public input and, furthermore, agreed to inform Friends of Romeo ahead of any future action. Notably, half of the text was dedicated to encouraging safe wildlife viewing practices around Romeo: maintaining appropriate viewing distances, controlling dogs and children, refraining from feeding, and so on. The issue of removing the wolf, at any location, would never come to the fore again, though Fish and Game could say that was more due to the wolf's actions and a lowered complaint level than anything else. No matter; it was a win-win deal. One more storm had passed, and the black wolf remained.

Harry continued in his self-appointed role as companion and guardian of the wolf he called his friend—less visible than the year before, but present as ever, accompanying Romeo on his rounds, several hours a day, often before dawn or after dark, regardless of weather. Their bond continued, closer than ever; they sometimes brushed against each other without thought. In public, he continued to set an example by walking Brittain on a leash and going out of his way to intercede in awkward or potentially dangerous situations on Romeo's behalf—sometimes facing down people who turned hostile. As a worst-case example, there was the man who made a regular practice of driving to the end of Skater's Cabin Road in his pickup truck at dusk, luring the wolf into the parking lot with his black Lab, then driving up the road slowly with his dog barking hysterically in the truck bed, and the wolf running along behind, sometimes just an arm's length from the rear wheels. I witnessed this bizarre rite twice, though the first time I wasn't sure what I was seeing, and the second, I wasn't in a position to even get a license plate number. Harry finally did manage to confront the man, who immediately squared off, chest to chest, enraged that any busybody smartass should interfere with what he called his "fun." Harry didn't back down, and the guy, though still defiant, thought twice about taking the first swing and stormed off. Several other people with reactive dogs continued to push their luck with the wolf on a regular basis. Harry, I, and others each did our best to steer them away, with varying success; a few folks didn't seem to get what was at stake or just didn't care. Forest Service law enforcement officer Dave Zuniga continued to exert his presence and hand out occasional tickets during heavy traffic hours out on the lake, with noticeable, positive effect. In a subplot with comic overtones, Harry relates that several times, Zuniga also trailed him, Brittain, and Romeo in vain, hoping to witness a violation; but the portly officer, huffing along, was unable to keep up with Harry's long uphill stride.

Almost everyone seemed to be finding a balance that worked, wolf included. Maybe Romeo would make it to old age, after all. But for all the never-ending danger humans posed, one of the wolf's greatest threats lay just ahead — not from us, not from the land, but from his own kind.

On a mild April morning in spring 2009, I leaned against my ski poles, as if they might support a sinking heart. I and a half-dozen others stood, transfixed, as howls echoed off the flank of Mount Mc-Ginnis — not Romeo's familiar, stately cadence, but the eerie, dissonant chorus of a pack in full cry, and less than a half mile away. I counted between four and six wolves, their intertwined voices rising and falling, filling the air, each individual modulating to avoid a note held by another. Small chance of coincidence that they'd chosen to announce their presence from an area where the open-timbered, steep-sided knolls on the southwestern shoulder of McGinnis form a natural amphitheater, one of Romeo's favored howling platforms. They surely must have encountered his carefully maintained scent posts, tracks, and trails and heard his own calls — all the signals wolves use to define territorial boundaries and reduce conflict. The newcomers weren't just slipping through an overlapping claim in the course of their travels. Their sudden, brazen arrival, down from the high country into the heart of the area Romeo had long claimed, amounted to a military invasion. Hopelessly outnumbered, the black wolf didn't have much of a chance if their intent was deadly; and considering the high rate of mortality caused by interpack strife — up to a third of all wolf deaths in some areas — that motive seemed more than likely. He might have been gone already, the pack celebrating over his torn remains.

Then, from farther down the West Glacier Trail, just a few hundred yards from where we stood, just inside the trees, a distinctive, drawn-out, and emphatic howl rose. Harry, who happened to witness at close range Romeo's response to the intruders, recalls, "I'd never heard him howl like that. He had his feet spread out, his back hair and tail up, and sort of huffed before each one, like he was pumping himself up, and just bellered back." But if the strangers were indeed coming for him with hostile intent, and homing in on the howl, it would be the cry of the doomed. At an instinctive and perhaps learned level as well, Romeo must have sensed the peril. At least he held the advantage of being an exceptionally large male wolf with an imposing voice, at the heart of his own territory.

Before and during Romeo's time, there had always been other wolves passing through—individuals that he must have known at least by scent and call, and vice versa. There was, of course, the black female, presumed pack mate of his, hit by the cab around the time of his first appearance. In late summer of Romeo's second year, three gray wolves had been spotted at the huge gravel mine across from our house. We can only guess whether they passed through quietly or made contact, sociable or otherwise. And despite the fact that never once did I identify wolf tracks on the lake other than Romeo's, now and then on quiet nights I'd heard his howls answered by distant replies—sometimes obvious human imitations (perhaps Harry attempting a late rendezvous), but others distinctly lupine and seeming to emanate from the surrounding mountain slopes.

In 2006, in ghostly ice fog along the lake's northwestern shore, I'd glimpsed Romeo trotting along the tree line less than one hundred yards away, with what I took to be a large, almost-white husky mix that I didn't recognize; when I skied closer, the light-colored animal seemed to evaporate, and there was no accompanying human. I still reckoned I'd seen a dog, until, the following November, at the Juneau Public Market, I met an elderly Eskimo woman who'd grown up in a remote western Alaska village. She studied the framed wildlife photos in my booth, which included, of course, a number of Romeo images. "I saw that one," she said, pointing with her chin, "with a white wolf." It was in her backyard, close against Thunder Mountain. When I suggested that it was probably some loose mutt, she fixed me with a withering glance that dismissed my impertinence. "I know a wolf," she said. The matter wasn't subject to debate. We could well have seen the same animal—a wolf after all. That possibility was strengthened several years later by occasional, confirmed-by-photo sightings of a bold, nearly white wolf in the upper Mendenhall valley.

There were other sightings of other wolves in country Romeo frequented, including Spaulding Meadows and those already noted near Amalga. All hinted that Romeo, far from being as isolated from his kind as most had assumed, might have had another life interacting with other wolves, in ways we scarcely imagined. Let's say Harry spent four hours a day with him, 365 days a year; Hyde, another two; everyone else put together, another six: twelve hours a day with people around. That average, including the many times when he was less visible for one reason or another, is surely an overgenerous total. But even twelve hours would still mean the wolf remained unobserved at least half of each day — and during his periodic absences and seasonal movements, far more than that. All we could claim to know is what he did and where he went when we were watching; the balance of his life would remain wrapped in mystery. And that was the part of the wolf I loved best: not what I knew, but all that I didn't.

Romeo could well have been one of those wolves that maintained loose ties to a pack but chose to spend large chunks of time alone. For all we knew, he might even have sired litters of pups in his time and played the unusual but not inconceivable role of absentee patriarch. Even dominant wolves have been known to wander from their family group, temporarily, periodically, or even permanently; the intense lure dogs held for Romeo may have been reason enough for such atypical behavior. In fact, our pets may have been closer to chosen social alternates than surrogates. Or maybe the wolf was indeed a pariah cast upon our strange shore, brushing against occasional visitors of his species that never remained, and facing down repeated, hostile probes from others — the latest of which was upon him.

Several mornings later, my friend Vic Walker and I stood just off the West Glacier Trail parking lot, peering into fog and a spattering cold drizzle. "There," Vic murmured, and lifted his camera. Romeo drifted into the open and lay down, facing us; and minutes later, a second wolf followed: a smaller but still broad-chested light gray animal with distinctive dark mask and saddle markings. It stared toward us, head low, ill at ease. Romeo glanced around, ears perked, relaxed as ever. It was as if he were playing handshake host between species, reassuring both that all could be well. He'd been leading the new wolf out onto the lake each morning, at about the same time; and at least once, it had appeared by itself, lying out on the ice, and overall seemed skittish, but curious all the same, and obviously drawn to Romeo. Fingers fumbling like my mind, I blew the focus on a series of rapid-fire shots before both wolves faded back into the trees. What the hell was going on? Was this a mate, after all these years? And where was the rest of the pack?

The smaller gray proved to be a male, as I'd initially suspected from his chunky head and build. Someone spotted him lifting a leg later on, effectively peeing on the happier-ever-after Juliet scenario (just as well; hard to imagine that a mated pairing with pups in this same limited territory could work). Instead, he seemed to be a lonely young wolf on the edge of dispersing, trying to figure out what next, and was accepted by his ever-affable senior. The two wolves and their tracks were observed both together and apart for a week or so, ranging at times into Dredge. No surprise, really, if the young gray were unable to adapt to Romeo's singular world; and sure enough, one day he was gone, either traveling alone or still following the pack. And we found what had probably brought them all: the wolves had taken down a pair of goats a half mile up the forested slope of Mount McGinnis and stuck around a few days, eating and digesting and socializing until the carcasses were cleaned down to hair and bone. Then it was time to move on in search of the next kill. Exactly what had transpired between Romeo and the others would never be known. Harry had glimpsed and heard them close by but never observed any direct social interaction between any other wolves except the gray male. The good news was, the black wolf showed no signs of combat—no limp or wounds. His peaceful, if brief, sojourn with the young gray, and the fact that he remained, hinted that they'd all managed at least some sort of truce, and perhaps more. Romeo led Harry and Brittain to the kill site several times that spring of 2009

and gnawed on bones with the same smug, look-what-I've-got satisfaction many a dog owner would recognize, though impossible to
say whether he'd taken part in the hunt or was merely lording over a
good find. Once more, the wolf had demonstrated his ability to survive against steep odds.

Meanwhile, our years living in the last house before the glacier,
with a wild wolf in our backyard, had wound to a close. With an eye
toward the future, we'd sold the house we'd built and moved to the
opposite end of the Mendenhall valley, downsizing with reluctance
into a more suburban ambiance. Despite the occasional black bear
strolling through our yard, and still being only a ten-minute drive
from the lake, life for us, in Juneau or anywhere else, would never be
the same. Of course we knew what we were giving up, and grieved
the loss, even as we looked forward to a new start several years
ahead in the mountain-framed wilds up the Chilkat valley — coincidentally, one of the places Fish and Game had considered relocating
Romeo. It was as if we'd sensed the coming darkness and taken leave
before it fell.

We often made that drive back toward the home ground that
would never be ours again. Sherrie, the dogs, and I went together;
more times I traveled alone. There we met the same Romeo, loping
across the lake, that wolfy grin and his head-on approach requiring
no translation. He knew there wouldn't be any play or even a sniff-
around with our short-leashed dogs, but he wanted to say hello all
the same. He'd trot up, tail high, keening that high, soft whine of
his, then circle behind to sniff our tracks. We'd settle in, and he'd
lie down a dozen yards away, everyone — dogs, humans, wolf — relaxed and content to hang out together for a few minutes, like old
friends on a park bench. Eventually Romeo would rise, stretch and
yawn, survey his surroundings, and trot off on his evening errands.
Sometimes he'd pause once or twice, looking back as if asking why
we didn't follow along.

It was the same even when Sherrie and I walked out without
dogs one mid-April evening in 2009. The black wolf trotted from
across the lake to stand near us, across from the Big Rock; together

we watched as shadows lengthened and pink alpenglow brushed the high peaks. We'd first met six years before, just yards from that very spot, in a moment that seemed then as it does now: caught like a leaf in glacial ice, each serration and vein frozen in perfect symmetry. If it had to end, it should have been there; but the fates had spun a different thread.

April 2009

13

THE KILLERS

September 2009

Harry Robinson lay awake, the edge between waking and dreaming swept away. "I felt Romeo scream," he said. "I could hear it inside my head. He was in agony. I saw him turn to bite at his side, and at that moment, I knew he'd been shot."

It was the third week of September 2009. He and Brittain had met Romeo as usual two mornings before and spent hours traveling, playing, and resting together. But when Harry pulled into the West Glacier Trail parking lot before dawn the next day, there was no wolf waiting. Neither did he respond to Harry's howls, or show up on the long hike he and Brittain took expecting to find him, or him to find them. There were times before when the wolf went missing for days or even weeks, but Harry, feeling that dream, was sure something wasn't right. Maybe Romeo lay wounded, or caught in an untended trap from the year before, and was waiting for their help. He and Brittain combed through Dredge Lakes and across the mossy woodlands above the West Glacier Trail—all the game traces and rendezvous points they'd followed over the years. They found nothing, not a single track or fresh scat to mark his passing. Harry widened his search, putting in long hours, eating and sleeping little, pushing through work and going back out again and again. Autumn colors glowed and faded; the first snows dusted the high country. The wolf he loved had simply vanished.

During those same few days, a similar dream came to my friend Vic Walker. Vic, a local veterinarian who had found his own quiet connection with the wolf over the previous three years, describes the scene: "Romeo was wounded, over near the visitor center. He'd been shot in the jaw. The bone was totally shattered. Harry was there. He said, 'He's done'; I told him, 'No, no, I can fix this.'" The words fall hard, and three years later, Vic's eyes still aren't right when he tells the story—less dream than haunted vision, so vivid it seems merged with the past. He didn't know about Harry's dream until years later—in fact, only knew the man by sight, out on the lake. Their only connection at that time was through the wolf. Of course, dreams could be just that—echoes of our fears, nothing else. Chances were Romeo would rise from the dead, as he had done before.

Meanwhile, I was traveling rivers a thousand miles to the north, my old home country of the western Brooks Range, straddling the Kobuk-Noatak divide—a place far from Romeo and the glacier, but enfolding one of the last strongholds for his species: a far expanse of mountains and tundra plains scarcely brushed by roads, none that lead outside. At least, not yet. One dawn in that same stretch of September, I woke from a hard sleep to sloshing just above camp, at a wide spot in the river—moose or caribou, maybe a bear, I thought. I slid barefoot out of my sleeping bag and out of the tent without camera or rifle, crept downhill toward the water, and nestled behind a clump of autumn-burned willows, wanting only to see. Less than fifty yards away, a gray wolf stood on the bank, framed against a sky of metallic turquoise and rose-tinted cirrus, the whole scene mirrored in water so clear that the reflection seemed to come from the river's bottom. I held my breath as the wolf, a young female with a delicate, thin face, probed a scent; then she lifted her head to find my gaze fixed on her. "Hello, wolf," I whispered. She stared back, her bright yellow eyes boring into me. I may well have been the first human she'd ever seen, though probably not the last; just over the next range lay three villages, all within fifty miles—home to Inupiaq hunters, some of whom I once knew as neighbors and traveling companions. She'd learn of them, with their hundred-mile-an-hour snowmobiles and assault rifles, soon enough. She turned and trotted off without a glance back; I watched her go, each of us complete in the moment, knowing nothing of what lay ahead.

When I returned to Juneau in early October, I scarcely had time to catch my breath before I was off again for weeks in the lower 48, making presentations about wolves and the politics of their management, in country bereft of any. Then Sherrie and I were off on a long-planned winter hiatus in her home state of Florida. She and I fretted about Romeo, along with Joel, Vic, Harry, and others who passed along updates. Our own fears were darkened by distance, but there didn't seem to be anything to be done. Maybe the wolf had finally taken that last wrong step into a trap or a rifle's crosshairs, or perhaps he had succumbed to any of the natural perils a wolf faces. No wolf lives forever, and Romeo, at least into his eighth year by then, was an old man by wild Alaska wolf standards. Maybe it just had been his time.

But why not another ending? He could have joined the pack he'd met that spring and returned to ranging the country; or found a mate on his own, and was raising a fat litter of pups in a perfect den — a granite alcove just below the tree line up some secret valley, a freshwater spring nearby, with a network of trails leading to meadows where marmots whistled, and down into a valley rich in beaver and salmon. Harry, after his nightmare, had been visited by such a dream, similar to my own waking vision. Romeo appeared, and he reached out and stroked his hand along Romeo's dark back, trailing through his thick, long-stranded mane, as he could have many times but never once did; then the scene dissolved and he saw a female gray wolf, giving birth to a black pup. Together and alone, we sought the same refuge in a world that should have been.

Harry continued his search as autumn deepened, his quiet persistence never wavering, even as hope withered with the leaves. His efforts to find his friend, whether in life or death, filled the space that had once been theirs together. Beyond the physical searching of the wolf's territory, he launched a tireless, single-handed investigation. Juneau was too small a town to hide such a secret; sooner or later, someone would give in to the urge to talk. And within weeks of Romeo's disappearance, a friend passed on an overheard snippet of conversation at Rayco Sales, a local outdoors and gun store: the wolf had indeed been shot. Of course, we all knew the rifts between talk and truth when it came to the black wolf. Harry posted flyers around town, offering a $1,500 reward. Turning to cyberspace—a realm he navigated with fluency in his professional work and as a beta tester for software—he strained through hunting blogs and websites, sending out pings like a submarine's sonar operator and listening for echoes. At last, he came across a chilling response, buried in the comment section of a YouTube tribute to Romeo: "He's dead, skinned, and stuffed.... Get over it people." The commenter went by an online alias, as is common in such venues. Using a cyber-sleuthing technique known as skip tracing (basically, following electronic bread crumbs to their source), Harry discovered the identity of the man through a surrogate email address and sent a veiled query his way. In an exchange with someone he took to be an interested hunter, and shielded by what he assumed to be online anonymity, the commenter replied, "I know the person that harvested the wolf. He is not from AK. I saw his photos from his trip up there. Romeo is currently at an Alaska taxidermist. This is not internet blah blah, ... it's the pure and simple truth. If you'd like I'll send a photo of the mount when he receives it."

The note implied a direct acquaintance with the killer, rather than some faceless electronic contact. Harry knew he was closing in, but he didn't want to press so hard that his unwitting informant shut down. Though burning to know, he bided his time. Then, just days later, he received a call from Libby Sterling, a reporter for the *Capital City Weekly* (a free Juneau paper, sister to the *Empire*). She'd been contacted by a Pennsylvania man who said he knew Romeo's fate. Instead of chasing down the story (surely a huge local news scoop), she decided to pass on a phone number to Harry; in exchange, he assured her she'd be the first to break the story—if the lead proved out—when the right time came. Harry made the call that evening and met Michael Lowman.

Lowman hadn't known of the online commenter's exchange with Harry; the timing may have been coincidence, but not the connection. Lowman happened to know the man from their work at R.R. Donnelley & Sons, a printing company in Lancaster, Pennsylvania. And they both knew another company employee, Jeff Peacock—a man whose last name suited his apparently uncontrollable urge to strut and squawk about his hunting exploits. Peacock had made a number of trips to Alaska since 2004, visiting a buddy who once worked at the plant and had moved to Juneau. Anyone who knew Peacock had been offered the opportunity to admire his dead zoo through images he kept handy on his cell phone, or through a work computer. As Nancy Meyerhoffer, another worker at the plant—and a self-described "dedicated hunter, trapper, and taxidermist"—later added, "All of Jeffs [sic] hunts have to be about the biggest and the best. He wants one of every majestic species to be tanned or mounted in his living room, so as he says, he can look around his room and people will see a great hunter."

Lowman, a stranger on the far side of the continent, confirmed to Harry the truth of his dream. Peacock had been boasting to anyone who'd listen that he'd killed "a famous wolf" on his most recent trip to Juneau that past September, and that before the year was out he'd have a full body mount of the animal as the centerpiece to his living room. At first, Peacock found an attentive audience in fellow hunters at the plant, Lowman and Meyerhoffer included. "He told everyone in our department," remembers Lowman. Peacock may have been a blowhard, but he'd hunted the land they'd all dreamed of. Knots of workers gathered in the break room to be regaled by his stories and to ooh and aah over photos of a huge black wolf—first alive, then dead. However, as Peacock dished the details, what the workers heard and saw shocked the most hard-core hunters among them. Considering his desire to be seen as a sportsman nonpareil, one might have expected Peacock to spin some self-aggrandizing tale of tracking the wolf up and down a mountain, and saving himself with a last-second shot as the animal leaped for this throat. Instead, he chortled over a truth as naked and troubling as the image he proffered of the wolf's bloody, skinned-out carcass.

As Peacock related to his listeners, he and his Juneau buddy, Park Myers III, had known exactly who Romeo was and what he meant to Juneau. Lowman wrote, "In fact, Peacock told me, one of the main reasons for killing this particular wolf was that it would cause a lot of anguish in the community. [He] seemed to derive a lot of satisfaction out of doing something specifically designed to hurt people in this way." Not surprisingly, Peacock's and Myers's plan bore far less resemblance to a sport hunt than a gangland hit. The idea was a quick, easy kill with no witnesses, and a body that vanished without a trace. The thrill, Peacock made clear to anyone who would listen, lay not in the chase, but in the killing and the suffering he caused. All that and more would be memorialized in the trophy that he would display as a supreme accomplishment. "He just didn't get it," said Lowman. "And he thought we wouldn't care."

Peacock and Myers had tried and failed to find and kill the wolf in the autumn of 2008. Though Peacock had returned in May 2009, they had decided to wait until the following September, when Romeo's coat would be more grown in, though short of full prime condition. Myers and Peacock did manage to kill a black bear that spring, in predictable style. They spotted the animal from The Road, grazing new shoots along the beach in a closed-to-hunting area between a home and a Catholic retreat park known as the Shrine of St. Therese. The stalk was hardly what the word might suggest; bears in protected areas often learn to ignore humans, discovering quickly that they pose no threat. Peacock blasted the bruin dead twice over with one shot of his prized Smith & Wesson .460 Magnum revolver (a caliber large enough to poleax a moose); then, according to what he told Lowman, Myers kicked and taunted the animal as it died, then gutted it and dragged it up the hill with a rope tied to the bumper of Myers's truck. Back in Pennsylvania, Peacock flashed around photos of the gaping exit wound, barely covered by a tennis ball held there for graphic illustration; and despite the illegal and unsporting circumstances, Peacock would point to the bear as one more emblem of his prowess.

Whatever his workmates thought of Jeff Peacock, his partner Park Myers III seemed determined to set a lower standard. Back in the days before he moved to Alaska, Donnelley staff recall two character-defining episodes. Once, in the plant parking lot, Myers pulled up for work with a pile of geese he'd just shot in the back of his truck. A few birds were still alive, gasping and struggling. As Myers sorted through the heap and wrung their necks, an upset onlooker asked him why he'd shot so many — more than he needed, and over the legal limit. "Because I can," he shrugged. Another time, workers watched as Myers chased down a possum crossing the parking lot, kicked it around like a soccer ball with his steel-toed work boots, then stomped it to death as people shouted for him to stop.

No surprise that Park Myers's attitude leaked into his social behavior. According to a 1999 police criminal complaint filed by the Commonwealth of Pennsylvania, Myers and his wife were accused of serving two juvenile girls (thirteen years old, one of them the family babysitter) "alcohol and marihuana [sic]," then playing a game of strip poker that ended up with everyone in their underwear, and one of the girls (in the words of the police report) being fondled by Myers in her "breast and pelvic area." In a plea bargain designed to shield the girl from traumatic cross-examination by a defense attorney, Myers pleaded guilty to two misdemeanors: corruption of minors and furnishing them alcohol. Local rumor was that Myers's wealthy, well-connected grandmother had not only funded his defense, but exerted influence behind the scenes. In any case, Myers escaped with four years of probation and no jail time, even though he was twice charged with violation of that probation. The ongoing fallout was apparently enough to persuade Myers, his wife Pamela, and their two sons to move somewhere far away, in search of a fresh start; and that somewhere ended up being Juneau, Alaska.

Park Myers found a job at Alaskan Brewing, helping to make the beer we all drank. Pam got hired to cut hair (at least once, mine included) and worked behind the counter for Southeast, the city's largest veterinary hospital, owned by admirers of Romeo. The boys enrolled in local schools, and the family, after trashing out and abandoning a rental trailer, put down money on a modest house on Birch Lane, in the heart of the Mendenhall valley. Park made a few friends with regulars at Channel Bowling and among local outdoors types, with whom he developed a reputation for killing to excess, talking freely about it, and shrugging at the law. In an odd, contradictory wrinkle, Myers often stopped in at Fish and Game headquarters to check on regulations and seek clarifications. "He was insistent, often borderline weird. He'd grill me about minor points and get pretty aggressive in his questions," remembers ex–Fish and Game sealing agent Chris Frary. Myers also hooked into the local drug subculture, set up his own commercial-scale indoor marijuana growing operation, and hosted whoop-it-up parties that were rumored to regularly include a variety of controlled substances, as well as minors of both sexes. Some, from troubled homes and situations, stayed at his place for days or weeks at a time. Cloaked beneath a veneer of normalcy, Park Myers III went right on being himself.

The exact circumstances of Romeo's death, in the third week of September 2009, will never be certain. On a grainy, blurred cell phone picture that Peacock showed to Lowman and others, a black wolf drifts along the edge of a gravel lot with some highway repair equipment in the background, later identified by Harry and confirmed by the Alaska State Wildlife Troopers to be the Herbert River parking lot near mile 28 of The Road, where a widening and resurfacing project was taking place. In Peacock's words, recounted by Lowman, "We saw him the one day, but we had only our large-caliber bear rifles with us, and were concerned about the noise. . . . When you are hunting an icon like this wolf, you got to be careful. We returned the next day with a .22 rifle and found him in the same place, where we then shot him. One shot—straight through the heart!" Peacock also told Lowman that they stalked him from their truck, which further confirms a near-road, illegal killing. Peacock told Nancy Meyerhoffer, "The stupid prick just looked at me, just stopped and looked at me, never had a more cleaner shot, fucking idiots, they didn't know how easy they made this one." Fatally struck, the wolf bounded off. The killers found him twenty yards away, curled in his last sleep. The one kindness was the relative speed of his death.

Myers would later swear under oath that he, rather than Peacock, shot the wolf, and not in the parking lot, but a mile or more up the trail network that began there; that the wolf was in the company of two gray wolves, so they never stopped to consider it might be Romeo; that his perfectly placed shot was "instinctive" rather than carefully aimed, let alone planned; and that they were actually carrying the .22 (a light-caliber weapon too small for legally shooting big game) to hunt ptarmigan.

Harry Robinson, though, believes that the wolf was shot miles away, in the West Glacier Trail parking lot instead, and he remains unconvinced that the shadowy lupine form on Peacock's cell phone camera was Romeo. He points to information gleaned from Lowman's conversations with Peacock, indicating Romeo was killed in the early morning, and that Myers and Peacock had a regular pattern that fall of first visiting the West Glacier Trail area—a detail that makes total sense, since it was just several miles from Myers's house—and heading out the road in the afternoon and staying into the evening. If so, Myers and Peacock would have claimed the Herbert River parking lot as the kill site to evade the additional charge of hunting in a closed area near the Mendenhall Glacier. Harry pointed to the killers' concern over noise in further support of his theory, bolstered by the fact that he'd recently been meeting the wolf there. It all makes sense; but the distinctive profile of the live wolf in Peacock's cell phone picture, obviously taken at the Herbert parking lot, seemed to me to be Romeo. He could have easily made a quick traverse between the two sites, and the abundance of salmon in the Herbert River at that time of year would have been a prime attraction. Keeping down noise at either place made sense.

Peacock and Myers slung the dead wolf in the back of Myers's truck, covered it with a tarp, and drove back to Myers's house, where they called taxidermist Roy Classen, who lived nearby. They hauled the carcass to his place, just a few blocks away, where they weighed the dead wolf and posed for pictures. According to Wildlife Trooper evidence files, the time imprint on the cell phone images indicates the skinning at Classen's house was recorded just before 8 P.M.; one could infer they hauled the carcass there as soon as they returned; or perhaps they'd waited all day for cover of darkness. In the end, who knows? That was just one issue in a complex case that would be marked by a hodgepodge of differing opinions, conflicting statements, and varying interpretations. In death as in life, the wolf that lived both beyond and among us would prove a magnet for human wrangles.

Classen skinned the carcass and placed the rolled hide and severed, skinned-out head (the latter to be stripped and bleached for a skull trophy, the former to be sent to a tannery) in his freezer, standard taxidermy practices. The naked, headless carcass would be disposed of — maybe in the woods somewhere, at the local landfill, or sunk in the ocean for the crabs to dismember. A full body mount of the wolf would be made with the tanned hide stretched over a wire-reinforced Styrofoam form; the agreed-on pose would be the wolf with a red sockeye salmon crosswise in his jaws. The raw hide was sealed with Peacock's locking nonresident big game tag (which could be used for either black bear or wolf), supposedly to deflect potential public anger away from Myers, a local resident, if the killing were discovered. According to Classen, Myers was considering keeping the original skull (not implanted in the mount) and having it bronzed.

Mum was the word, except that already the pair couldn't resist talking. According to Myers's neighbors Douglas Bosarge and Mary Williams, Peacock and Myers showed up at their house that same day or the next. In Bosarge's words, "Myers stated to me that he had just killed Romeo the wolf. He appeared to be very excited and pleased that he had done this, dancing around. He acted like he had been out to get him. . . . These acts disturbed me to the point that I no longer associated with Park Myers." Williams added, "I asked him why he did it but he didn't really answer me." Classen, too, blabbed around that he was mounting Juneau's black wolf — including to

U.S. Fish and Wildlife Service Special Agent Chris Hansen, who had stopped by his studio on other business. As far as Classen was concerned, no one had done anything wrong, and he couldn't resist telling the story.

The ill-advised, seemingly compulsive lip-flapping didn't stop there. A Tlingit woman working as a safety flagger for the widening project along The Road near Herbert River that fall approached me more than a year later with a story she needed to tell. Peacock and Myers, stopped at her checkpoint that September, had showed her the same cell phone images the Donnelley workers would see. She described the same odd, gleeful excitement that Bosarge noted, and felt a similar personal revulsion. Peacock went down the line of several waiting cars and showed the drivers, strangers all, the same photos.

Soon after Peacock's departure from Juneau, Myers was talking up the Romeo killing to his bowling league crowd, just as Peacock, back East, launched his own tell-all campaign, the intensity of which seemed to grow as winter set in, the lake froze solid, and Juneau reacted to the black wolf's absence. According to Lowman, "For months after the killing, Peacock bragged about the effects his and Myers's actions had on the community. . . . Peacock would get online in the break room and invite others of us to come with him. . . . He would go on YouTube and also read the comments to the stories about Romeo in the *Juneau Empire*. . . . He would say, 'Those morons! Ha! What idiots! I killed their beloved wolf! Ha!' He would shout at the screen, saying, 'You fucking idiots! Sobbing over your poor missing wolf!' A lot of us at the plant were disgusted by his behavior, and after a while it got pretty strange, to see him gloat over this." In a conversation with me two years later, Lowman reflected, "What amazed me was how stupid he was to give us all the details. That really surprised me. . . . If he hadn't talked, he'd have gotten away with it. He really thought he was superior to the rest of us."

Peacock apparently took particular delight in a January 22, 2010, *Juneau Empire* article titled "Where Art Thou, Romeo?" Nancy Meyerhoffer (with less than perfect spelling and so forth) relates Peacock's words as she heard them: "Yeh I know wherefor is your Romeo, he is gonna be in my living room, why don't ya tell Juliett to put her head on my lap and tell me all about it." And around that time, I received an online order for my collection of Southeast Alaska essays, *The Glacier Wolf*, which featured Romeo's silhouetted, howling image on the cover, as well as several short pieces describing the wolf's life among us. A request for a special inscription accompanied the order: "Wherefore art thou, Romeo?" The commonly misinterpreted phrase (rather than *where*, it actually means *why* are you called Romeo) stuck in memory, as did the unusual name, Peacock. At the time, the name meant nothing to me, and of course I didn't know of his plan to accent his trophy display with my book, to prove both the wolf's fame and his own sadistic cleverness. All that would snap into focus soon enough.

Though in retrospect, the chattering of Myers and Peacock seems voluminous, most of it was disconnected, confined to limited circles, and far beneath the radar of enforcement agencies, state or federal. The myriad but scattered dots between Romeo and his killers would depend on the unflagging persistence of Harry Robinson, backed up by Michael Lowman, whose own dedication to solving a wildlife crime thousands of miles away, affecting people and a single wild animal he'd never seen, stands as a singular act of altruism — and not without personal risk, either. In February of 2010, Lowman and Peacock traded words as they worked in the Donnelley plant: "Peacock mentioned a $1,500 reward being offered for information leading to the identification of Romeo's killers. I jokingly told him that 'for enough money, I would turn you in myself.'" Peacock looked me dead serious in the eye, and said, 'If you did, I would shoot you!'" Unfazed by the threat, Lowman recorded Peacock's words and added them to a growing, damning pile.

Through the winter of 2009–2010, Harry Robinson persevered. Matching up information he received from Lowman with research into public records and Alaska and federal statutes, he compiled a veritable grocery list of violations Myers and Peacock might be charged with, complete with names, dates, and other specifics. These extended far beyond Romeo, as far back as 2006 when Peacock killed a rare, blue-gray phase black bear known as a glacier bear. He bragged back East he had killed "Juneau's spirit bear," a title he apparently invented to augment his personal legend. The rug of the two-year-old juvenile (the size a buddy of mine used to call a suitcase bear, because if it had a handle on its back, you could pick it up and walk away with it) was so small that some Donnelley workers snickered. Other potential violations included illegal killing of that larger black bear in 2009, illegally mailing a handgun across state lines, making numerous false statements, multiple counts of possessing and transporting illegally taken game, Peacock's hunting and fishing without a license in some years, and several more.

With the input of local attorneys and Romeo watchers Joel Bennett and Jan Van Dort, Harry opted to present his findings to federal rather than state authorities. The potential charges at that level were far greater—notably, violation of the Lacey Act, which targets transport of illegally gotten animal parts across state lines. Special Agent Sam Friburg of the U.S. Fish and Wildlife Service was impressed by the thoroughness of Harry's documentation. He'd been handed far more than the usual citizen's tip; the pile of evidence amounted to a blow-by-blow journal of activity for two serial poachers. And, thanks to Michael Lowman's continuing reportage redirected through Harry, there were details of Peacock's upcoming return to Alaska in the spring of 2010, and so the opportunity to catch Peacock and Myers, red to the elbows.

When Peacock arrived as scheduled in early May, he lacked any clue that he and Myers were being tailed. In fact, they were the focus of a cooperative investigation by the U.S. Fish and Wildlife Service, the U.S. Forest Service, and the Alaska State Wildlife Troopers. (Such joint investigations are common in Alaska, whenever jurisdictions overlap.) Federal agents Friburg and Chris Hansen staked out a baiting station (an area where food is left to attract bears, with a blind or tree stand nearby) that Myers had established Out The Road, weeks before Peacock's arrival. The idea, of course, was to set up Peacock for another easy kill or two. As a guy who poked at the regulations, Myers surely knew that bait stations weren't permitted in the Juneau area, but he and Peacock stoked it with stale bread and burnt honey all the same. Friburg and Hansen watched and video-taped the poachers at the site and, late on the evening of May 14, heard a single gunshot. They recorded Myers and Peacock on video carrying and loading yet another suitcase bear into the back of My-ers's rig—a scrawny, dog-sized two-year-old, perhaps even a year-ling. Peacock was set to leave on May 23 with one more conquest recorded on his cell phone camera. He had no idea that his aura of invincibility was about to implode.

Running an errand, I happened to be driving past Alaskan Brew-ing on the afternoon of May 20. As soon as I saw the enforcement SUVs pulled up, I knew the bust was going down—long-awaited among a handful of us who knew. Inside, Park Myers was being in-terviewed by Alaska State Wildlife Trooper Aaron Frenzel and Fish and Wildlife Service Special Agent Stan Pruszenski. Search warrants had already been served at the Myers house and at taxidermist Clas-sen's home. Troopers and agents seized a large, tanned black wolf hide and skull, plus a black bear skin and Peacock's cell phone. They also discovered Myers's marijuana-growing operation inside My-ers's garage: in the words of the state trooper report, "approximately twenty-seven" high-grade, expertly tended plants with an estimated street value in the tens of thousands. In addition, Myers was found in possession of a .30/.30 carbine stolen while being shipped by the U.S. Postal Service—a potentially serious federal crime in its own right. Meanwhile, across the continent, Fish and Wildlife Service agents executed a warrant in Pennsylvania and seized Jeff Peacock's work computer, packed with evidence. Peacock was charged with unsworn falsification, taking big game in a closed area, baiting bears without a permit, plus three counts of unlawful possession of game. My-ers's warrant specified taking big game by unlawful methods, bait-ing bears without a permit, and three charges of unlawful game pos-session. Each one of those charges carried a possible maximum fine of $10,000 and three hundred days in jail—times five for Myers, six for Peacock. That total was just Alaska bringing the hammer down. What would upcoming federal charges add to the already-daunting

heap? Myers and Peacock, arraigned separately with private repre-
sentation from defense attorney David Mallet, pled the standard not
guilty. Peacock was allowed to leave the state after posting a $10,000
bail bond. The two seemed destined for some serious legal worries,
major payouts, and time behind bars.

The arrests and arraignments, covered by the *Empire* and local
radio, catapulted the case into public view. While many Juneauites
had speculated for months about the wolf's fate, by spring most had
sighed and gone on with their lives. No one expected to ever know
anything, let alone find the wolf's killer staring out at them from the
morning daily: a slight, unremarkable man with a baggy sweater,
blank face, wire-rimmed glasses, and a bad haircut. I was among
those who recognized the face: that guy with his sons at my Public
Market booth, three years before, who talked loudly about Romeo's
resemblance to a wolf he'd skinned.

Even though most citizens knew just what little the paper reported, you'd expect some sort of visceral outcry: drive-by rock-
throwing at the Myers house, tire-slashing on his gaudy blaze-
orange Jeep with its roof-mounted floodlights, public curse-outs,
and maybe more. But instead, I, like most involved Juneauites, utterly ignored and avoided him, treated him as a nonperson, even
when I glimpsed him at Fred Meyer.

Meanwhile, there was scattered but steady pushback as well from
the crowd who saw Myers and Peacock as ordinary joes and stal-
wart sportsmen, unjustly crucified by the greenies. *Just a damn wolf
and a punk bear or two, the rules a little bit bent—what was the big
deal?* However, aside from a sometimes-bitter spatter of emails, *Empire* letters, and blog entries both ways, restraint and social decorum
echoed in an almost eerie quiet. Maybe we were all in shock, but one
truth held sure: we were law-abiding citizens bound by a sense of
community, confident that the law would deliver a measure of justice—maybe not perfect, but something we could recognize.

Overlooked by almost all onlookers were two omissions in District Attorney Gardner's affidavit of counsel and other court records:
no mention anywhere of Myers's marijuana operation, and Gardner

(who had been presented with Myers's past criminal record when the Fish and Wildlife Service shared their evidence cache with the state) maintained in that affidavit that Myers had no prior record. Neither Myers's past history with the Pennsylvania babysitter and subsequent probation violations, nor the pot farm was public knowledge; and to those who knew, both seemed swept under the rug by an invisible hand. We'd later discover that Myers had made a plea bargain with the court, getting the drug charges dropped for turning informant; and perhaps there had been other side bargains as well. Somewhere along the way, mention of the .30/.30 stolen from the mail (potentially a federal felony) evaporated, too.

Meanwhile, the identity of the dead wolf—the heart of the case, as far as most Juneauites were concerned—remained uncertain to the general public. They didn't have access to Lowman's affidavit and other particulars that Harry, Joel, I, and others had known for months. A May 26 *Empire* headline asked the question many wondered: WAS IT ROMEO? The hide in Peacock's possession had, according to its plastic seal, been duly presented for inspection by Fish and Game as required; but department records labeled the skin as gray, though the skin bearing the recorded seal number was in fact black. The rather startling discrepancy gave birth to the immediate suspicion among some that Fish and Game or even enforcement agencies might be involved in a cover-up. To this day, Fish and Game sealing agent Chris Frary remains perplexed. He doesn't recall examining a black wolf hide at any time that September, though his handwriting is on a form dated 9-23-09. He was later grilled on the topic by Agent Friburg and Trooper Frenzel, which seems to let enforcement off the conspiracy hook. Having myself interviewed Frary—now retired, and still chagrined by his word being called into question—I buy his story. Quite possibly Peacock's tag was first affixed on a gray hide of unknown origin and later removed and transferred to Romeo's. Thus the black wolf's hide may well have never been inspected, yet the tag validated. It was just the sort of gambit a poacher who studied and poked at regulations might try.

In a postarraignment interview with the *Empire*, Myers flailed like a man snared in his own alibi. True to form, he adamantly denied shooting a black wolf, despite having just been caught with its tagged skin: "You'd be a complete moron if you thought it was Romeo. A complete moron. I know a gray wolf from a black one. I know a 70-pound wolf from a 140-pound wolf." Never mind that just days earlier, under oath, Myers had told District Attorney Gardner that he'd "panicked" when he realized the wolf he'd killed might be Romeo, which indicated the wolf in question was in fact large and black; and some of Peacock's cell phone images of the wolf had also been titled with "Romeo." However, no court document, nor any source other than the Fish and Game sealing record, mentioned Myers or Peacock shooting a gray wolf, and there was no matching skin ever offered to anchor the excuse. And where did that specific weight for each animal come from? Myers seemed to have fallen into the standard liars' club faux pas of introducing details he shouldn't have known. All added credence to some sort of calculated sleight of hand. The contradictions, questions, and omissions in the case continued to pile up, with the trial still months away.

Legal constraints further shaped the course of events. As far as the state was concerned, a wolf was a wolf; there was no law or penalty addressing the killing of a specific individual, no matter how well known or regarded. Several citizens had samples of Romeo's shed hair that could have been used in a DNA match, plus access to at least a half-dozen people—including Harry, John Hyde, and me—who knew Romeo well enough to identify the hide through specific scars and markings. But even if the state had the means to positively identify the skin as Romeo's, they had zero legal reason, and far less incentive, to do so. Such an ID could only lead to awkward complications, not the least of which might be a public uproar, when the available penalty couldn't possibly match the public perception of the crime. For perspective, consider the fine Myers would pay in direct compensation for a wolf, if found guilty of illegally depriving Alaska of said resource: $500. Each black bear was worth $600. And though the total potential penalties in the two cases indeed were fairly severe — nearly $20,000 combined and years in jail for Myers and Peacock — the violations they were facing were all misdemeanors.

This was still a good start, we told each other. Soon enough, the Feds would add their own crushing charges to the legal dog pile. But the weeks passed, and the second wave of indictments never came. Behind doors, the decision passed to pursue the cases only at the state level — supposedly, we were later told, because that was the stronger legal route. That rationale seemed questionable at best, given that Lacey Act violations (the illegally taken wolf hide and skull, like the two bear hides, had crossed state lines) and the firearm charges could pin on a felony or two apiece. Surely, state and federal charges could both have been brought; they complemented rather than duplicated each other. Of course, the call wasn't up to the investigating agents. Years later, Agent Friburg would express to me his own disappointment at the prosecutorial decision. Pursuing a case that spanned thousands of miles and state lines was a huge drain of resources, and there were surely bigger fish to fry. This was, after all, just a two-bit poaching case involving some wolf and a couple of black bears, in a state where their lives came cheap.

Peacock and the suitcase bear

Park Myers in court

THE WEIGHT OF DREAMS

November 2010

Spring merged into summer and gave way to autumn. The court dates for both Myers and Peacock were twice set back at the request of defense attorney David Mallet: a solid if cynical strategy, based on the premise that the more time passed, the more public interest would wane. The wolf had already been gone for a year, after all. Court scheduling conflicts resulted in additional postponement. But though judgment was delayed, and Myers (by his own later in-court admission) encountered surprisingly little day-to-day rancor, local justice did, in small ways, assert itself. Myers reportedly got shoved around and roughed up outside a bar for bragging about the wolf; and a grocery checker told me she'd watched mall security summoned at Super Bear to protect Myers from a guy who recognized him from the paper and started making threats. A woman I didn't know also approached me, months later, with the story of her own Myers encounter. She'd had a flat tire near the airport, and a man stopped to aid her. As he was setting up her jack, he asked her how she felt about being helped by Romeo's killer, and she recognized him from the *Empire* photo. Taken aback, she refused his assistance. Other repercussions were far more direct. Park Myers lost his job at Alaskan Brewing, for reasons undisclosed to the public.

After that, Park scrounged and found odd jobs, and Pam Myers, no longer working at Southeast Veterinary Hospital, found work as a checker at Super Bear. A handful of Juneauites offered support — everything from food to work opportunities — and Park Myers played the sympathy card to the hilt. He seemed expert at telling a sob story, featuring how he'd been framed, suffered persecution (which in fact, he scarcely encountered), and faced a looming bank eviction that was apparently never imminent. Park was also heard to brag that they were scamming the bank and living rent-free. "He had me fooled," said neighbor Jon Stetson, who had extended a helping hand that was later bitten. "I learned the hard way."

More than five months after his arrest, more than a year after Romeo's death, Park Myers's judgment day arrived. About forty spectators, plus another dozen participants, crowded into the chambers of the Juneau District Court on a clear, early-November morning — an unprecedented crowd for a 9 A.M. misdemeanor hearing on a midweek workday. Harry, Joel Bennett, Vic Walker, Sherrie, and I sat within whispering distance, surrounded by many faces the wolf would have recognized. Someone had been concerned enough about order to summon a pair of state troopers to stand at the back, pistols on hip and broad-brimmed hats pulled low over their foreheads; but the crowd proved quiet and well mannered, awed by the unfamiliar setting and the moment. The Myers entourage — Park, Pamela, one of his sons, and several scruffy teens who obviously considered him a great guy — bunched together at front right, profoundly alone. Myers's defense attorney, David Mallet, appeared via speakerphone from Washington State. Presiding over the *State of Alaska v. Park Myers III* sat District Judge Keith Levy, by all accounts a fair-minded man, sensitive to the community. On this morning, he bore the quietly exasperated, fatalistic visage of a modern Pontius Pilate, and with good reason.

This wasn't a standard trial, roiling with real-time drama: attorneys sparring over evidence and witnesses; the judge ruling on points of procedure and law; the guilt or innocence of the accused hinging on a jury's verdict, culminating in the final act of sentencing. Such a piece of theater — rife with blow-by-blow detail, laden with catharsis — had never been in the cards. Defense attorney Mallet knew better than to publicly expose his client to the facts and the winds of emotion. This change of plea hearing, planned all along, was the final step in a purposely dull, well-choreographed procedural dance. By originally pleading not guilty, Mallet had given Myers every possible chance to gain from any legal loophole; facing a slam dunk case, he'd also created a bargaining chip out of nothing. A revised plea of guilty would spare the state the impending expense and trouble of a trial and also demonstrate a change of heart by the defendant — one that would position him for the best possible chance at leniency. Immediately following this calculated mea culpa, the imposition of a just and fair sentence would then fall upon a single man. Keith Levy must have known what sort of box he was in.

The prosecution's presentation was brief; the change of plea and the specific nature of the charges had rendered most details moot. District Attorney Gardner called just one witness: Wildlife Trooper Aaron Frenzel, who fielded some slow-pitch questions and narrated a brief evidentiary slide show, including images from Peacock's phone. To those familiar with the case, the state's version of events seemed closer to a Japanese kabuki show than summation. Neither Harry Robinson nor Michael Lowman would be called to the stand, though Harry was present and Michael Lowman had volunteered to fly across the country at his own expense to testify. No public acknowledgment of their key roles in the investigation (starting with the fact that they had uncovered the crime and then furnished specifics that had made the prosecution possible) would ever be made. Gardner concluded his presentation with a sentencing request for substantial fines and incarceration — sincere, perhaps, but still part of the dance. If the prosecution's case was brief, the defense's was all but nonexistent. Attorney Mallet just wanted the hearing to end — the quicker, the better. Without challenge from the prosecution, he reiterated Myers's lie that the wolf in question was seventy pounds and gray, insisted that his client had no previous criminal record, and concluded by arguing that such small offenses didn't call for jail time.

Pared to its legal essence, the case before Judge Levy indeed amounted to this: overlapping wildlife misdemeanors, committed by a contrite perpetrator with a clean Alaska rap sheet. Observers ignorant of procedure, as most sitting in the courtroom surely were, supposed that the judge had the power to sentence Park Myers to the maximum on each and every count, or at least assign some time behind bars, as the district attorney had requested. But District Judge Keith Levy, as arbiter of justice for the Commonwealth of Alaska, was constrained by a funnel of sentencing guidelines. Despite lip service paid to the high value of Alaska's wildlife, state law and the record of its application tell another story. Court records show that no one serves time for first-time misdemeanor wildlife violations in Alaska, and full fines on all possible charges are seldom, if ever, imposed. If Judge Levy had exceeded those boundaries set by precedent, his sentence would have been appealed and overridden. So it was that the judge meting out justice on our behalf had no choice but to let Park Myers walk free with little more than a hand slap. He explained that much in his sentencing preamble.

Though some of us had known how it would go, we all sat in numb silence as Judge Levy, stumbling over words and making little eye contact with anyone, worked his way through the various counts, assigning and suspending time and dollar amounts. The end result: Romeo's killer was sentenced to a total of 330 days in jail, all of them suspended, and $12,500 in fines, all but $5,000 canceled out. Including compensation for one bear and a wolf, plus miscellaneous fees, Myers was ordered to pay a total of $6,250. In addition, he was required to complete one hundred hours of community service and forfeit three firearms (one of them actually Peacock's .460). He also lost Alaska hunting privileges for two years, in case the legal constraint had ever mattered, and was placed on probation for an equal span. The suspended portions of the sentence were somewhat more than symbolic; if Myers violated the terms of probation, those penalties or portions of them could be reimposed — small consolation at best, and less so if we had known then how little Park Myers would ultimately pay.

There was one added disappointment beyond the sentence and Myers's jump-through-the-hoops apology that ended by suggesting everyone should "move on." If Judge Levy meant to make up for his legally tied hands with at least a public tongue-lashing on behalf of the citizens of Juneau, he fell pathetically short. Here are Levy's words, quoted verbatim from the court transcript: "I think the main—the other main goal here is community condemnation. I think it is—I think you knew what you were doing. I think you did show a lot of disrespect for the laws. I think it isn't fair to others, and I think it, you know, certainly affects the conservation efforts."

Around the courtroom, people traded glances, some incredulous, others hard-eyed. At that moment, we understood the full extent to which we'd been marginalized. The wolf belonged to the state. Paradoxically, we, its law-abiding citizens, were nonentities—observers without importance or voice in the proceedings. There was no provision for any member of the community to take a turn at the microphone and address Romeo's killer, as nearly the whole gallery would have done. As Myers walked free, passing close enough to where I stood near the door that I turned my shoulder to let him pass, a thick-throated silence hung in the air. No doubt the letter of the law had been served in the matter of *State of Alaska v. Park Myers III*, but what about justice? Even a child would know there was none, and never would be. We might as well have trusted some clumsy machine to restore life to a flower, reattach each petal, breathe life into its wilted stem.

That failure, though, couldn't forgive our own. On the drive home, Sherrie stared straight ahead, tearless, jaw quivering. "What was wrong with us?" she muttered. "What the hell was wrong with all of us, just sitting there, saying nothing? We could have all jumped up and started shouting, *'You bastard! You murdering bastard!'* All of us together. That was our chance. My only chance to say or do something that mattered, and I just sat there. We all just sat there." What would the court have done with such an outburst? Arrested us all, charged everyone with contempt, fined us, thrown us in jail? Any penalty would have been worth it, a moment we would have carried with us always, a story to remind ourselves of who we truly were. Instead, we're condemned to the echoes of our own silence.

District Attorney Gardner had made one beau geste to those who knew the wolf. At the end of Judge Levy's pronouncement of sentence, the prosecution introduced a final piece of evidence — one that had no direct bearing on the case, yet was everything to us. As Trooper Frenzel unfurled the contents of a black plastic trash bag and draped it over a display easel, a collective gasp rose from the courtroom. There was no mistaking the grizzled patterns around the jaw, the minor scars and marks here and there, the patches of gray behind his forelegs. Before us, empty of life, hung the husk of the wolf we called Romeo. After the gavel came down, the tanned hide was moved to the courthouse foyer, with a trooper standing guard a few feet away. We gathered there, speaking in low tones, taking turns to stand near, brush a hand along his back, peer into sightless eyes, and whisper farewell. Though we'd known the wolf was gone, now we felt the ache of forever.

Jeff Peacock's legal reckoning would provide even less satisfaction. Though Judge Levy had originally insisted that Peacock would return to Juneau to face the court in person, he ended up appearing via telephone from Pennsylvania, due to health issues we guessed had been exaggerated and seemed conveniently timed. The change of plea hearing, also orchestrated by David Mallet, snuck into the court docket in early January of 2011 with so little fanfare that most Juneauites didn't realize it had occurred until they read about it the next day. With eighteen months in jail and $13,000 in fines suspended, Peacock was ordered to pay $2,600 in total fines and restitution, serve three years' probation, forfeit Alaska hunting and fishing rights for that same period, and endure one of Judge Levy's mild-mannered rebukes. That was the best the state could manage: it provided justice to neither wolf, nor dead bears, nor us — just to itself, on its own terms. The system had taken care of itself; it was up to us to do the same.

Of course we mourned — then, as now, with more pain sweeping ahead down the trails we'd all walk over the years, glimpsing in a flicker of shadow a familiar shape, straining to hear a distant howl in the wind. We mourned for what we knew was as lost as any miracle could ever be, mourned, too, for what each of us might have done or not done, a small choice, maybe, passed at the time with scarce notice: picking up a ringing telephone instead of walking out a door, making a snap decision about what trail we might hike on a given day — hell, stopping for coffee? Who knows what act, by whom, might have shifted a million interwoven sequences so the wolf would have trotted on? As for me, if saving this one wolf had somehow offered a glimmer of redemption, I had utterly failed. Harry Robinson, perhaps more than any of us, is visited by the ghost of all he might have done. His self-condemnation rings simple, absolute. "I let my friend down," he said quietly. "I wasn't there when he needed me." A fond thought, to believe that any small act, from any of us, might have saved the wolf. Like his Shakespearian namesake, Romeo's die was cast by his nature, shaped by forces beyond his and our horizon. In the end, Harry, and all who loved Romeo, were fortune's fools.

We endured the head shaking, pontificating, and outright ridicule of those who didn't know or understand, and never would. *Just a wolf,* they said, as if he were a rusted-out truck or a pile of rotting wood. *Move on.* One snide comment to the *Empire* suggested Romeo's end as a tanned hide was a "perfect" example of resource utilization. The official version of things — the story we heard in snippets, passed down from authorities — was pointed in its blame. People had loved the wolf to death, lured him by thoughtless, selfish behavior toward a doom so sure they all saw it coming. There are men wearing the uniforms of four agencies — two state, two federal — who more than believe that; they call it true. I pass them in lines at the bank and hardware store; I may nod and chat with some, and not recognize others. This is the story they know, the one that's almost always right.

On its surface, the saga of Romeo the wolf may well seem a cautionary tale of wildlife habituation gone wrong. Wolves and people just don't mix, and that maxim was once more proven. However, the

facts don't match the narrative. The black wolf didn't become habituated over time, but arrived the way he was: engaging our dogs
and snatching toys in those first days among us. Nor did he seem the
product of food conditioning; he bore none of its negative marks.
And there was no driving him off; when we tried, he returned. If we
had succeeded, he would have been pushed into even more perilous straits. As a sentient, intelligent being, he made a choice to live
where he did, and to interact with us and our dogs—not only on his
own social terms, but through an adaptive understanding of our
rules. While Myers and Peacock may have taken great pleasure in
killing a "famous" wolf, they would have shot him or any other animal just the same, as they poached nameless, tiny bears most hunters would be embarrassed to shoot. The wolf's celebrity, rather than
causing his death, shielded him for an astounding reach of time. Too,
according to the court's own accepted evidence, Romeo was killed
in the company of other wolves, in wild country, not in someone's
backyard, and not because of any identified behavior related to habituation. Thus the party line of blame contradicts itself; the state
can't have it both ways. But regardless of where or how he died, one
essential fact seems clear: the black wolf wasn't killed by love, but by
its determined, malignant inverse.

How safe was Romeo among us? Not very, is the short and obvious answer, one that I would have given at any moment over the
years. In retrospect, though, consider that he was close to tripling
the measured life span of an average wild wolf in Denali National
Park—a startlingly brief three years—in a place where wildlife is
afforded wide chunks of habitat protected from our kind. Not for
weeks or months, but years, the city of Juneau and the black wolf
set an unprecedented standard for coexistence and mutual safety between two species conflicted as any on this planet. His survival was
not due to the actions of a few, but the tolerance of many, and the
restraint of state and federal agencies—not to mention the actions
of the wolf himself. If not for two warped outsiders, he might well
still be there, waiting by the Big Rock for his adopted pack mates to
appear.

I look back over my shoulder to that black shape curled against the snow, to that spring day years ago that I saw him, as if for the last time. Alone in the stillness of night, Sherrie and the dogs breathing about me, the weight of dreams press against my chest. I try to weep silently, so I don't waken anyone; I cry not for myself, nor the black wolf, but for all of us, adrift in an increasingly empty world. What can we hope to carry away from such sorrow? But there is another side to the story, a faint glow that flickers and returns, a pulse of auroral fire across a dark sky. Nothing can take away the miracle that was Romeo and the years we spent in his company. Love, not hate, is the burden we carry. But that fact makes it no lighter.

During the black wolf's time among us, he brought wonder to thousands, filled a landscape to overflowing, taught many to see the world and his species with fresh eyes. Without knowing or caring, simply by being what he was, he brought people closer: friends and families, but also those who might have never met, if not for his presence. Across the years, I watched hundreds and finally thousands of Juneau residents—two here, a half dozen there, one group after another, out on the broad sounding board of the lake—lean on their ski poles and chat as they watched the wolf playing with dogs, trotting across the ice, or lying in one of his spots at the lake edge; and many times, I took part in such conversations. Talk may have anchored around him, but it percolated outward to include the myriad matters, trifling and larger, that create a woven sense of community—everything from local politics to who got married to where winter-run king salmon might be biting. Thanks to the black wolf, I and many others met, or got to know better, Juneauites from all walks of life—friendships and acquaintances that have endured his passing and the passing of others. He spun context into our lives, drew us closer without our realizing any more than he did. Even those of us who didn't agree, including on what should and shouldn't be done with, or to, or around this wolf, had a chance to shape words and thoughts face to face, gain added sense of who we were, individually and collectively, and of what we held as true. So it was that the wolf melded into Juneau's story and became part of us.

Two weeks after the trial, its pain still sharp as frost, we stood in the cold bright silence of a late-November day, staring out over the frozen expanse of Mendenhall Lake. Beyond, the mountains rose, cradling the glacier, and all of us, in their arms. More than a hundred people had gathered near the Big Rock to remember and mourn — and many more in spirit. For months afterward, strangers and friends approached me, apologizing that prior plans on a busy weekend, just before Thanksgiving, had drawn them away. Though this was probably the first memorial service for a wolf in Alaska, and maybe in human history, it seemed natural enough — in fact, what circumstances demanded. The crowd included dogs, of course, and construction workers, lawyers, taxi drivers, young and old, hunters, trappers, and vegans. We stood together, air sharp in our lungs, the flow of time transparent, each moment of the wolf among us a stone in a clear-flowing river. I recall standing on a rock and speaking, in turn, after Joel and Harry. I can summon back the emotion, but not my words; and I remember holding up the heavy bronze plaque Joel had commissioned from sculptor Skip Wallen, to be installed on a boulder at the far side of the lake, on a path where it would be seen by tens of thousands of visitors each year, and perhaps — just maybe — a passing wolf. The memorial bears an image of Romeo reclining on the Big Rock, and below, a simple inscription to remind us — one you should read for yourself. As his recorded howls rose into a vacant sky, dogs joined his song, twining a chorus more perfect than human voices could have been.

Years from now, we'll tell this story: Once upon a time, there was a wolf called Romeo. Together, we watch him trot across the lake and fade into twilight. And we remember.

EPILOGUE

November 2013

Years pass, and Romeo is still with us. His name rises often in conversation, and his image adorns walls in dozens of homes. Out near the glacier, you can turn onto Lone Wolf Drive and Black Wolf Way, or sit on the lakeside cedar bench Joel Bennett placed where his wife, Louisa, used to pause and watch for the wolf in her last days. We pass his memorial, mounted on a granite boulder, as we walk toward Nugget Falls, and sometimes pause to visit our memories. The plaque hasn't become a shrine as some feared; nor has it been vandalized. It's simply merged into the landscape, become part of Juneau's story. And, in a town that places high value on coffee and beer, there's a brand of each named in Romeo's honor: Heritage Coffee's Black Wolf Blend and Alaskan Brewing's Black Wolf IPA (India Pale Ale). At just the right time of a late-winter afternoon, people glimpse what some claim to be Romeo's ghost: the silhouette of a wolf's head cast in shadow on a mountainside above downtown Juneau. Back out toward the glacier, many of us who used to wander the west shore of the lake and Dredge now go elsewhere instead. When we do walk those trails, we can't help looking for those familiar paw prints, or listening for his voice in the wind. As Harry says, it's too lonely.

Of course, other wolves pass through. In the year after Romeo's death, there were repeated sightings of an almost-white wolf in the

Montana Creek and glacier area. I wonder if it was the same light-colored animal the old Eskimo woman saw and that I glimpsed in the fog, with Romeo, several years before. Sometimes alone, sometimes in the company of a gray wolf, it approached cars and followed hikers with their dogs. However, those who encountered the white wolf described an unsettling, bold-verging-on-menacing behavior and, instead of relaxed sociability, a cold, inscrutable stare. It was, after all, another wolf, and after a few weeks, it and its pack mate had drifted on.

A few months after his sentencing, Park Myers III was back to being himself, peddling a strain of high-grade marijuana he called Romeo's Widow and bragging that he was untouchable, as he truly seemed to be. Nonetheless, he ran afoul of the law again — this time, for unemployment fraud, a felony offense and a violation of his probation. Unlike the first time, he ended up in jail for several days; but after much behind-doors folderol and legal proceedings that are a story in themselves, the state declined to pursue the case or to enforce any of the suspended fines and prison time from the Romeo trial. Once more, Park Myers walked free. A few months later, he and his family were gone, back to Pennsylvania. Aside from $2,000 of forfeited bail money, he never paid a cent of his original fines for killing Romeo, nor performed any documented community service. As for Jeff Peacock, his health problems were real enough, rather than feigned. His hunting days seemed to be over. We don't dwell on either of them. In the end, they don't matter much at all.

As I write on a rain-spattered, late-autumn day, Romeo's hide lies draped over the couch, close enough that I can reach over and run my hands through the silk-smooth guard hairs along its shoulders. When I first opened the box containing the tanned skin and bleached skull, I didn't know how I'd react; but I've taken a quiet comfort from their presence. They're here for a few days, on the way to a museum-quality taxidermist. At the request of Mendenhall Glacier visitor center director Ron Marvin, Harry, Joel, and I gave input to the design of an installation for the center — an educational exhibit featuring the wolf reclining on a boulder and his recorded howls. Some, including Joel, thought his remains should be destroyed — perhaps in a fire, high on Mount McGinnis. I almost agreed, but the nod toward preservation prevailed. As Sherrie said quietly, "It's all we have left of him." I volunteered to find the right person to breathe the illusion of life back into his eyes. The mount will take at least a year to complete, and its placement at the center will surely face opposition from some, and support from many. Romeo's future among us is far from certain; but then, it never was.

Left to right: *Joel Bennett, Harry Robinson, Nick Jans, Vic Walker*

NOTES

Chapter 1

For more on the black wolf as a genetic marker leading to dogs, see "Molecular and Evolutionary History of Melanism in North American Gray Wolves," by Tovi M. Anderson and others, *Science*, vol. 323 (March 6, 2009).

Ballard's far-ranging doctoral dissertation, "Demographics, Movements, and Predation Rates of Wolves in Northwest Alaska," is available at http://arizona.openrepository.com/arizona/handle/10150/186483?mode=full.

For more on the wayward wolf OR-7 and his rambles (as of autumn 2013 he's still alive and well) a quick Internet search keying OR-7 will come up with tracking maps and more. See the California Department of Fish and Wildlife information page for more information on OR-7, http://www.dfg.ca.gov/wildlife/nongame/wolf/. He also has his own Facebook page.

For more on Alexander Archipelago wolves, see http://www.adfg.alaska.gov/index.cfm?adfg=wolf.aawolf and http://akwildlife.org/wp-content/uploads/2013/02/Alexander_Archipelago_wolves_final.pdf.

Vicious: Wolves and Men in America (Yale Press 2004), by Jon T. Coleman, is one of many sources giving detailed coverage to wolf eradication efforts in North America and its underpinnings. His work also details Audubon's encounter with the trapped wolves that I describe.

For a catalog of quotes from Lewis and Clark's journals related to their wolf encounters, see http://www.mnh.si.edu/lewisandclark/index.html?loc=/lewisandclark/journal.cfm?id=984.

For more on the effects of wolf reintroduction on the greater Yellowstone ecosystem, see William J. Ripple and Robert L. Bestcha's excellent article "Trophic Cascades in Yellowstone: The First 15 Years After Wolf Reintroduction," http://fes.forestry.oregonstate.edu/sites/fes.forestry.oregonstate .edu/files/PDFs/Beschta/Ripple_Beschta2012BioCon.pdf.

Alaska's figures on total wolf populations are based on extrapolations — basically, well-educated guesses. Counting wolves over such a large area is an all-but-impossible task. However, the latitude between high and low ends of the estimate — five thousand — is large indeed and indicates a huge amount of uncertainty by any scientific standard, raising significant management questions.

Chapter 2

"Black Wolf Near Glacier Brings Locals Delight — and Some Concern," *Juneau Empire,* January 11, 2004, http://juneauempire.com/stories/011104/ loc_wolf.shtml.

For more on wolf play, see the index in *Wolves: Behavior, Ecology, and Conservation,* edited by L. David Mech and Luigi Boitani (University of Chicago Press 2007).

Evolutionary divergence between dogs and wolves continues to be a topic of ongoing debate and conflicting evidence — when, where, and how? See Tina Saey's article in the June 10, 2013, online issue of *Science News,* http://www.sciencenews.org/view/generic/id/350913/description/Now -extinct-wolf-may-be-ancestor-of-modern-day-dogs. DNA evidence indicates that dogs may have descended from a line of wolves that no longer exists.

Science Nordic's online magazine, June 13, 2012, http://sciencenordic .com/dna-reveals-new-picture-dog-origins, gives an accessible report on results from a major European genetic study that examined DNA from thirty-five dog breeds and concluded from the results that dogs evolved from wolves in a number of independent locations between fifteen thousand and thirty thousand or more years ago.

Chapter 3

My Inupiaq friend Nelson Greist, whom I'd known since 1979, died in 2012 at age ninety. He once cautioned me after I'd camped alone near a pack of relaxed, amicable wolves for several days: "Maybe they try to eat you. You just never know it."

For a summation on the research regarding wolf territory size, boundaries, and so on, see the index in *Wolves: Behavior, Ecology, and Conservation,* edited by L. David Mech and Luigi Boitani (University of Chicago Press 2007).

For a good summary of research on interpack strife, see *Wolves,* pp. 176–81.

Haber, Mech, Van Ballenberghe, Ballard, and many others have studied dispersal, since it is a key factor in both wolf conservation and management. Haber hypothesized that predator control actually may increase wolf populations at a faster rate than if groups are left undisturbed, since more dispersing wolves means more free-ranging breeders with fewer constraints.

A study summarized by Nikos Green and others in "Wolf Howling Is Mediated by Relationship Quality Rather Than Underlying Emotional Stress" (*Current Biology,* vol. 23, issue 17, 2013) has indeed confirmed that wolves howl to express separation from pack mates—the closer the bond between two animals, the more howling.

Chapter 4

Author interviews: Pete Griffin, Juneau District Ranger, U.S. Forest Service, retired; Harry Robinson; conversations with Gordon Haber; Inupiaq informants including Dwight Arnold, Joseph Arey, Sr., Nelson Greist, Sr., and Clarence Wood.

Research by Gordon Haber in *Among Wolves* (see suggested reading list) is especially strong regarding social cohesion and interactions of wolf family groups.

See Layne Adams and David Mech's study of wolf mortality within Denali National Park, http://www.nps.gov/dena/naturescience/upload/wolfmonitoring2011-2.pdf.

Also see studies on mortality summarized in *Wolves: Behavior, Ecology, and Conservation,* edited by L. David Mech and Luigi Boitani (University of Chicago Press 2007).

Csanyi's work contrasting the learning patterns of captive wolves and dogs is nicely summarized and thoughtfully analyzed in *Animal Wise* (see suggested reading list). See also the article "A Simple Reason for a Big Difference: Wolves Do Not Look Back at Humans, but Dogs Do," by Ádám Miklósi and others (*Current Biology,* vol. 13, issue 9, 2003), http://www .sciencedirect.com/science/article/pii/S096098220300263X.

Chapter 5

Author interviews: Alaska State Trooper Dan Sadloske; Alaska Department of Fish and Game area biologist Lem Butler; Judith Cooper; Joel Bennett; conversation with Inupiaq informant Zach Hugo.

Wolves indeed seem the man-eating beast du jour in recent television and film efforts, including a number of TV commercials selling everything from coveralls (an attacking wolf breaks a tooth on the tough pants) to deodorant (men wearing "meat shirts" being pursued by hungry wolves).

Solid documentation for individual attacks in remote areas of India, Afghanistan, and other Asian countries are difficult to come by; many are presented through clearly antiwolf Internet links and are impossible to verify. No doubt some are exaggerations or total fabrications. However, the preponderance of reports over centuries forces one to conclude that if even a fraction are accurate, many fatal attacks have indeed occurred, with the victims being predominantly children of poor herding families. A 2001 online edition of the *Hindu,* India's national paper (apparently authentic), presents a book review detailing a spate of twentieth-century attacks in one province, http://hindu.com/2001/05/08/stories/1308017f.htm.

Stanley P. Young's 1944 book, *The Wolves of North America,* parts 1 and 2 (Dover Publications), provides a snapshot of lore, attitudes, research, and knowledge from sixty years ago. Young himself worked for several years for the U.S. Department of Agriculture in predator and vermin control. The fact that even he had trouble corroborating solid evidence of fatal wolf attacks in North America speaks for itself.

Alaska Department of Fish and Game biologist Mark McNay's 42-page publication is titled *A Case History of Wolf-Human Encounters in Alaska and Canada* (Alaska Department of Fish and Game Wildlife Technical Bulletin 13, 2002), http://www.adfg.alaska.gov/static/home/library/pdfs/ wildlife/research_pdfs/techb13p3.pdf.

Alaska Department of Fish and Game's report on the Candice Berner killing, titled "Findings Related to the March 2010 Fatal Wolf Attack Near

Chignik Lake, Alaska" is available at www.adfg.alaska.gov/static/home/ news/pdfs/wolfattackfatality.pdf.

The death of Kenton Joel Carnegie, like Candice Berner's, has received extensive media and online blog attention, much of it heavily slanted by antiwolf advocates. The official report, difficult to find, is titled *Review of Investigative Findings Relating to the Death of Kenton Carnegie at Points North, Saskatchewan,* by Dr. Paul Paquet, University of Calgary, Calgary, Alberta, and Dr. Ernest G. Walker, University of Saskatchewan, Saskatoon, Saskatchewan (August 8, 2008).

The Wikipedia article on Carnegie's death and the following investigation is exhaustive, detailed, well referenced, full of quotes from those who testified, and by far the best and most inclusive single source of information on the subject, http://en.wikipedia.org/wiki/Kenton_Joel_Carnegie_wolf_attack.

The nonprofit organization Wolf Song of Alaska (see suggested reading list) provides archived news articles from 2001 to 2011 regarding wolf-human conflicts; these are well organized and accessible. Go to the home page and click the Browse Our Archives button, lower right, http://www .wolfsongalaska.org/.

Chapter 6

Author interviews: Harry Robinson; John Hyde; Neil Barten, Biologist, Alaska Department of Fish and Game; conversations with Inupiaq informants, especially Clarence Wood and Nelson Greist; and Robert Armstrong, Biologist, Alaska Department of Fish and Game (retired).

Estimates of wolf life span in the wild vary and are subject to constantly fluctuating local conditions. What holds true in one area may not in another. Most data is compiled from radio- and satellite-collared wolves, which may skew data sets. The three-year figure from Adams and Mech's work in Denali Park (http://www.nps.gov/dena/naturescience/upload/wolfmonitoring2011-2.pdf.) is quite an eye-opener.

Murie, Van Ballenberghe, and Mech, among others, have done extensive work on hunting strategies and tactics used by wolves. Again, the indispensable *Wolves: Behavior, Ecology, and Conservation,* edited by L. David Mech and Luigi Boitani (University of Chicago Press 2007), offers a summation of peer-reviewed research on the subject. See especially pp. 119–25.

Haber has also documented hunting behavior, including the extensive scavenging and small-game hunting efforts by wolves (see the suggested reading list for *Among Wolves,* pp. 119–45).

Adams and others have documented the considerable amount of salmon that some interior Alaska wolves may consume, http://www.esajournals.org/doi/abs/10.1890/08-1437.1.

Person and others found considerable levels of fish consumption among wolves, coastal and interior, http://www.adfg.alaska.gov/index.cfm?adfg=wildlifenews.view_article&articles_id=86.

Watts, Butler, Dale, and Cox documented coastal wolves' heavy use of marine resources, http://www.wildlifebiology.com/Volumes/2010+-+Volume+16/2/814/En/.

Chapter 7

Author interviews: Anita Martin; Joel Bennett; Harry Robinson; Pete Griffin, District Ranger, U.S. Forest Service, retired.

For the entire Tim Treadwell story (quite different in perspective from Werner Herzog's documentary film *Grizzly Man*), see my book *The Grizzly Maze* (Dutton 2005).

Chapter 8

Author interviews: Neil Barten, Biologist, Alaska Department of Fish and Game; Matt Robus, Alaska Department of Fish and Game, retired; Harry Robinson; Joel Bennett; Vic Van Ballenberghe, U.S. Forest Service, retired; Elise Augustson, a local with regular contact with Romeo.

"Lake Wolf Apparently Kills Beagle," *Juneau Empire,* March 20, 2005, http://juneauempire.com/stories/032005/loc_20050320004.shtml.

"Safety More Important Than Wolf," letter to the editor, *Juneau Empire,* March 27, 2005, http://juneauempire.com/stories/032705/let_20050327018.shtml.

Chapter 9

Author interviews: Harry Robinson; Joel Bennett; John Hyde.

Person and Russell have studied the considerable vulnerability of wolves to human hunting and trapping in road-accessible populations, http://onlinelibrary.wiley.com/doi/10.2193/2007-520/abstract.

Chapter 10

Author interviews: Harry Robinson; John Hyde; Kim Turley.

The debate over Alaska's wolf control program ranks among the most contentious in the history of wildlife management programs in the United States. Well-regarded biologists have lined up on both sides of the issue. A 2007 technical report by the Alaska Department of Fish and Game represents the pro side, http://www.adfg.alaska.gov/static/home/about/ management/wildlifemanagement/intensivemanagement/pdfs/predator_ management.pdf.

A strong science-based rebuttal of the program was produced by Defenders of Wildlife (and yes, that's Romeo on the cover, less than one hundred yards from our back door), http://www.defenders.org/sites/ default/files/publications/alaskas_predator_control_programs.pdf.

A nonpartisan analysis of Alaska's predator control program was conducted in 1997 by a blue-ribbon panel of the National Research Council at the request of then governor Tony Knowles, http://www.nap.edu/openbook .php?record_id=5791.

In 2008 Alaska state senator Kim Elton was named special undersecretary of the interior for Alaska and presented President Obama with a photo portrait of Romeo, which is said to hang in the White House.

Search YouTube for "man and crocodile best friends" to locate a series of videos on these two, including Pocho's funeral in 2011. Equally interesting are the sneering, nay-saying comments that follow some of the clips. Also search YouTube for "Christian the lion" and "JoJo the dolphin" for videos on those interspecies friendship stories.

Kim Turley's wife, Barbara, died suddenly just a few weeks later, in a delayed reaction to a fall—one of a growing list of those who knew Romeo and are no longer with us.

Chapter 11

Author interviews: Pete Griffin, District Ranger, U.S. Forest Service, retired; Harry Robinson; John Hyde; Ryan Scott, Area Biologist, Alaska Department of Fish and Game; Lynn Schooler, Amalga area resident, writer, and naturalist; Nene Wolfe, DVM; Denise Chase, Amalga area resident and employee, Alaska Department of Fish and Game; Steve Kroschel, wildlife park owner and expert wolf handler, Haines, Alaska.

"One Solution to the Wolf Problem: Bean the Lamebrains," *Juneau Empire,* letter to the editor by Anita Martin, February 14, 2007, http://juneauempire.com/stories/021407/let_20070214026.shtml.

"Mendenhall Wolf Snatches Small Dog," *Juneau Empire,* Alaska Digest, April 4, 2007, http://juneauempire.com/stories/040407/sta_20070404009.shtml.

Chapter 12

Author interviews: Denise Chase, Amalga area resident; Ryan Scott, Area Biologist, Alaska Department of Fish and Game; Neil Barten, Biologist, Alaska Department of Fish and Game; Doug Larsen, Research Biologist, Alaska Department of Fish and Game, and at the time, director of wildlife management; Vic Van Ballenberghe, Ph.D., Wildlife Biologist, U.S. Forest Service, retired, currently independent wildlife biologist; Kim Turley, cofounder, Friends of Romeo; Vic Walker, DVM; unknown Yu'pik Eskimo woman.

"Juneau and the Wolf," *Juneau Empire,* February 14, 2008, http://juneauempire.com/stories/021408/loc_246928335.shtml.

Chapter 13

Author interviews: Harry Robinson; Vic Walker, DVM; Michael Lowman, co-worker of Jeff Peacock; Ginger Baker, co-bowler of Park Myers at Channel Bowling; Chris Frary, Sealing Agent with Alaska Department of Fish and Game, retired; Jon Stetson, neighbor to Park Myers; Sam Friburg, Special Agent, USFWS; Chris Hansen, Enforcement Officer, USFWS; Aaron Frenzel, Alaska State Wildlife Trooper; Harriet Milks, attorney at law; Joel Bennett; anonymous Tlingit woman who worked as construction flagger near Herbert River.

Nancy Meyerhoffer, sworn affidavit submitted to Juneau Trial Court.

Michael Lowman, sworn affidavit submitted to Juneau Trial Court.

Douglas Bosarge and Mary Williams (neighbors to Park Myers), sworn affidavit to Juneau Trial Court.

Police Criminal Complaint and Affidavit of Probable Cause, Docket Number CR-271-99, Commonwealth of Pennsylvania, Lancaster County, December 21, 1999, and Sentencing Order for Park Myers III.

"Where Art Thou, Romeo?" *Juneau Empire,* January 22, 2010, http://juneauempire.com/stories/012210/loc_553296141.shtml.

"Man Arrested for Killing Black Wolf," *Juneau Empire*, May 25, 2010, http://search.juneauempire.com/fast-elements.php?querystring=Man%20 arrested%20for%20killing%20black%20wolf&profile=juneau&type=stan dard.

"Was It Romeo?" *Juneau Empire*, May 26, 2010, http://juneauempire .com/stories/052610/loc_644797986.shtml.

Juneau Trial Court public records, including evidence images, charging documents, and transcripts, *State of Alaska v. Park Myers III*, 1JU-10-651 CR, November 3, 2010.

Addressing Peacock's claims of having killed Juneau's "spirit bear": The general term "spirit bear" refers to a very rare, white-phase black bear. Though such an animal did frequent an area near Amalga Harbor during roughly that time frame, and did disappear, it's clear from photos that Peacock's bear wasn't that individual.

Chapter 14

Author interviews: Harry Robinson; Michael Lowman; Joel Bennett; Jeffrey Sauer, attorney at law; Harriet Milks, attorney at law; anonymous grocery checker, Super Bear Supermarket; anonymous woman with flat tire; Cindy Burchfield, Alaskan Brewing; Jon Stetson, neighbor to Park Myers; Joel Bennett; Tina Brown, President, Alaska Wildlife Alliance; Alex Simon, ex-professor of social sciences, University of Alaska Southeast.

Juneau Trial Court public records, including evidence images, charging documents, and transcripts, *State of Alaska v. Park Myers III*, 1JU-10-651 CR, November 3, 2010.

Following are a number of links to *Juneau Empire* articles during the period, to give a sense of the case's importance to Juneau. Here, as elsewhere, the anonymous comments that follow most articles provide as much insight as the stories themselves:

"Romeo Trial Delayed," *Juneau Empire*, September 21, 2010, http://juneau empire.com/stories/092110/loc_710505630.shtml.

"Myers' Court Appearance Set for Nov. 2," *Juneau Empire*, October 14, 2010, http://juneauempire.com/stories/101410/reg_720410479.s html.

"Guilty Plea Expected Today in Myers Hunting Violations," *Juneau Empire*, November 1, 2010, http://juneauempire.com/stories/110110/loc _729241648.shtml.

"Hunter's Plea Hearing Moved to Wednesday," *Juneau Empire*, November 2, 2010, http://juneauempire.com/stories/110210/loc_729751503.shtml.

"Juneau Man Receives Suspended Sentence for Hunting Violation," *Juneau Empire*, November 4, 2010, http://juneauempire.com/stories/110410/loc_730859127.shtml.

"Helping Juneau Move On by Honoring Romeo," *Juneau Empire*, November 7, 2010, http://juneauempire.com/stories/110710/opi_732535770.shtml.

"Spirit of Romeo Rises over Old Roaming Grounds," *Juneau Empire*, November 21, 2010, http://juneauempire.com/stories/112110/loc_739556163.shtml.

"Second 'Romeo' Assailant Sentenced for Game Violations," *Juneau Empire*, January 6, 2011, http://juneauempire.com/stories/010511/loc_765565209.shtml.

Epilogue

Author interviews: Harry Robinson; Joel Bennett; Vic Walker, DVM; Ron Marvin, Director, U.S. Forest Service, Mendenhall Glacier visitor center, retired; Laurie Craig, Interpretive Naturalist, U.S. Forest Service, Mendenhall Glacier visitor center.

Juneau Trial Court records and transcripts, *State of Alaska v. Park Henry Myers III*, Case No. 1JU-10-651-CR.

Again, *Empire* articles focused on Myers's return to court:

"White Wolf Encounter," *Juneau Empire*, March 19, 2010, http://juneau empire.com/stories/031910/out_592882717.shtml.

"Wolf Country," *Juneau Empire*, May 28, 2010, http://juneauempire.com/stories/052810/out_645917431.shtml.

"My Turn: It's Not About the Wolf," opinion piece, Harriet Milks, *Juneau Empire*, January 6, 2011, http://juneauempire.com/stories/010611/opi_765993847.shtml.

"Probation May Be Revoked for Man in 'Romeo' Case," *Juneau Empire*, January 23, 2011, http://juneauempire.com/stories/012311/loc_774966703.shtml.

"Wolf Killer Back in Court as Judge Weighs Facts of Legal Filing, Previous Criminal History," *Juneau Empire*, April 5, 2011, http://juneau

empire.com/local/2011-04-05/wolf-killer-back-court-judge
-weighs-facts-legal-filing-previous-criminal-history#.UkSsP4Y
WJR0. The comment section that follows this story (and others related to the wolf) is especially interesting.

"Myers Sentenced for Probation Violation," *Juneau Empire,* July 17, 2011,
http://m.juneauempire.com/local/2011-07-16/myers-sentenced
-probation-violation. This is a very strange *Empire* piece with no by-
line that mischaracterizes facts, doesn't even mention why Myers
was really in court, and carries obvious sympathy for Myers. See also
blog comments.

SUGGESTED READING

Of Wolves and Men, Barry Lopez, Charles Scribner's Sons, 1978.
Though dated in some respects (much has occurred in both the wolf-related political and scientific realms since its publication), this book remains a cornerstone of nonfiction wolf literature. An eclectic and cerebral combination of research summations, wolf lore and legends, history, philosophical musings, and polemic.

Wolves: Behavior, Ecology, and Conservation, L. David Mech and Luigi
    Boitani, editors, University of Chicago Press, 2007.
This massive, 448-page compendium of wolf research, illustrated with photographs, diagrams, and tables, is the most comprehensive and up-to-date resource on wolves available. Accessible and highly recommended.

Among Wolves, Gordon Haber and Marybeth Holleman, University
    of Alaska Press, 2013.
The research and observations of Alaska wolf biologist Gordon Haber, in his own words, with added writings by Holleman and others who knew him. Haber's four decades of research on wolves within Alaska's Denali National Park includes some of the longest and most detailed personal field observations of wolf family groups and individuals ever conducted. His writing is lucid and compelling. Haber's refusal to formally publish his findings in

peer-reviewed journals, his abrasive, sometimes contradictory personality, and his fearless advocacy for wolves made him a controversial figure. Haber died in a plane crash in 2009 in Denali while studying the wolves he loved.

The Wolves of Mount McKinley, Adolph Murie, University of
     Washington Press, 1985.
Biologist Murie's book is based on studies of wolves he made in Denali National Park in 1939–1940 and is full of vivid observations and analysis of wolf behavior in the wild.

The Wolf Almanac: A Celebration of Wolves and Their World,
     Robert H. Bush, Lyons Press, 1995, updated 2007.
A useful, well-illustrated, and well-researched compendium of wolf information with an extensive bibliography.

Arctic Wild, Lois Crisler, Harper and Brothers, 1958.
A classic narrative featuring keen personal observations and detailed interactions with captive-raised, free-ranging wolf pups in remote Arctic Alaska.

The Arctic Wolf: Living with the Pack, L. David Mech, Voyageur Press, 1988.
A beautifully photographed and well-written record of personal observations by eminent wolf biologist David Mech, detailing his experiences studying a pack of human-habituated white wolves in the high Canadian Arctic.

Romeo: The Story of an Alaskan Wolf, John Hyde, Bunker Hill
     Publishing, 2010.
Photographer John Hyde's book features superb color images of Romeo, along with a six-thousand-word text relating the story of the wolf from Hyde's perspective.

Unlikely Friendships: 47 Remarkable Stories from the Animal Kingdom,
     Jennifer S. Holland, Workman Publishing, 2011.

A series of true anecdotes of friendships between animals of different species, with color photos of the actual animals involved. Light, heartwarming, and a fast-paced read.

The Emotional Lives of Animals, Marc Bekoff, New World Library, 2008.
Biologist Marc Bekoff explores the abilities of animals to express emotions once thought the sole province of humans, and their abilities to establish emotional connections with others.

Animal Wise: The Thoughts and Emotions of Our Fellow Creatures,
    Virginia Morell, Crown, 2013.
This thought-provoking and far-reaching examination of animal sentience by noted science writer Morell is bolstered by the latest research. Chapter 10 specifically addresses the similarities and differences of the inner workings of wolves and dogs.

The Last Light Breaking, Nick Jans, Alaska Northwest Books/Graphic
    Arts Center, 1993.
This collection of personal essays set in Arctic Alaska includes stories of my life among the Inupiat, including wolf encounters and hunting referred to in this book.

A Place Beyond: Finding Home in Arctic Alaska, Nick Jans, Alaska
    Northwest Books/Graphic Arts Center, 1996.
My second collection of Arctic essays, including a three-part story of camping near a pack of wolves, referred to in this book.

Never Cry Wolf, Farley Mowatt, Atlantic/Little, Brown, 1963.
While numerous questions have been raised regarding the veracity of Mowatt's story, this account of human-wolf interactions in the Canadian Arctic nonetheless remains an entertaining classic.

Wolf Song of Alaska, a nonprofit organization located in Eagle River, Alaska, maintains a huge online library covering wolves within a huge range of contexts, from wolves in art and literature to specific articles, editorials, and so forth, from both Alaska and around the world, including antiwolf materials. Highly recommended and worthy of support. For Alaska articles spanning 2001–2011, search their archives for titles, http://www.wolfsongalaska.org/.

The Alaska Department of Fish and Game maintains a website with links to its research on Alaska wildlife, including wolves, http://www.adfg .alaska.gov/index.cfm?adfg=librarypublications.wildliferesearch.

INDEX

Page numbers in italics refer to illustrations.